INNOVATION IN LIBRARIES AND INFORMATION SERVICES

ADVANCES IN LIBRARY ADMINISTRATION AND ORGANIZATION

Series Editors: Delmus E. Williams and
Janine Golden

Recent Volumes:

Volumes 13–20:   Edited by Edward D. Garten and Delmus E. Williams

Volume 21–24:   Edited by Edward D. Garten, Delmus E. Williams and
James M. Nyce

Volume 25:   Edited by Edward D. Garten, Delmus E. Williams,
James M. Nyce and Sanna Talja

Volume 26:   Edited by Edward D. Garten, Delmus E. Williams,
James M. Nyce and Janine Golden

Volume 27:   Edited by William Graves III, James M. Nyce, Janine
Golden and Delmus E. Williams

Volume 28:   Edited by Delmus E. Williams, James M. Nyce and
Janine Golden

Volume 29:   Edited by Delmus E. Williams and Janine Golden

Volume 30:   Edited by Delmus E. Williams and Janine Golden

Volume 31:   Edited by Delmus E. Williams and Janine Golden

Volume 32:   Edited by Delmus E. Williams and Janine Golden

Volume 33:   Edited by Delmus E. Williams, Janine Golden and
Jennifer K. Sweeney

Volume 34:   Edited by Samantha Schmehl Hines and Marcy Simons

ADVANCES IN LIBRARY ADMINISTRATION AND
ORGANIZATION   VOLUME 35

INNOVATION IN LIBRARIES AND INFORMATION SERVICES

EDITED BY

DAVID BAKER

University of St Mark & St John, Plymouth, UK

WENDY EVANS

University of St Mark & St John, Plymouth, UK

Emerald

United Kingdom – North America – Japan
India – Malaysia – China

Emerald Group Publishing Limited
Howard House, Wagon Lane, Bingley BD16 1WA, UK

First edition 2017

Copyright © 2017 Emerald Group Publishing Limited

Reprints and permissions service
Contact: permissions@emeraldinsight.com

British Library Cataloguing in Publication Data
A catalogue record for this book is available from the British Library

ISBN: 978-1-78560-731-8
ISSN: 0732-0671 (Series)

Printed and bound by CPI Group (UK) Ltd, Croydon, CR0 4YY

ISOQAR certified
Management System,
awarded to Emerald
for adherence to
Environmental
standard
ISO 14001:2004.

Certificate Number 1985
ISO 14001

INVESTOR IN PEOPLE

CONTENTS

EDITORIAL ADVISORY BOARD

LIST OF CONTRIBUTORS

David Baker	University of St Mark & St John, Plymouth, UK
Chris Batt	Warlingham, UK
Laurel Sammonds Crawford	University of North Texas Libraries, Texas, USA
Karen Harker	University of North Texas Libraries, Texas, USA
Masanori Koizumi	University of Tsukuba, Tsukuba, Japan
Tibor Koltay	Eszterházy Károly University, Eger, Hungary
Derek Law	University of Strathclyde, Glasgow, UK
Derek Marshall	Mississippi State University, Mississippi, USA
Mike McGrath	Leeds, UK
Chloe Persian Mills	Robert Morris University, Pittsburgh, USA
Valentini Moniarou-Papaconstantinou	Technological Educational Institute of Athens, Athens, Greece
John Robinson	SOAS University of London, London, UK
Jo Smedley	University of South Wales, Pontypridd, UK
Evgenia Vassilakaki	Technological Educational Institute of Athens, Athens, Greece
Graham Walton	Loughborough University, Loughborough, UK
Paul Webb	Bradford, Salford, Sheffield & Sheffield Hallam Universities, UK

PREFACE

This volume of *Advances in Library Administration and Organization* takes as its underpinning theme the whole subject of innovation in Library and Information Services. It considers the various types of innovation through case studies and exemplars both from within the Library and Information Services (LIS) sector and other cognate industries and environments. It looks at both the last and the next 30 years by charting major technology developments and the ways in which they have not only been adopted and adapted by library services but also how the resulting improvements and enhancements have impacted upon key user communities. But more importantly, the volume projects these developments forward and in addition forecasts and analyses likely future inventions and innovations and how LIS leaders and managers should not only respond but also actually help to create and shape our future world.

All web links were correct at the time of checking (June 2016).

David Baker
Wendy Evans
Editors

ACKNOWLEDGMENTS

The editors are especially grateful to all who made this volume possible; to the authors of the various chapters for their contributions and their willingness to be involved in the project; to Eileen Breen and Emma Stevenson for their advice and assistance throughout the development of the proposal and the production of the volume, to Sharon Holley for her help during the various stages and also to the University of St Mark & St John for their support.

MAKING SURE THINGS CAN NEVER BE THE SAME AGAIN: INNOVATION IN LIBRARY AND INFORMATION SERVICES

David Baker

ABSTRACT

Purpose — *To provide an in-depth survey and review of innovation in library and information services (LIS) and to identify future trends in innovative research and its practical application in the field.*

Methodology/approach — *An in-depth review and summation of relevant literature over the last twenty years, along with an analysis and summary of the other papers in the volume.*

Findings — *Innovation in library and information work varies between the evolutionary and the discontinuous. A taxonomy of innovatory approaches to development and provision in the sector is provided, along with a detailed listing of the key elements of successful and not-so-successful innovative practice.*

Research limitations/implications — *The work is dependent on existing literature rather than direct empirical work. However, because it draws*

Innovation in Libraries and Information Services
Advances in Library Administration and Organization, Volume 35, 1–44
ISSN: 0732-0671/doi:10.1108/S0732-067120160000035007

together all major aspects of the topic, it has the potential to be used as a springboard for further generic studies and also specific programmes of work.

Practical implications — *The need for innovation in LIS will be ever more pressing. The present chapter provides a necessary and rigorous overview of the necessary elements required for success in this area. It will be useful as a reference tool for intending researchers in library and information provision in a wide range of environments.*

Originality/value — *Because the chapter brings together a substantial body of information on the topic of innovation, it provides a comprehensive study of major developments and likely future trends in the field.*

Keywords: Innovation; invention; improvement; technology development; strategic positioning; investment

INTRODUCTION

'The more things change, the more they can never be the same'. Thus wrote Allen B Veaner (1982) in the first paper in the first volume of *Advances in Library Administration and Organization (ALAO)*. This statement is as true now as it was then, despite the fact that much has happened since the very first page of ALAO was published. 'The ... library world has been transformed beyond all recognition ... There is no turning back: indeed, the pace of change quickens' (Baker, 2007) and product innovation and change are faster than ever before (Brindley, 2009), while the speed at which the public is accepting new products and services also grows apace; 'many have no problem with keeping up with the speed of the innovation lifecycle' (Porter, 2015). 'Technological innovation is creating exciting opportunities to do things differently and also, to do different things' (Smyth, 2015). But the challenges are significant. Smyth continues:

> The task of evaluating or appraising what is happening in the field of digital information is not to be underestimated, especially considering the rapidity of change that confronts citizens around the world. There is substantive complexity at various levels, whether at the global, national, regional and local levels as well as within and between commercial, public and citizens in terms of activities and modes ... Review[s] of key principal trends and perspectives [should be] undertaken in the widest possible context, cognisant that there are often substantive differences around the world, due to variances in socio-economic, political and cultural factors.

However, it can also be argued that:

> One of the main reasons for change is to preserve the best aspects of the organisation —
> to change in order to remain the same: this can often be a powerful argument when per-
> suading people to alter the ways in which they work, not least as something on which
> to 'anchor' change, to rally people behind and to help explain the need for something
> new and different. (Baker, 2007)

The significant transformation in Library and Information Services (LIS) some 34 volumes after Veaner codified the essence of change, in all its forms, has come about through innovation, both major and not-so-major, and this is the subject of this edition of the *Advances* .... But innovating has never been — and never will be — easy. As will be seen later in this chapter, the last 30 years have seen major disruption in LIS provision, beginning with a state where libraries existed 'in two worlds — the world of Gutenberg and the world of Gates ... [and where] the transition from one to the other [would be] extraordinarily painful, enervating, morale-crushing, and expensive' (Lee, 1997; see also Mike McGrath's chapter in this volume). But it was at a time of financial setbacks and industrial decline in many areas that it was deemed especially important 'to encourage, recognise and reward innovation in ... library/knowledge services, particularly in the new economic climate, when access to knowledge will be crucial — as will cost and smart ways of providing it. If library/knowledge services are to rise to the challenge, innovation will be essential'.[1]

That challenge — present for several decades now, as Koizumi points out in his chapter — remains, and the imperative to innovate is as strong as ever:

> New technologies are enabling the provision of increasingly diverse information pro-
> ducts and services with embedded location capabilities. In addition, a wide range of
> technical and business drivers are having significant impacts on existing and new sec-
> tors. Opportunities and challenges abound, provided by economic, social and environ-
> mental factors that are likely to prove as important, if not more so, than the
> technological changes in the near future.
>
> We are witnessing a paradigm shift, creating a dynamic geospatial ecosystem in which
> information and technology are not only integrated in mainstream enterprises, but such
> information and unlimited applications extend beyond, to consumers and citizens,
> and ... the increasing role, and harnessing the value of 'data' — from the public sector
> and corporations alike — is set to revolutionise and bring about further societal and
> economic change, in part through transformational change agendas with increasing
> data transparency and openness. (Smyth, 2015)

In consequence, as Curtis Brundy (2015) stresses, 'libraries are facing times of unprecedented challenge and unparalleled change. Innovation has moved from a consideration to a necessity'. Librarians need to innovate as never before if library and information services (LIS) are to have a vital and vibrant future.

> Libraries of all kinds are likely to need to adapt for two basic reasons: firstly, they need to survive; secondly, they must enable their users to get the support and advice that they require within the new information architecture that has been brought so rapidly to the fore through the development of, and pervasive connectivity to, the Internet. (Baker & Evans, 2009)

They have an opportunity as well as a requirement in doing so, for '[libraries] should not merely move with the times but make the pace. [They] should lead rather than follow' (Baker & Evans, 2015; see also Molaro & White, 2015). This volume of ALAO aims to codify and summarise the key elements of recent and likely future innovation in LIS, and to provide exemplars and case studies of when, where and how innovation takes place – and should take place – in LIS.

INNOVATION

The editors of this volume have long been interested in innovation, both in general and with regard to LIS in particular. Together and separately David Baker and Wendy Evans have written and edited a number of books and papers in the field of strategic library management and digital developments (see, e.g., Baker, 2004, 2006; Baker & Evans, 2007, 2009, 2011, 2013a, 2013b, 2015). In all this work, innovation – typically driven by economic imperative and financial need and usually underpinned if not led by technological developments – has been to the fore. This may have been in relation to major discontinuous change or as a result of the many and varied incremental improvements that the editors have observed and charted over the last twenty years and as noted in Walton and Webb's chapter later in this volume. Witness all the case studies in *Handbook of Digital Library Economics* (Baker & Evans, 2013a, 2013b) and the ways in which financial imperatives have driven invention and innovation. Take the EZID project, described in the *Handbook* ... and the 'benefits' of being hard pressed financially in terms of being forced to innovate:

> Running a library service while recovering its costs can be a daunting enterprise. But being budget driven can provide some real advantages. EZID's economic imperative has been a strong teacher about marketing, teaching the team to talk about library services in new ways. Equally, it has given priority to the formal improvements in procedures, documentation and infrastructure that are necessary for business continuity under any circumstances. And, it has opened doors to new kinds of partnerships with new kinds of partners. EZID is in the process of tracking costs and income so that, over the next couple of years, it can determine whether or not the service can indeed pay for itself, but, meanwhile, the process of trying has already generated returns. (Starr, 2013)

Innovation – in the context of information provision – is defined in more detail later in this volume by Jo Smedley and Evgenia Vassilakaki and Valentini Moniarou-Papaconstantinou in their respective chapters, but some explanation of the term is necessary here also. Innovation takes place in all walks of life: public, private, third sectors; commercial, charitable; for profit, not for profit. It has been taking place for some considerable time, and on occasion leads to technological revolution resulting in fundamental changes to every aspect of life, including society itself, as for example 'the full-scale breakthrough of the steam engine in the early 1800s' (Van de Pas, van Bussel, Veenstra, & Jorna, 2015) or the Internet over the last 30 years. 'It is [a concept] that can be traced back to at least the eighteenth century and the beginning of the industrial revolution. The "spinning jenny" was a piece of [innovative] technology; so were the canals ... Innovation ... is [now] widely regarded as the norm' (Baker, 2004). That technological revolution changed production and transportation, and caused massive societal changes. As already noted, and as discussed and analysed by Smedley, technology has underpinned most if not all of these changes and developments, and there is no indication that this will change. For that reason, there is an inevitable and necessary emphasis on technological innovation in the development of LIS provision throughout this volume.

There is no single approach to, or type of, innovation, but rather there is a broad spectrum of innovative approaches and innovatory thinking, as noted in Walton and Webb's chapter, amongst others in this volume.

> Invention, innovation, improvement and integration are not four separate activities, but form points on a continuum on which individual organisations will have to find their position (which may vary depending on the particular technology, product or service). (Baker, 2004)

In this context, 'innovation' is typically categorised into four different types. These are:

- Revolutionary innovation, where the technology and the markets are new
- Radical innovation, where the technology is new, but the markets are the same
- Market niche, where the technology is not new, but it is applied to new markets
- Regular innovation, which is the further development of existing technology within existing markets (Baker, 2004).

Evgenia Vassilakaki and Valentini Moniarou-Papaconstantinou discuss different types of innovation further in their chapter. Innovation may be based on a new idea, concept, product, system or service which is applied to a specific situation, such as library and information provision (Baker, 1991, 1992, 1994a, 1994b, 1998, 2006, 2007, 2008, 2013, 2014). 'The interaction between markets and technology is an important one and can affect the way an invention becomes a successful innovation' (Baker, 2004).

In the United Kingdom (UK), the £60m eLib programme of research and development in higher education LIS provision − complemented by public library sector programmes The People's Network[2] and the New Opportunities Fund (NOF) NOF-digitise programme (Woodhouse, 2001) − that lasted from 1995 until 2001 and emerged from the Follett Report of 1993 (Carr, 2007; ESYS Consulting, 2001; Follett, 1993; Greenaway, 1997; Rusbridge, 1998; Tavistock Institute, 1998, 2000) was a good example of the ways in which innovation in LIS work came about through a rich combination of the application of (then) relatively recent inventions through prototyping, technology integration,[3] evolutionary and, occasionally, revolutionary change, resulting in advancement and improvement (Abrahamson, 2000; Baker, 2004, 2007; Eccles, 1996; Smyth, 2015); all supported nationally and internationally by the injection of significant financial, technological and specialist resources.[4] Other countries could point to similar initiatives (see, e.g., Ball, 2009; Chan & Spodick, 2015; Savenije, 2009).

The required major transformation of LIS provision that these programmes aimed to achieve would only come about through invention, innovation and improvement, notably through the application of new and emerging technologies. But it was not just the challenge of technology management that arose in the 1980s and 1990s:

> The application of innovation is challenging, and needs to take account of a number of critical success factors. Technology cannot itself solve problems, it can only assist in their solution; re-engineering [processes, systems, services and even whole organisations] may be the necessary fundamental shift that is required in order to ensure that the problem really is solved ...
>
> What is important is to try and forecast ... trends and likelihoods before they happen There is no single best way of managing invention, innovation or improvement. Different stakeholders will have differing perspectives, for one thing; the climate in which an innovation is to be made will also have a considerable effect on the success of the innovatory change. This requires a high degree of risk management at all levels of innovation and improvement in order to maximize both the chances of success and the return on investment. (Baker, 2004)

Nor were there any hard and fast rules about how to innovate during the 1990s and 2000s when the LIS provision was being radically transformed; the chaotic and disruptive nature of major economic, societal and technological changes meant that novel approaches to innovating had to be developed:

> There is no single way to innovate or improve. Organisations will need to determine their approach and to assess and, as necessary, develop their capacity and capability. However, innovation and change can be harder in service than in manufacturing sectors, for the 'product' is often less easy to define and therefore to improve. (Baker, 2007)

Evgenia Vassilakaki and Valentini Moniarou-Papaconstantinou discuss some of the particular challenges of innovating in service provision rather than product development in their chapter, while Graham Walton and Paul Webb enumerate the key criteria for success – discussed also in more detail later in this chapter – in their contribution to the volume.

Much of this volume – and this chapter, as already noted – focusses on technology innovation in LIS; that is, the application of technologies (typically information and communication technologies – ICT) to create, develop and enhance innovative approaches, services, products and more in library and information provision, as foregrounded, for example, by Evgenia Vassilakaki and Valentini Moniarou-Papaconstantinou and Tibor Koltay in their respective chapters later in this volume. But this is not the full story; there is much more than just technological innovation, even though technology often underpins, influences or even drives other modes of invention, innovation and improvement, as discussed below (Smith, 2015). The whole concept of the library – physical as well as virtual – is being disrupted, changed and transformed.

But while some things can never be the same as a result of transformation through innovation, there are also things that are being reinvented and renewed in consequence of the major movements that have taken place to date. 'There is nowhere quite like [the library] and there is so little quality social space – that third place between home and work – in many countries' (Baker & Evans, 2015). 'The Library' is also still a physical as well as a virtual space (Watson, 2011), despite some commentators' views, as analysed by Derek Law in a later chapter of this volume and as discussed by Vassilakaki and Moniarou-Papaconstantinou in their study of modern Greek public libraries. With regard to 'library space' not only is there a continuing need to innovate, but there are also many exciting exemplars of innovation by LIS workers and, more importantly perhaps, visions of how the library of the future should look, feel and be experienced by the user, again as discussed and developed by Law in his contribution (see also Chan & Spodick, 2014, 2015). As summarised by Baker and Evans (2015):

> The balance between space for collections and space for people will need to be carefully considered by every library in the context of its locality, context, community and aspirations. For the library to continue as successful 'space' then members will need a reason to go there ... Library space will be used as a place to get work done in a wide variety of forms – personal learning, group learning, co-working, personal research, video creation and so on. Space needs to be configured to stimulate creative and imaginative enterprise.

But current technology developments are set to be more disruptive than simply making librarians rethink their physical spaces, as noted amongst others, in John Robinson's case study. 'Digital media [are not only] influencing the design of libraries – changing the way users occupy spaces within them – and the role libraries play as cultural buildings' (Smyth, 2015) and as noted in Vassilakaki and Moniarou-Papaconstantinou's study of innovation in service provision in Greek public libraries later in this volume. 'Digital media are [also] influencing the architectural design of libraries and the contribution they make towards the civic fabric of our towns and cities ... Digital media collections can change the way users occupy space within libraries, and what the broader implications of this are on library design, as well as the role libraries have as a cultural building' (Smith, 2015). Now, with the development of the 'Internet of Things' (IoT) there is even the prospect of 'smart' linking of the physical and the virtual in ways previously undreamed of:

> The IoT is evolving fast, enabled by the development of (wireless) networks without human or centralised components. The IoT includes everything from power and energy meters that report usage data automatically, to wearable heart monitors that send health data to a doctor, and to traffic sensors and cars that will automatically report their position and condition to authorities in the event of an accident. (Van de Pas et al., 2015)

> The 'Internet of things' is a concept where ... everything can be connected to the Internet, as the self-powered wireless enabled computers or sensors become ubiquitous, such as the concept of the 'smart electric grid', where appliances are wired to the Internet is becoming commonplace in the energy consumption sphere ... While the IoT is reported to be beneficial to society, enabling many things to be possible, including both applications and services, it will, however, present new challenges ... As the IoT becomes more pervasive, questions over the invasiveness of the technologies will undoubtedly abound, particularly in relation to the information content, and end users (or indeed reselling or re-supply to third parties), as well as

the capabilities of mega companies such as Google and others to 'mine' or query information to their benefit. Ubiquitous surveillance is most definitely real and ever closer. (Smyth, 2015)

Thus will develop the smart city, a place 'where information technology is combined with infrastructure, architecture, everyday objects, and even our bodies to address social, economic, and environmental problems' city (Townsend, 2013). As with all major innovation, ultimately, 'the solution ... lies, fundamentally, in taking a different approach to the way we do things ... many of the problems ... are ... cultural, not technological' (Carpenter & Milloy, 2007). In the case of IoT and Smart Cities, a whole new approach to Information Management – as also discussed by Jo Smedley in her chapter – will be required, in order to ensure that maximum value is created from the ever-increasing amounts of data produced and at our collective disposal (Smyth, 2015).

IMPERATIVES

The impetus to invent, innovate, improve or enhance has a number of imperatives. The ability and capacity to innovate is fundamental to maintaining and developing a vibrant service or sector. In the case of LIS, a key imperative is almost always to improve efficiency and effectiveness because of financial, political or user need (see, e.g., Mcgrath, 2009 with regard to one major area of change in LIS – document delivery, taken up also later in this volume by McGrath himself and also Derek Law; Estelle, 2009 regarding another – digital collection development; Savenije, 2009 for a third – improved academic library provision):

There is always the need to juggle diverse needs with limited resources in a constant quest for sustainability. Libraries of all kinds ... must be efficient and productive along with the rest of the economy. As a result, they have to increase efficiency and decrease costs in order to survive in any economic climate, and to ensure that information is available as cheaply as possible ... Libraries of all kinds ... must be efficient and productive along with the rest of the economy ... They have to increase efficiency and decrease costs in order to survive in any economic climate, and to ensure that information is available as cheaply as possible to wider society. (Baker & Evans, 2009)

In a later chapter of this volume, Evgenia Vassilakaki and Valentini Moniarou-Papaconstantinou look at how the economic, political and social crisis in present-day Greece has forced public libraries to make significant innovations in order to remain viable by providing what their local user communities need at a time of major disruption in people's lives. By changing the ways of working they have been able to embrace change and turn difficulties into opportunities. This has allowed the libraries not only to innovate, but also to encourage and promote innovation amongst their user communities.

However, apart from market pull, certainly over the last 50 years, there has also been 'technology push'. 'The strategic imperative in an ever more competitive environment is to act sooner rather than later in order to ensure that institutions are able to take advantage of new technology when the time is right, rather than being left behind' (Baker & Evans, 2009; see also Baker & Evans, 2015). Koizumi discusses this imperative further in a later chapter in the context of his theory of management strategies for libraries. In the early days of major innovation in LIS, there was 'mechanisation' of library operations in order to improve efficiency and reduce costs – a simple, basic 'market pull', supported by improving and occasionally new technology (notably the advent of computers that could process library data).

Since the massive and pervasive development and implementation of information and communications and technologies (ICT), and especially since the advent of the Internet and the ever-increasing speed of change and innovation, the emphasis has moved towards significant 'technology push': there is simply no alternative but to embrace change through technology implementation and application (Chan & Spodick, 2015), as discussed throughout this volume. However, it should be stressed that there is also almost always a tension between technical innovation and 'the broader issues associated with the role of institutions within a changing social fabric', as well as one between public encouragement and constraining of 'the ability of practitioners genuinely to think collectively about strategic futures' (Batt, 2015).

What is clear from a study of innovation in LIS work in recent years is that the relationship between library content and services and the various technologies that have been/are being applied is changing. What were once strategic, pacing or leading edge technologies have now become the norm across much if not all of the sector, while former 'base' technologies are now obsolescent if not obsolete. An alternative categorisation of technologies that we have used in much of our work and which we believe remains valid (though technologies can move between different categories over time) can be found in Baker (2004).

Table 1.   Standard Technology Typology.

Critical	Those that are central to an organisation's competitive position, which are proprietary to some degree, and which differentiate it from the competition.
Enabling	Those that are not proprietary to the same degree, are broadly available to all members of the industry, but are essential to the efficient design, manufacture and delivery of the organisation's product or service, and its level of quality.
Strategic	Which can be emerging or already existing technologies, whose salience arises from their ability to provide new competitive opportunities when combined with or substituted for existing critical or enabling technologies.

To the list in Table 1 may be added the concept of the 'sustaining innovation', a technology, product, service or approach that will 'work alongside' existing and more traditional modes of provision and delivery to strengthen both the offering and the institution. As Porter (2015) summarises, 'those institutions that are able to adapt to, and embrace, the new technologies will be best placed to continue with what is excellent and special about what they do already, whilst taking best advantage of what is new ... One of the biggest challenges. is to move forward at an appropriate rate of change − to keep moving fast enough to maintain momentum, but not so fast that many people are left behind'. Smedley explores this also in her chapter.

Thus, the challenge for LIS leaders and managers is to ensure that the choice of key technologies for future application will put the organisation or the sector into the best possible position to remain competitive and hence sustainable in the longer term while at the same time ensuring that the organisation is fully behind the changes and there is the capacity to implement the innovations effectively and efficiently and to longer term best value and maximum benefit. This is not easy when there is significant continued 'churn' in the technologies that are − or could be − applied to LIS activities.

'In reality, however, the distinction between the pull and the push is not normally ... clear cut' (Baker, 2004). As Feather (2004) points out:

> The growth of some of the key areas of the information sector ... is associated with technological innovation and the widespread adoption of new technologies ... The issue is whether this change is a fundamental re-conceptualization of activities and their purpose, or whether it is merely a change, albeit very significant, in techniques and mechanisms. Another way of expressing the problem is to ask whether technological change drives social change, or social change demands new technological solutions to new and newly identified problems ...
>
> The issue is not whether there has been technological change and innovation ... It is rather whether the change has been led by the needs of users and of society at large, or

whether technologies and systems have been developed for which uses have then been found ... [Some] writers have identified a consistent delay between the development of information and communication technologies and their large-scale adoption ... It is argued that there is a consistent pattern of invention followed by a search for an application. The application often turns out to be quite different from that envisaged by the inventor ...

As Reg Carr put it:

The main questions for us therefore seem to be: 'Can we, as information brokers in a digital world, keep up with what our users want?' And, 'How much smarter can we get at making it affordable, for them and for us?' (Carr, 2009)

As ICT has affected every aspect of life, the user has had ever greater choice and control over how to create, store and retrieve information. In consequence, ultimately, innovation is shaped and driven by people – 'users need to feel in control' (Baker, 2006) – and library management strategies have had to adapt to respond to this development, as Koizumi analyses in a later chapter. However, it should be stressed that there is no such thing as a typical user, though a number of cognate if not coherent user generations can be determined. But the challenge is more complex than just satisfying a single block of user needs. By 'identifying trends and factors leading to the emergence of the various generations of library users', Evgenia Vassilakaki 'aims to assist information professionals and libraries in keeping up to date with users' information needs, assisting in the formulation of their strategies for collection management and the offering of competitive information services' (Vassilakaki, 2015; see also Smith, 2015). Vassilakaki and Moniarou-Papaconstantinou return to this theme later in this volume, as does Mike McGrath. The proactivity of the LIS staff is important given the fact that:

It is, by and large, users who determine the success or failure of particular systems and devices. Choices may be based on social convenience (the mobile phone), business efficiency (electronic mail), or economic necessity (financial information systems), but they are essentially choices. Technology does not determine what happens; it only determines what *can* happen. (Feather, 2004; see also, e.g., Baker & Evans, 2015; Porter, 2015)

Porter's work – and Koltay's chapter in this volume – suggest that many users have no difficulty keeping up with technological change and, indeed, often demand rapid development:

Consumers increasingly expect rapid change in online services, with new products and services appearing regularly, and new features and added value with those services that they already use. (Porter, 2015)

But it is not just about users and technology, important though this is, and as discussed by Smedley later in this volume. Changing usage is just as important:

> People have not stopped using the physical library, but they do so in new ways. A significant trend in library design is increasing informality; they are becoming the 'civic living rooms' of our towns and cities. The move toward more informal spaces, facilitated in part by greater emphasis on digital collections, is a positive step in further democratising library spaces. This repurposing of spaces reflects changing relationships between the library and its users. (Smith, 2015)

So 'libraries must continue to plan for and position themselves where the users are, and that requires constantly changing decisions and skill sets' (Chan & Spodick, 2015; see also Mike McGrath's contribution to this volume). That is not to say that innovative products and services in LIS are always what the user wants or even needs. When the technology push is too distant from the market pull, as noted above, there is often a tendency to produce a 'solution' that is in search of a 'problem' (Baker, 2004; Hamilton, 2004; Smith, 2003). 'There is, then, a vital need to make sure that the product or service is valued by the end user or it will be under or sub-optimally utilised. It is essential to make sure that the technology adds value and is seen to have a purpose that stakeholders can appreciate' (Baker & Evans, 2009; see also John Robinson's extended case study later in this volume for an exemplar of decision-making processes in technology management and application).

A BRIEF HISTORY OF INNOVATION IN LIS WORK

As a prelude to the later parts of this chapter and the volume as a whole, it is necessary to look at where and how innovation in LIS work has developed and been transformed whether by technological, cultural, societal or economic change. Derek Law continues and adds to this short history in his contribution to the volume, with special reference to UK higher education libraries, as does Mike McGrath in his focus on inter-library loan and document supply, while Masanori Koizumi concentrates 'on 16 detailed management cases involving U.S. and Japanese academic and public libraries from the 1960s to the 2010s … analysing documents related to strategic management, organisation, and operations, collected through surveys and interviews with library directors and managers. Based on those case analyses, the researcher identified the strategic patterns of libraries; a strong relationship of services, organisations, core skills and knowledge and environments'.

As the present author has described elsewhere, writing of the UK's academic library sector (Baker, 2004):

> By the early 1990s, the UKHE LIS sector had got to that final 'specific pattern stage of innovation ... [where it was] vulnerable to the possibility of a revolutionary new product introduction' (Noori, 1990). The development of Internet-based resources and services and the breakdown of the old dominant design was a 'landmark' change (Kingston, 2000). On the one hand, new technology was being applied to existing markets; on the other, new markets were being tapped once new products and services were fully developed. Existing suppliers, such as traditional libraries and document delivery services (and, indeed, users) began to find it 'difficult to adapt to environmental changes with ... an ageing product'. (Noori, 1990)

In other words, the old ways of providing library services were at the end of their lifespan. Existing ways of doing things were simply neither affordable nor justifiable, though this was not for want of trying:

> Simple and even insignificant changes to a product or service may make it possible for it to be used in markets other than those for which it was originally intended ... This process typically occurs when the original product or service market is almost saturated and there is a need to diversify into other markets in order to maintain viability. Such changes can also, of course, be used to ensure that the product or service remains attractive within existing markets, at least until radically innovative ones can be launched. That is why we often see advertisements for 'new, improved' versions of existing products when, in fact, the changes made are mainly cosmetic ones. (Baker, 2004)

Adopting new technology may have extended the life of traditional library provision, as for example with regard to the 'automation' of the creation of catalogue records, may have extended the life of the traditional library, but ultimately, the model was becoming unsustainable, as Derek Law and Mike McGrath both remark later in this volume. John Robinson also covers the ways in which librarians first embraced computers to assist the task of organising and administering libraries. Writing of a project that was a relatively early attempt to move things forward in the UK academic library sector, Chris Awre (2009) could say:

> The systems that now exist have greatly helped libraries to cope. It is, however, noticeable that these systems and roles often are about coping, reacting to changes and providing a way of keeping heads above water. The work of the CREE project specifically looked at how to be proactive in the presentation of search services, a situation that requires the coping mechanisms to be well embedded so that focus can be given to options for presentation and meeting the needs of local end-users. Hence, there is a need for libraries to be confident of their strategies and mechanisms for dealing with the information they manage so that they can then afford to look at ideas beyond this.

Change was obviously needed and there were LIS staff ready to rise to the challenge of significant innovatory change. It was − and still is − 'make or break' time.[5] In his contribution to this volume of ALAO, Derek Law even goes so far as to say that librarianship had reached a dead end by the 1990s. Certainly at the start of that decade, and even more recently, the key question related to the extent to which LIS staff would be able to anticipate decline while more traditional provision was still relatively successful, accepted and valued:

> Change may be necessary to avoid stagnation in an age of changing external circumstances: even if the organization appears to be performing well, it will become relatively worse off if it does not adjust where possible and certainly in advance of any predicted future change in circumstances or even a crisis point ... Anticipating decline and acting at a 'peak' point in the organization's life will pre-empt enforced change brought about by the need to react to decline. (Baker, 2007)

But it was not just about the need − and perhaps also the inevitability − of radical change and significant transformation in LIS work. It also involved substantial change in the role of the LIS worker, a theme taken up later in this volume by Derek Law:

> When online searching in distant databases started in the 1970s, an elite group of information professionals achieved a prominent position − nearly as a 'priesthood' of searchers who could translate the users' requests into the 'mysterious language' of the machine. These special searchers were able to tap into an almost 'magical world' of information largely on their own ... Indeed, the users were seen as pure clients in those days. When the CD-ROM was introduced in the mid-1980s, the professionals' status as 'priests' and 'magicians' [was] probably shaken, as a significant and self-confident end-user culture was emerging. However, it was first the arrival of the Internet in 1993−1934 that seriously transferred the control of searching to the end-user, thereby radically changing the status of the user from client to active participant. (Johannsen, 2015)

LIS workers have had to innovate in terms of their own roles as a result (Bitter-Rijpkema, Verjans, & Bruijnzeels, 2012; Parry, 2008; Partridge, Lee, & Munro, 2010). However, Johannsen (2015) looking at 'how certain technological trends concerning information and literature searching have changed the demand for the work and competencies of librarians and information specialists', found that technological development has influenced the position of the library professions in the eyes of its users, and also has changed the way the profession has looked upon its users. He continues:

> With regard to how technological developments may influence a profession, one obvious assumption could be that information technology advances are usually likely to diminish the role of the information professional and to empower the user. However,

the opposite opinion seems also probable: that every time the technology gets more complex and advanced, the information professionals will gain an advantage. The point of view that will be promoted here is, that the relationship between information technology developments and the relationships between information professionals as mediators and the (end)-users very much depend on the particular setting and situation. (Johanssen, 2015)

As Chloe Mills discusses in her contribution to this volume of ALAO, LIS workers continue to have an important role to play at a time when 'unfortunately, technology dependency often can become problematic, reducing traditional skills, especially when consumption typically is via digital means' (Smyth, 2015). What is especially interesting about Mills's work is the way in which the portfolio approach offers a way of evaluating the performance of LIS staff in a way that can be adapted to a range of environments and contexts as well as being integrated with the performance management of other related staff working in cognate institutions. Walton and Webb's contribution to this volume also looks at the importance of LIS staff training and development at a time of major, discontinuous change – as does John Robinson's case study – in order to ensure that innovative approaches can properly come to the fore, while Koltay's chapter considers the need for 'new' kinds of LIS workers, ready and able to work innovatively in the future digital world.

Major and sometimes discontinuous change is therefore inevitable and necessary (Curtis, et al., 2012; Hyams, 2010; Porter. 2015). Significant technological invention, innovation and application in LIS work has resulted in a number of radical and discontinuous changes, leading to the irrevocable collapse of the previous 'dominant design' (Baker, 2008) of traditional volume-on-shelf library provision. No amount of new technology application or substitution can preserve a way of storing and retrieving information that many now believe has outlived its relevance in all but a small number of specialist scenarios.

However, the developments in LIS over the last 20 years or so have for the most part been 'not so much a series of step changes as a curve of continuous advancement and improvement' (Baker, 2004). Indeed, Feather (2004), commented that:

The society of the 21st century is critically dependent on information and communication technologies for a huge number of activities. Very few of these, however, are genuinely and inherently new. Some have displaced older systems, as paper-based correspondence has been largely, although by no means entirely, replaced by e-mail. Some operate in parallel to existing systems, as online databases sit happily alongside traditional reference books.

It is certainly the case that there has been a good deal of 're-innovation' in LIS work, with existing products and services being redeveloped and reengineered, notably by 'new' technology application, and especially through the integration of technologies. So for example, by the time of the eLib programme, it was already commonplace for ICT solutions to be applied to the retrieval of increasing amounts of information (the so-called 'data deluge' was already under way in the 1990s), content itself was scanned, stored and, in due course created digitally. Within five years of the eLib programme – and the parallel initiatives in the US (such as the National Science Foundation) and elsewhere – finishing, the prospect of a world without print-on-paper was under serious contemplation (Buchanan, 2010; Castelli, 2006; Higher Education Consultancy Group, 2006; Savenije, 2009). It had taken just over a decade to get to that point.

There were also times in the 1990s, as programmes such as eLib began to develop, when drives to alter the market, and to 'break' the dominance of certain suppliers came to the fore, heralding an ongoing trend for technological innovation to 'disrupt' existing supply chains:

> In the UK, for example, the British Library [was] the major force in document delivery. It had ... a near unique service that represented good value to organizations keen to reduce their own high fixed costs (as for example storage space) and from which it would have been expensive to decouple. However, the increased availability of alternative sources of supply, not least through more advanced and differentiated use of technology, increased the power of the buyer (whether individual user or LIS unit) and reduced the dominance of the key supplier. (Baker, 2004)

The rise and fall of document supply (where the British Library was once such a dominant force) is discussed further in Mike McGrath's chapter. eLib in particular sought (amongst other things) to develop alternative means of document delivery in order to create choice for the end user and to develop new and more cost-effective ways of providing a service, just as, more recently, new for-profit providers are seeking to disrupt the traditional model of teaching and learning in higher and further education and, by implication at least, LIS provision with it (Porter, 2015).

The Joint Information Systems Committee (JISC) had already been set up in the 1990s alongside eLib and its work continued beyond the original experimentation and prototyping phases of the programme; in particular, JISC helped to make the digital library a reality through resource discovery and delivery, digital subscription, digitisation and content creation and preservation initiatives, underpinned by much more sophisticated tracking, analysis and decision support systems than ever previously thought possible. This ably demonstrated 'the UK's ability to work at a national level in a coordinated programme of development, which at the same time fostered a cadre of people with new and highly relevant skills ... In parallel with this development programme, JISC was spearheading impressive work on national shared services and national site licences for electronic content delivery' (Brindley, 2009; see also John Robinson's reference to JISC's Pathfinder work, discussed later in this volume). Few similar national organisations to JISC were set up in other countries – surprisingly, given the organisation's signal success over the years. SURF,[6] the Dutch equivalent, is a notable exception.

In retrospect, it is clear that much of the development of products and services in the wake of eLib and similar initiatives could be described as a classic 'reverse product cycle' (Barras, 1986, 1990), also referred to by Smedley in her chapter here in ALAO 35:

> The key point to stress with regard to the ... cycle is the fact that the new product or service comes at the end of the cycle rather than at the beginning. The drive for improvement begins with increments and it is the cumulative effect of improvement and innovation that leads to the discontinuity of radical change through the appearance of a new dominant design. In other words, while radical innovation was not intended when computers were first used to improve basic technical operations in libraries, banks or other service industries, those applications started an incremental innovation process that resulted in radical, discontinuous change. (Baker, 2004)

eLib may have been a catalyst and a watershed, but it was not the beginning. Reference was made earlier to technological advancement in the 18th and 19th centuries. The pace of change quickened in the 20th century. Since 1945, there has been continuing if not continuous incremental development until by the 1960s technology applications were beginning to predominate in all walks of life (Tanner, 2009). It was – and still is – to the credit of the LIS profession that there has been much 'early adoption' – discussed both in this chapter and elsewhere in this volume – of new ways of working, especially using computers, right from the time when machines were introduced to ease the burden and improve the efficiency of 'housekeeping' operations (Savenije, 2009). Because things changed more and more, there was no going back, as Veaner rightly concluded, nearly 35 years ago (Veaner, 1982).

STRATEGIC POSITIONING

David Baker has written elsewhere (Baker, 2004, 2006, 2008; Baker & Evans, 2015) about the need for effective strategic decision making in innovation within LIS. This is closely linked to strategic positioning, as discussed later by Koizumi, amongst others. It is heartening to note that, as already stressed, LIS organisations and their staff have often been pioneers and leaders as much as they have been laggards when it comes to innovation. As a minimum, there has regularly been a strong impetus amongst many library and information service managers to ensure that they are 'fast followers':

> The information world is populated by a naturally collaborative set of innovators ... [who] have slowly grappled with transient technology, developing and changing standards, whilst absorbing huge shifts in the forms and nature of communication. But throughout it all they have begun to create linkages which allow us to begin to perceive the emerging shape of a viable information new world, where no one group dominates, where collaboration is to the advantage of all and where we still have valuable products and services to offer users in the prosecution of their lives. (Law, 2013)

> While there is often a tendency towards inertia, there is also much innovative development that is already transforming library and information provision because our society, culture and economic are transforming, technology is developing and the library as an institution of society has to respond to the challenges. (Baker & Evans, 2015)

Mike McGrath's chapter in this volume talks of the value of collaboration as a way of innovating, particular in terms of resource sharing, while John Robinson's extended case study provides a valuable exemplar of shared service development, especially where the whole can become significantly greater than the sum of the parts. As another example of LIS organisations' ability to collaborate, writing in the *Handbook of Digital Library Economics* (Baker & Evans, 2013a, 2013b) Jennifer Johnson and Kristi Palmer (Johnson & Palmer, 2013) highlighted 'three of over 30 community partnered digital projects led by Indiana University – Purdue University Indianapolis (IUPUI) University Library':

> Our success in these collaborations is a result of openness to thinking innovatively about digital collection creation and levels of ownership (a community partner owns the original but IUPUI University Library supports the digital version). The fact that IUPUI's mission is rooted in a connection to local community makes these collaborations all the more relevant and our local partnerings increase the types of funding sources to which we have access. As with many digital library projects, our initial years were spent primarily looking for partners, promoting our services, and building our technology core. Over time, we have become a sought after collaborator, with local cultural heritage institutions and for-profit entities (the Indianapolis Motor Speedway being the newest partner) seeking us out as a means of creating digital access to their valuable (often deteriorating) collections. Overall, our allowance of organic relationship development has been wildly beneficial.

This emphasis on engagement with local user communities and the fulfilment of their needs was evident in earlier significant work — such as CREE,
noted above — and the success of the work at IUPUI is clearly linked to
such an approach, which obviously remains both popular and valued.
Derek Mills and colleagues describe later in this volume a project that combines a national approach to standards with what on-the-ground users are
likely to value most. What may have started out as a collection development
tool for LIS staff has been transformed through innovative thinking into
something 'based on the information needs of the user population' and
through which the library can communicate with its key stakeholders. And
while the project described here in ALAO volume 35 is specific to a veterinary medicine library, it has the virtue of using techniques that can be repli-
cated and applied across a whole range of subject disciplines and types of
library. It should be noted that the value of this approach has been much
enhanced in recent years by the librarian's ability to access significant
amounts of usage and related activity data in electronic form, thus reinventing and reinvigorating the traditional collection development role of LIS
staff, albeit in a digital context. Chris Batt's chapter develops this theme
further in the context of future collecting in libraries, archives and museums,
given the likely future push to digital only content in many contexts. John
Robinson's case study also refers to the topic, as does Koltay's contribution,
with special reference to research data curation and management.

Tough financial environments continue to loom large in case studies
such as that written up here by Derek Mills and his colleagues. 'Libraries
continue to operate in a climate of declining budgets and increasing costs'
and this is one key imperative in John Robinson's narrative later in this
book. In such a resource-scarce environment, academic library leaders are
under pressure to make wise decisions in regards to how innovations are
adopted and implemented in their libraries' (Brundy, 2015). Being first or
early in the field always means taking risks. This is true in any field; it is
always clever to be second rather than the first to try something.[7] As Tony
Hall, current Director General of the BBC, has recently stressed, 'the risk
of failure is the price of success'.[8]

Knowing when to make change and at what pace is one thing. Making sure that there
is sufficient time to make the change properly is another. Time to prepare, time to
make the changes and time to evaluate them once made: these time requirements all
need to be taken into account. Short or unrealistic timescales are a major reason for
failure in change management projects ... not least because trying to find immediate
solutions can inhibit more long-term change and fundamental learning. At the same
time, people have differing ideas of time and organizations may be under pressure to

change more quickly than they would prefer, especially where the external environment or even the sector itself is moving quickly ... 'Customers', in particular, have increasingly high expectations of public services and systems, and are unlikely to tolerate steady development and especially the lack of it. Staff also may be impatient for change, perhaps because they see improvements elsewhere that they wish to see introduced in their own organization or because they themselves want a more rapid personal development than is currently on offer. (Baker, 2007)

Carr (2009) analysed the many projects undertaken in LIS in the 1990s and more recently primarily in the UK and the USA, some of which were, ultimately, an 'act of faith', with institutions learning 'the hard way' including by making (sometimes costly) mistakes and getting it wrong:

It became clear on both sides of the Atlantic that library managers − under pressure perhaps from their local user communities, but ambitious also to 'move with the times' − were not generally prepared to wait for published research outcomes before embarking on digital library initiatives ... Most institutions were willing to accept the risks of 'learning by doing' in the digital environment. It was almost as if the question was not 'Can we afford it?', but rather 'Can we afford not to do it?'

The more innovative a new product or service − especially when it is technology based, the more time it will take to get to the point where it is capable of serious, widespread and robust application and takeup. Substantial demands are placed on organisations engaged in significant Research and Development (R&D).

Timing is also crucial: the point at which a new product or service is introduced can have a significant impact on its success. A launch that is too early may result in low take-up and withdrawal of the product or service because the market was not ready for it − perhaps the demand was not there or there were insufficient add-on benefits or support tools to make the product sufficiently attractive. On the other hand, launching a new product or service at a late stage in the development or lifecycle of the underlying technology may be equally unsuccessful − too many other suppliers are already in the market, or the market itself is growing tired and looking for novel products or services. (Baker, 2004)

In retrospect, it may have seemed more than a little foolhardy for some of the initiatives that were launched in programmes such as eLib to be undertaken without proper plans or strategies and little or no appreciation of the likely cost or the economic implications. Prototyping (the 'green shoots' of innovation, as Jo Smedley describes it in her chapter) is nevertheless an essential element of R&D work, not least as a means of providing practical demonstrations of the original innovative idea or concept, though there is normally still a long and often difficult journey to be made to the point of general application and often the involvement of commercial organisations:

> Where LIS departments are involved with R&D projects with external partners over a period of time, there has been a cumulative development of expertise in, for example, electronic document delivery, though it has taken a considerable time for these new products to be fully integrated into mainstream activity. Where this is happening, it is a result of further development by commercial partners rather than in-house work by LIS departments for the simple reason that they (or their parent bodies) do not have the capacity to maintain and further develop the systems past the prototype stage. (Baker, 2004)

As Carr (2009) points out, these first-in-the-field projects nevertheless achieved much in terms of innovation, despite − or perhaps even because of − the significant risks involved in doing something that had not been done before, or had not been done previously on a substantial scale. 'The investment and risk-taking required by a pioneer will be very high, but the rewards will be equally significant if the decision is a good one' (Baker, 2004). For example, 'Michigan [University] ... "spawned" the enviably successful JSTOR electronic journals experiment, whose economic sustainability as a worldwide service was by no means certain in its early years' (Carr, 2009). What is not clear, judging by Batt's research, described and discussed later in this volume, is the extent to which collecting organisations (libraries, archives and museums), at least in the UK, but by implication at least in many other countries, are ready for a digital future.

INVESTING IN INNOVATION

Innovation can be challenging, then, and major investment, support and determination is likely to be needed in order to improve the chances of success (Savenije, 2009).

> Any and all new developments cost money, in addition to which there is the significant resource associated with researching, evaluating and testing any new technology before it can be provided as a mainstream service. (Baker & Evans, 2009)

Resources are not always easily available for the necessary research and development that forms the underpinning of so much innovation. 'This is because there is always the need to juggle diverse needs with limited resources in a constant quest for sustainability' (Baker & Evans, 2009). Would the eLib programme have even started, let alone been so successful, if there had not been significant government funding and support over a long period of time, however pressing the need to change and regardless of the ambition and drive of the leading libraries and staff of the era? Certainly, it is unlikely that the major software development programmes (involving a number of commercial partners) that formed an integral part of many eLib projects would have occurred if there had not been significant political and financial backing at national level. Equally, it is just as improbable that the significant R&D work and product and service proto-typing carried out by the UK's JISC that led to a number of substantial commercial 'spin-offs' would have happened without the major government-backed programmes of work over a number of years. As Carr noted:

> The key role of JISC and of eLib in accelerating the move towards a digital library approach in the UK has been widely recognised and well-documented. Experimentation of any kind is necessarily expensive; and the exceptional scope of innovation which took place within eLib was possible only because of the sustained investment made at national level. (Carr, 2009)

Looking back at academic library innovations, there was certainly a need for culture change in some areas, and not all LIS staff or their organisations were always as proactive as they might have been, as Walton and Webb note later in this volume:

> We often underperform. We have not done a good job of really understanding what our students are doing or what they expect from us. We've done a very bad job of collaborating with campus IT organisations. We have not even worked well with each other to form liaisons or collaborations to pursue common aims. Finally, we have not taken as much responsibility as we might have done – or done better. (Brantley, 2008)

This is not to say that LIS and their staff have let technology developments or external (to their institutions and sectors) initiatives more broadly drive change, or to believe that they have waited for initiatives to 'come along'; although Derek Law comments later in this volume on the way in which some academic librarians in the UK at least, feeling threatened by significant change, 'waged war' on those who most sought to unseat LIS staff from their premier position (see also Johannsen, 2015 and Mike McGrath's chapter in this volume). However, there were many librarians in leadership roles at the time who took the opposite position, as evinced by the examples cited in this chapter, as well as many of the chapters in this volume of ALAO (as for example Walton and Webb's contribution) and much of the LIS literature, including the many papers to be found in the *Journal of Library Innovation*. In the UK, for example, librarians were innovating before the eLib initiative began, and their 'early' work contributed to the formulation and development of the main R&D programmes, as well as demonstrating the benefits that might accrue from serious investment in electronic library initiatives. Take Lynne Brindley's work at Aston University:

> In the late 1980s I was involved in early initiatives around the now quaint sounding 'electronic campus' developments, and an important national conference of the same title was held in 1998 bringing together key players at that time, sharing experience of trying to bring the electronic campus to reality ... At Aston University we installed the first ubiquitous broadband network on campus, preparing a richer technology infra-structure upon which the electronic library might begin to flourish. We were working at wiring up campuses, wiring up student residences, preparing for desktop delivery of information, and being prepared to consider new methods of teaching in this context ...
>
> The concept of the information strategy was emerging, whereby information and libraries were seen as important knowledge resources to be harnessed and increas-ingly treated as a strategic asset − to underpin teaching and learning and research activities − which needed to be valued and managed ...
>
> Information strategies emerged in the 1990s in universities, with more or less enthu-siasm, and beyond universities the focus was on the discipline of knowledge manage-ment, the concepts of knowledge exploitation for competitive edge. There was a recognition of the increasing economic value of information − of knowledge, both tacit (in people's heads) and explicit (more formal), as a key element of the corporate, assets of the business. (Brindley, 2009)

As evinced by Lynne Brindley's whole career, LIS staff have typically been early adopters of new technology, as demonstrated by programmes like eLib and Jisc's many initiatives over the years and as discussed by Derek Law in his contribution to this volume. *Digital Library Economics* (Baker & Evans, 2009) contains descriptions of other similar national initiatives across the globe. In consequence, librarians evolved 'from mere content providers to sophisticated service suppliers' (Markscheffel, in CILIP, 2007). So there were opportunities − often well taken − as well as threats.

Writing in volume 32 of *Advances in Library Administration and Organization*, Buchanan (Buchanan, 2010) argued that, as trusted provi-ders, librarians were in an advantageous position to respond to the much-changed environment already described here and in many other places (see, e.g., Chowdhury, 2010). Once libraries entered the online world, they were 'moving from a relatively sheltered environment, operating at the pace of the academic enterprise, into one that operates at the speed of web com-merce' (JISC, 2008) and away from the 'dependency culture' that mitigated against exposure to risk and the need to be adventurous (Law, 2013), as noted also in Walton and Webb's chapter. However, it needs more than just innovative approaches and a willingness to take risks to be successful. As Buchanan continued, it requires 'integrated strategic and enterprise architecture planning' across a complex matrix of variables ... While challenging, such integrated planning should be regarded as an opportunity for the library to evolve as an enterprise in the digital age, or at minimum, to simply keep pace with societal change and alternative service providers' (Buchanan, 2010).

Once major technological developments began to impact seriously upon LIS provision, then librarians could no longer innovate without serious help from other sources. Partnership working came to the fore, as for example at the University of Hull, a library service long involved in the development of services in association with the institution's computing service (Wallace, 1989), though, rightly, the project leaders recognised where the most important partnership of all would lie:

> A key part of investigating options for proactive presentation of resources within institutional environments is identifying where staff and resource outside the library can assist, and where there are likely to be dependencies. Libraries already depend on computing services for many aspects of their electronic resource infrastructure. Where the library does not have control over institutional environments, working in partnership with those who do is likely to open up potential for incorporation of library resources in ways that the library itself would not have been able to do alone. The ultimate partnership is with those end-users who require and will use the resources. Bringing the resources to them in a way that invites them to try them out and adds value to their information gathering offers great potential. (Awre, 2009)[9]

John Robinson's case study later in this book offers a valuable insight into similar partnership working. In addition, therefore, a whole range of strategic alliances, whether arranged 'vertically' between organisations from different sectors or 'horizontally', integrating different elements of one *organisation* or a group of similar organisations have developed:

> Organisations that engage in 'vertical' relationships with suppliers and collaborations with suppliers are better placed ... than others. At the same time, strategic 'horizontal' relationships (eg with other LIS departments in the same region, or covering the same subject areas) allow institutions to harness technology collectively ... This development of a critical mass is particularly valuable where emerging technologies require a standards base. (Baker, 2004)

Collaborations and partnerships, then, have done much to ensure that LIS as a subject area has been in the lead in terms of the application of new technologies, ways of working and delivery of content and services to users, especially where there has a been a critical mass of innovation and development, though it should be noted that this has not always been the case:

> It is, however, a matter of debate as to the long-term cognitive value of the 'scatter-gun' approach adopted by [some] initiatives: the activities were spread so thinly across the country that the expertise gained was perhaps not as effectively disseminated or retained as it might have been. (Carr, 2009; see also Ball, 2009)

As Brindley (2009) comments:

> The scale of ... these challenges is such that solutions are not going to come through small projects and experimentation that so characterised the digital library work of the 1990s, or indeed through independent institutional investment. We have to submerge autonomy and move towards much wider organisational collaborations and a much greater mix of players, whether from the private or from the public sector. The concept of national or international shared services – which for reasons of economy need to be conceived and delivered at scale – should be a fundamental part of our thinking ... This combination of individualisation and local engagement and global partnerships appears necessary for future success.

Brindley (2009) continues by determining that collaborative solutions will be needed increasingly, often – especially in larger projects – through public and private partnerships, together with 'open innovation and the participation of expert amateurs':

> There are interesting parallels between private sector developments and the LIS sector. Over the last fifteen years, there has been a move towards the 'extended firm', where communications networks in particular have enabled several organizations to work closely together to spread the risks involved in research and development through close strategic alliances. This approach has also become popular in the UK LIS sector, for example, with the strategic aim of co-operation between libraries, notably through the Internet, both to improve performance (as for example in respect of access to special collections) and to spread the costs of provision. (Baker, 2004)

Thus the many and varied case studies in this volume of ALAO and other publications by the present editors such as A *Handbook of Digital Library Economics* (Baker & Evans, 2013a, 2013b) provide evidence, amongst many other recent studies, of significant innovation in LIS. But even at national and international levels in LIS work, it is more about innovation rather than invention and about application rather than design, for the simple reason that:

> The global nature of technological change means that it is virtually impossible to control or channel technologies; it is more a question of managing their impact and integrating them to best effect within our organizations whilst trying to influence the wider future development of those technologies. (Baker, 2004)

SUSTAINABILITY

Studies of digital library economics (Baker & Evans, 2009, 2013a, 2013b) show that while the involvement and intervention of major agencies — including government — can enable new inventions or innovations to develop, there comes a point when the product or service being developed has to become sustainable without such support (Guthrie, Griffiths, & Maron, 2008). As Derek Law points out (Law, 2013), even projects that are set up for the public good have to be sustainable, for 'without sustainability there is no long term, and any benefits envisaged can either not be realised, or only fleetingly … It is about thinking and planning for the long term, not least in order to ensure that up-front investment results in long-term benefit for the key stakeholders — funders, users, subscribers, and so on' (Baker & Evans, 2013a, 2013b):

> Ensuring sustainability requires taking long hard looks at the environment and the service or collection required, including in relation to costs … sustainability is also about preservation and the risks associated with losing data if financial sustainability is not achieved. (Baker & Evans, 2009)

Even universities, often deeply conservative institutions (Porter, 2015) are being challenged with the development of disruptive alternatives to their provision of learning and teaching, as Smedley discusses later in this book. While the MOOC (Massive Open Online Courses) phenomenon may pass into oblivion in due course, it certainly has the potential to challenge higher education institutions (Christensen, 2013) in the way that the development of the Internet in the 1990s and more recently led to discontinuous transformation of LIS provision:

> MOOCs are the latest step in the development of the disruptive online learning technology continuum. Although the systems that are used in MOOCs may not be particularly new or advanced from a technical perspective … the scale at which they are being used, with class sizes typically in the thousands, and the large numbers of institutions that are investing significant resources and reputation in them, mean that they are having a marked impact on how we think about higher education. (Porter, 2015)

Thankfully, as already stressed, LIS leaders are good innovators (Rowley, 2011; Walton, 2008) and continue to be so, as noted throughout this volume and, for example in Walton and Webb's chapter with reference in particular to leadership and creativity in innovation. Take project MUSE, whose approach to collaboration is echoed and supported by Walton and Webb's conclusions later in this volume of *Advances* and reinforced by John Robinson's extended case study:

The critical success factor has been the organisation's vision, strategy and ability to evolve 'in dynamic ways', supported by collaborative approaches and tiered pricing structures. MUSE leaders were – and are – also willing to take risks. The end result has been an attractive product that people want to buy into because – as for example in the case of libraries and the need to make savings – it gives them what they want and need. In other words, it adds value at a price or a cost they can afford. (Smith, 2013)

'Begin work on planning for sustainability as soon as possible' is a key lesson from successful innovatory projects, as for example Chronopolis (Minor & Kozbial, 2013). Implicit in this dictum is the need to be flexible (much as discussed by Smedley later in her chapter), and to accept that organisational change – as for example from public to private or from 'free' to 'fee' – has to be embraced in order to ensure sustainability. Iterative approaches to economic and business modelling will also be essential at all stages of the product cycle – from early prototype to final, finished, mature offering (as e.g., Kirchhoff & Wittenberg, 2013).

As Lynne Brindley comments 'business models are in flux and likely to remain so for some time' (Brindley, 2009). But in the coming years there will be an obvious need to respond to what might best be termed macro-sustainability; that is, the need to be sustainable at national and international or indeed global levels as much as at institutional, local and regional ones.

From a global perspective, sustainability is an area requiring much consideration. Such is the pace of technological change that it poses a range of questions relating to societies and indeed, nations ... The world is witnessing new challenges, and redefinition of 'norms' [and] the shifting of powers from once powerful nations to nations whose development is very much founded upon and supported by technological developments and the digital age, garnering new capabilities and new positions in the global rankings. Indeed, given that information is power, increasingly, shifts in power from nation states to individuals may be more commonplace.

Socio-cultural change into the future is very much inevitable, and resources, security, privacy, digital literacy and learning, employment, digital data preservation are among ... the areas requiring more significant attention ... There are undoubtedly many new challenges evolving that require our attention as we continue our journey through the post-digital age, as individual citizens, as well as organisations and national institutions. For certain, it is recognised that 'cyber' raises many security questions, with knowledge and information a source of competitive advantage for nations, institutions and individuals. There is an ever growing challenge to retain control as mobility, and the democratisation of everything increases, with the potential for cybercrime and war becoming more realistic in the divide between digital freedoms and 'big brother'. (Smyth, 2015)

Digital literacy and learning are covered in more detail in Tibor Koltay's chapter.

SUCCESS, FAILURE, RISK, APPETITE

With hindsight, it is possible to have perfect vision, as Derek Law notes in a later chapter. It is tempting to look back on previous innovations and innovative applications and assume that the path of progress was smooth and the road to success easy. Quite the contrary: there is no shortage of examples of significant investment in new products or services − typically technology based − that have disappointed the investors (Baker, 2004). It is frequently the case that the innovation has not been fully understood; nor has the application been managed and developed in the broader organisational, cultural and even political contexts that are such important factors in sustainable success (Akintunde, 2015; Baker, 2006; Baker & Evans, 2013a, 2013b).

Take eLib. In many ways, despite the fact that the programme was 'the envy of the world' (Brindley, 2009) there were many ways in which the initiative was less than successful, especially in terms of the various projects actually meeting their original stated aims (Baker, 2004; Duke & Jordan Ltd, 2006; Pinfield, 2004). But then it was a very ambitious and in some ways radical programme, so there is little surprise that not everything worked, especially when it has long been understood that 'even among the best performers, forays of more than moderate reach [in terms of innovation] quite frequently lead to problems' (Peters & Waterman, 1982). Take the question of technology integration:

> ... the fundamental issue ... is of join-up from the start. Earlier electronic and digital library developments were cumulative − incremental and single advances that did not create innovation over the whole. Prior to e-Lib phase 3 and later, integration was often an afterthought ... Given that current work in one area (as for example content creation) will spread into other areas, it is of paramount importance that integration is at the heart of future library development. The emphasis should be on innovative integration from the point of view of the user rather than the service provision, with long-term market research from the start. (Baker, 2005; see also Ball, 2009; Dolphin & Walk, 2008)

Referring back to an earlier major theme of this chapter, Lynne Brindley (2009) comments:

> There are of course many gaps in our understanding of what may be sought in the future and the precise nature of user needs ... And yet if we have learned anything

it is that the market decides. The most advanced technological products have a strong history of failure if they do not excite and please potential customers at a mass level.

But this criticism of innovative approaches is arguably unfair, whether the development has been incremental or radical, as defined earlier. How many inventions have never been successful; how many innovations have failed? Derek Law talks later in this volume of the many technological 'dodos' that came and went or, indeed, never ever arrived. More importantly, how often has failure been a prelude to – and, indeed, a prerequisite for – success? Failure is typically the best lesson that can be learned. JISC's many research and development programmes over the years have allowed for projects not to succeed. Indeed, there are those who have consistently said that 'if it works, it's not research' (Greenstein, 2002). To a certain extent, the CREE project was one such example of a project from which a good deal was learned, even though the original aims were not all fully met:

Many of the issues arising from the opportunity that CREE offered ... take as their starting point that the outputs from the project can be used as delivered. For many projects delivering software there is often a gap between what suffices to meet a project's objectives and what is required for delivering robust services to end-users. This was partly true in the case of the CREE project. The embedding of search boxes in web pages did not require any technical work other than a commitment to implement the approach. The portlets developed, though, were a different matter, as they had been developed largely as proof of concept services due to the emerging nature of the portlet standards. They did offer workable search services, but their usability was affected by a number of factors ... The CREE project always had the intention of developing services that can be used in production. Potential conflicts between the expectations of a project (which may have wider aims and objectives to benefit the community as a whole) and what it can deliver for local use need to be carefully managed when projects are being set up. (Awre, 2009)

Not only this, but the lead institution in the case (the Library at the University of Hull) was unable to take advantage in the first phase at least of the outputs from the project in terms of improving services for its own users. With regard to the eLib programme, Reg Carr (2009) comments: 'the learning process within the projects, as well as more widely through the dissemination of results, was quite considerable. The experience gained by the community, in relation to economic issues as well as to many other aspects of the digital library, became an important feature of eLib's continuing legacy'. This was even – if not especially – where the specific projects did not always complete to best effect. Learning how not to do something is always a valuable process (Baker, 2004), though some projects were almost certainly always destined to fail because of the inappropriate and ineffective ways in which they were set up, as for example the ill-fated e-University project in the UK.[10] One of the many mistakes made in this instance – and many others – was 'not to take into account skills and behaviours, attitudes and cultures' (Baker, 2004) alongside the technological and systemic imperatives and developments. Smedley develops some of these points about failure in her chapter later in this volume.

So these major programmes and projects – successful or otherwise – had an appetite for risk, perhaps the most essential ingredient in any innovatory work (Deiss, 2004). When asking for submissions for *A Handbook of Digital Library Economics* (Baker & Evans, 2013a, 2013b) the editors were looking for hard-hitting case studies that told the full story – success and failure – and that told of all the lessons learned from the projects undertaken, however risky or unsustainable they might have been, and even (if not especially) where the transition from prototype to full-blown product or service has yet to be made, assuming it actually will be. The editors were not disappointed (yet more evidence of the innovatory energy and risk appetite amongst LIS staff when given the opportunity). It is instructive to identify the key verbs from the 'lessons learned' section of the case studies that appeared in the *Handbook*. To begin with, the 'MUSE message' (Smith, 2013) of 'evolve, expand, engage and embrace the future' offers a motif for much of the innovatory work carried out – and still being carried out – in LIS work. Table 2 summarises

Table 2. Key Actions in Innovatory Work.

Action	Area
Allow	Time to innovate; to implement; to manage change
Assess	Requirements to be fulfilled
Believe	Technology can be harnessed to provide solutions
Budget	In detail and with care, continuously evaluating and refining
Build	Best approaches for particular environments when innovating
	Critical masses, of expertise, users
	Robust groups of stakeholders from all key communities and user groups
	Relationships based on trust
Commit (to)	Market research
	Robust teams
	Users
	Usability testing
Communicate (with)	Key stakeholders – notably users and staff – at all stages
Demonstrate	Leadership

Table 2.   (*Continued*)

Action	Area
Determine	What is possible Synergies Extent and nature of innovatory change over a particular time period, where possible
Develop	Rationales for ongoing investment/compelling value propositions
	Robustness Links to other strategies Business and costing models Business continuity plans Roadmaps for improvements and enhancements
Differentiate	Between different business models needed for the requirements of different environments and markets
Embrace	Future chaos
Engage	Continuously with key stakeholders – and especially user groups
Explore	Future approaches and services that will respond usefully to need
Extend	Service delivery models
Fill	Gaps in markets or services
Focus	On quality
Fuse	Expertise and competencies
Identify	Feedback from target user groups
	Minimum viability for a new product or service Gaps in markets or services Relevant expertise Key responsibilities
Integrate	Innovation and improvement into 'normal' work
Invest	Sufficient resources
Involve	Constituents, participants, customers, users
Know	Communities, stakeholders, users, environments, marketsLimitations – of technology, product, service, markets
Learn	From both failure and success
Listen	To users/customers, other key stakeholders
Plan	Continuously
Recognise	Stability and continuity are also important at times of (major) innovatory change
Respond	To users, markets, technology, change more generally
Review	The environment
	Competitors Significant current and likely future ICT developments
Strengthen	Partnerships
Target	Key User Groups

the key actions that evidently form much of the core of innovatory work, as based on an analysis of the case studies in the *Handbook of Digital Library Economics*, those in this volume of *Advances* ... (as for example Koizumi's chapter and his analysis of a number of case studies of library innovation) and Baker and Evans's other collections of essays, papers and reports.

Walton and Webb's chapter in this volume focuses in more detail on the key prerequisites for successful innovation. Most important of all is obviously leadership and creativity – two criteria that are much in abundance in many of the programmes and initiatives discussed here and throughout the volume and much of the other literature cited.

THE FUTURE OF INNOVATION

There is no shortage of writers willing to forecast the future, and this volume also includes many comments and suggestions about what might happen in future years, as for example Derek Law, who also makes reference to Lorcan Dempsey's significant work in the area. John Robinson discusses horizon scanning as well. It is certain that there will be continued turbulence in the relevant markets and sectors, even if the pace of (technology) innovation slows. One lesson to be learned from a study of innovation in LIS over the last thirty years must surely be that technologies and their integration and application have a limited lifespan. However much they may be developed and enhanced, they will eventually be replaced by 'next generation' systems, products and services. Technological innovation – as discussed here and elsewhere in the volume, as for example by Tibor Koltay – will continue to be a major driver in what for many will be a chaotic future environment. Competition will be to the fore as much as collaboration, as Jo Smedley discusses further in her chapter.

But what does 'competition' mean in terms of LIS provision? In the private or commercial sectors, competitiveness comes at least in part from the ability of an organisation to differentiate itself from its rivals However, 'innovation is rarely a source of competitive advantage on its own ... [success also depends on an organisation's] capability, their depth of technical expertise, their marketing skills' (Henry & Mayle, 2002). Indeed, LIS work the world over is characterised by collaboration rather than competition

(Tanner, 2009). Perhaps this is why library innovators have been so successful in making a difference:

> Major debates are taking place around different models of innovation − open and closed paradigms. Rather than relying entirely on internal ideas to advance the business an open approach to innovation leverages internal and external sources of ideas. The knowledge environment of the early 21st century and the changing context of the Internet are enabling and encouraging more openness. Manifestations come in various forms of openness − the open access movement in publishing; the open software movement and also increasingly in open models of creativity and development. This is often contrasted with the closed model of innovation, with an emphasis on protection of rights, protection of Intellectual Property (IP) to ensure just reward for invention, just recompense for investment and appropriate encouragement for new invention. (Brindley, 2009)

Innovation through technology application and enhancement has enabled libraries to continue to add value in the face of alternative sources of information provision that threaten to render them obsolete (Baker & Evans, 2015). Indeed, as already noted, LIS departments are often to the fore when it comes to developing the future 'state of the art', not only within their specific sectors, but also more generally through the provision of technology exemplars that have relevance more broadly.[11] Smedley develops the idea of 'organisational innovation' and its three main components (recognised need, competence with relevant technology and financial support) in her chapter later in this volume, while Vassilakaki and Moniarou-Papaconstantinou and Walton and Webb in their chapters look at the need for creativity amongst LIS staff and how it manifests itself to best effect in a range of environments, as for example the major challenges facing Greek public libraries at a time of significant economic turmoil.

But will that situation obtain in the future? There seems little prospect of many more national programmes such as eLib and their equivalents in other countries at the time of writing. Indeed, the sorts of organisation such as Jisc (now a company limited by guarantee rather than a publicly-funded body per se) talk of consolidation rather than development in terms of both their research and development work and their service provision.[12] Public−private partnerships between institutions (whether individually or collectively) and vendors (system suppliers, publishers and so on) would seem to be one way forward, looking in particular at future supply chains and the likely best and most cost-effective ways of adding sufficient value to attract and retain users at a time when markets − and also products and services (as Derek Law and John Robinson both comment later in this volume) – are ever more differentiated and fragmented. On the one hand, suppliers are often aiming for integrated models of provision to their customers, while on the other, 'unbundling' (Porter, 2015) is also developing as an approach, with product and service segmentation appearing as a response to increasingly diverse market needs and user wants.

But just because collaborative ventures flourish in the future (if they do) does not mean that the priorities identified by LIS organisations and their staffs will be met. What works for commercial organisations – and especially ones that wish to bind in their customers through integrated products and services – does not necessarily fit with the social good that typically drives library and information provision. There is still a need to identify the 'gaps', as Lynne Brindley (2009) described with regard to the eLib programme and more recently and for governments and other related national organisations to empower organisations to fill those gaps that otherwise 'the market' would leave alone. Indeed, Derek Law argues in his contribution to this volume that some LIS staff still remain too closely and unhealthily wedded to 'dead tree' formats – a topic also covered by McGrath in his chapter – even though the (former) users of the library are way ahead of the staff in terms of their ability to see the potential and value of new formats. Smyth (2015) provides a useful description of the previous and likely future phases in the development of our digital world:

> Many commentators refer to the 'post-digital' era – a period of consolidating on embedded technological change where information and the data landscape become more important. While global 'connectivity' was central to the first phase of the digital revolution, bringing people and institutions closer, improved access to information and efficiencies, digital data and information – from a variety of sources, and the capacity to process and learn from such data is considered to be crucial to the next 'revolutionary' phase in our digital world, allowing us to adapt, improve services, and enhance our way of life across a spectrum of areas (health, education, transport, governance and so on).

But there is still the major issue of the digital divide, as described by Akintunde (2015) and as forecast to continue by Smyth and, to a certain extent, at least, by McGrath in his contribution to this volume:

> Since advances and trends are developing at a rapid pace, it is important to recognise that there are substantive differences in the pace of change affecting countries and people, including varying adoption rates and/or impacts, within and between countries

that has led to the use of, and debate around, the term 'digital divide'. The next digital phase will focus on the abilities of nations [and] institutions ... to use information to make decisions, embracing areas such as 'data-driven' medicine, education, resource allocation and economic growth. (Smyth, 2015)

Porter (2015) quotes a helpful categorisation by Ernst and Young of the reasons why an institution might want to engage with a new technology (in this case MOOCs). It has been adapted here to apply to any kind of future innovation:

- Defensive − to be ready if/when the technology takes off
- Offensive − to become a leader in the field
- Marketing − to market the institution, to gain more users/customers, to reach new markets
- Enhance existing provision
- Change existing provision − to offer novel and attractive ways of providing the product or service
- Financial − to reduce costs and hence the price
- Research − to explore the technology in practice and to become a leader in the field

As Porter (2015) summarises:

In many cases, an institution will be driven by more than one of the motivating factors, and [it] is often interested in exploring many of them at the same time. This is understandable, but can lead to a situation where there are multiple strategic drivers that are being explored at the same time, and it can be difficult ... to identify how successful the experiment has been in achieving its objectives.

There is already a well-known categorisation that summarises approaches to the adoption of innovation. Institutions tend to fall into one of a number of types, from leading edge innovator or adopter, through fast follower right down to the last-in-the-field laggards, who normally benefit least from the application of an innovation, technological or otherwise (Baker, 2004). Porter has developed this approach in respect of the extent to which universities have engaged with MOOC technology and its development as a mainstream tool for learning and teaching in their current and future strategies (Porter, 2015). This helpful summary of adopter types, which combines the technological with the business and user-driven aspects of innovation, can be adapted to a range of other scenarios, including those relating to LIS provision. The perceived categories proposed are as follows (adapted from Porter, 2015).

Just as with the more traditional adopter typology, each of these categories of institution has challenges to face in the way it handles innovation, whether it is the advantages and disadvantages of being the ones to lead the way or, at the other end of the spectrum, being in a group which chooses not to embrace the innovation in any significant way at all. Each type of innovator (or perhaps better described as non-innovator when considering the 'laggard' category) will need to determine when, where and how it innovates, bearing in mind that any innovation is best carried out within mainstream activity rather than as a discrete add-on (Baker, 2004, 2007). Not adopting a new technology or a novel approach is a perfectly valid decision to take and, in some circumstances, may be the appropriate one to take. Having said that, how many LIS units now survive which have not in some way been affected by, and responded (through some form of change and development) to the advent of the Internet over the last thirty years? (Table 3).

There is much evidence — as presented here in terms of the descriptions of the major innovative initiatives such as eLib — that co-ordinated programmes of work are likely to yield the best results in terms of both impact and return on investment, especially when, as Jo Smedley describes later, when communities of engagement, especially at the intersections between subjects and disciplines are encouraged to interact. Yet in its early days, e-Lib at least aimed to foster a good deal of local initiative as well, using the 'let a thousand flowers bloom' approach, with all its benefits and disadvantages, as noted earlier in this chapter. Certainly, whatever the merits of

Table 3.   Types of Innovator.

Confident entrepreneurs	Who are investing heavily ... and leading the way in shaping the landscape
Old hands	Who have a long pedigree of investing ... and are applying their experience ... which lends competitive advantage but also brings baggage and some limitations with it
Institutional innovators	Who are investing ... as part of a holistic strategy for institutional innovation
Opportunists	Who have spotted the potential ... to gain specific strategic advantage ... without necessarily making long-term commitment
The cautious	Who are dipping their toe in the water but not willing to take risk or invest heavily
The old guard	Who are circumspect about investment in any innovation because their current elite position makes them believe that there is little or no need to make major changes to their current ways of working

'bottom up' developments, there is no escaping the fact that the building of capacity, understanding and expertise will almost certainly continue to need some form of overarching coordination, even if that comes after the initial experimentation and prototyping. Bottom up and top down approaches are discussed later in this volume by Jo Smedley. Early adopter innovation is unlikely to result in a 'big bang', discontinuous transformation of an organisation, but as the new technology, product, system or service gains momentum, then later adopters will have the option to make wholesale changes in a relatively short space of time. It is a question of whether the adopter wishes to go for 'stall out' or 'stand out' innovation (Chakravorti, Tunnard, & Chaturvedi, 2015). In this context, Batt's research, set out in his contribution to this volume, suggests that many collecting organisations in the UK public sector at least are not yet ready for the digital future that has been forecast here and by many other writers, including Walton and Webb later in this volume. Indeed, even more worryingly, the approaches that have worked to date in terms of innovation in LIS may well not be fit for purpose in the future and new approaches may be needed urgently, judging by Batt's work.

END NOTE

These, then are some of the key considerations concerning innovation in LIS work. But, more than anything, while 'we can count on no shortage of new technologies and delivery options, and new organizational theories and structures ... without vision and implementation by the people in the library none of these advances reaches the [users]' (Chakraborty, English, & Payne, 2013). As Smyth (2015) summarises:

> The future digital landscape is undoubtedly unclear and while future developments are hard to predict, they are likely to come about with the convergence of a number of acting and often competing forces; it is widely recognised that many trends of today have the capacity to shape tomorrow − the 'post-digital' era ... Planning ICT needs in the future will be more difficult, with the inevitability that fixed content becoming of lesser relevance is ever-increasing, especially as the technological change windows are ever smaller, and adoption and investment by organisations requires significant attention by way of decision making and expected needs in the near future.

Above all, therefore, 'the ability to demonstrate leadership ... will be essential ...' (Brazier, 2015; see also Walton and Webb's chapter and John Robinson's case study later in this volume) in order that LIS provision continues to evolve and (re-)innovate as an 'iconic element', in Derek

Law's words at the end of his chapter, especially in a completely different environment from that in which libraries currently exist and operate. The best LIS organisations will survive, develop, sustain and be sustainable through innovation and improvement. They will do this by ensuring that they see themselves in ways which the users want and need them to be seen; and by maintaining and sustaining the best of all that they have ever been with the best of all that they can and should be in the future.

NOTES

1. http://www.libraryservices.nhs.uk/document_uploads/LQAF/Recognising_and_Rewarding_Innovation_in_NHS_LKS_June_2012.pdf.
2. http://www.ukoln.ac.uk/services/lic/newlibrary/full.html.
3. Here defined as 'the bringing together of different technologies, processes, systems, activities, organizations or all of these to form a new product, process, service or technology, the aim being to progress by improving, innovating or even inventing' (Baker, 2004).
4. There were three basic phases to e-Lib (Baker, 2007):

Phase	Description
1	The 'let a hundred flowers bloom' period, with a wide range of programmes and projects being approved or commissioned in the wake of the Follett Report's recommendations. The aim was to look at the many ways in which ICT could be applied to library services to best effect
2	This was a time of turning projects into products or services, and of ensuring a complete portfolio of activities that covered the whole spectrum of library activities. The emphasis was frequently on scalability, and on co-operative solutions
3	This was the integrative phase, designed to bring together the various strands and initiatives, and to continue the push towards viable and coherent digitally-based services.

5. http://www.artscouncil.org.uk/media/uploads/pdf/Envisioning_the_library_of_the_future_phase_1_a_review_of_innovations_in_library_services.pdf.
6. http://www.surf.nl.
7. https://en.wikipedia.org/wiki/Advanced_Passenger_Train.
8. http://cardiffbusinessclub.org/product/tony-hall/.
9. See also http://www.researchgate.net/publication/238324864_Service_innovation_in_academic_libraries_Is_there_a_place_for_the_customers.
10. House of Commons, Education and Skills Committee, 2004–5. *UK e-University*. 3rd Report, 3.

11. Many writers have stressed the need for a full appreciation of the 'state of the art' when dealing with strategic technology management and technological innovation and improvement. This state is also difficult to define at any one moment for the simple reason that, as already stated, invention and innovation in technological environments is moving so quickly that any description would be out of date by the time it was written! There is also a need to differentiate between the *current* state of the art (i.e., what the best organisations in the field are using or doing) and the *advanced* state of the art (what research and development and 'cutting' or 'leading' edge institutions are using or doing, and which may well become the current state of the art when the technology is adopted more widely. One of the key aspects of strategic technology management, of course, is to anticipate what future current states of the art will be and anticipate that altered state accordingly (Baker, 2004).

12. https://www.jisc.ac.uk.

REFERENCES

Abrahamson, E. (2000). Change without pain. *Harvard Business Review, 78*(4), 75–79.

Akintunde, S. (2015). People's technology: Where is the line? In D. Baker & W. Evans (Eds.), *Digital information strategies: From applications and content to libraries and people* (pp. 117–130). Oxford: Chandos.

Awre, C. (2009). The CREE project: A case study on the novel delivery of search-related library services and its economic implications. In D. Baker & W.Evans (Eds.), (2009) *Digital library economics: An academic perspective* (pp. 247–264). Oxford: Chandos.

Baker, D. (1991). From inter-library loan to document delivery. *Assignation: ASLIB Social Sciences Information Group Newsletter, 8,* 24–26.

Baker, D. (1992). Access versus holdings policy with special reference to the University of East Anglia. *Interlending and Document Supply, 20*(4), 131–137.

Baker, D. (1994a). Document Delivery: The UEA Experience. *Computers In Libraries International 1994: Proceedings of the 8th annual conference,* London, Meckler.

Baker, D. (1994b). Document delivery: The UEA experience. *Vine, 95,* 12–15.

Baker, D. (1998). The multimedia librarian in the twenty-first century: The viewpoint of a university librarian. *Librarian Career Development, 6*(10), 3–10.

Baker, D. (2004). *The strategic management of technology: A guide for library and information services.* Oxford: Chandos.

Baker, D. (2005). *Digital library development to 2010.* Unpublished final report and routemap. Joint Information Systems Committee, Bristol.

Baker, D. (2006). Digital library futures: A UK HE and FE perspective. *Interlending and document supply, 34*(1), 4–8.

Baker, D. (2007). *Strategic change management in public sector organisations.* Oxford: Chandos.

Baker, D. (2007). Combining the best of both worlds: The hybrid library. In R. Earnshaw & J. Vince (Eds.), *Digital convergence: Libraries of the future* (pp. 95–106). London: Springer.

Baker, D. (2008). From needs and haystacks to elephants and fleas: Strategic information management in the information age. *New Review of Academic Librarianship, 14*(1–2), 1–16.

Baker, D. (2013). Beyond space: Access is all — Or is it? In L. Watson (Ed.), *Better library and learning space: Projects, trends and ideas* (pp. 151–158). London: Facet.

Baker, D. (2014). Guest editorial — Resource discovery and delivery: Back to the future. *Interlending and Document Supply, 42*(4), 144–146.

Baker, D., & Evans, W. (2007). From holdings to access — And back. *Interlending and Document Supply, 35*(2), 85–91.

Baker, D., & Evans, W. (2009). *Digital library economics: An academic perspective.* Oxford: Chandos.

Baker, D., & Evans, W. (2011). *Libraries and society: Role, social responsibility and future challenges.* Oxford: Chandos.

Baker, D., & Evans, W. (2013a). *A handbook of digital library economics.* Oxford: Chandos.

Baker, D., & Evans, W. (2013b). *Trends, discovery and people in the digital age.* Oxford: Chandos.

Baker, D., & Evans, W. (2015). *Digital information strategies: From applications and content to libraries and people.* Oxford: Chandos.

Ball, R. (2009). Digital library economics: International perspectives — The German perspective. In D. Baker & W. Evans (Eds.), *Digital library economics: An academic perspective* (pp. 130–144). Oxford: Chandos.

Barras, R. (1986). Towards a theory of innovation in services. *Research Policy, 15,* 161–173.

Barras, R. (1990). Interactive innovation in financial and business services. *Research Policy, 19,* 215–237.

Batt, C. (2015). Strategic futures for digital information services. In D. Baker & W. Evans (Eds.), *Digital information strategies: From applications and content to libraries people* (pp. 23–38). Oxford: Chandos.

Bitter-Rijpkema, M. E., Verjans, S., & Bruijnzeels, R. (2012). The library school: Empowering the sustainable innovation capacity of new librarians. *Library Management, 33*(1/2), 36–49. doi:10.1108/01435121211203301124

Brantley, P. (2008). Architectures for collaboration: Rules and expectations of digital libraries. *Educause Review, 43*(2), 30–32, 34, 36, 38. Retrieved from http://connect.educause.edu/Library/EDUCAUSE + Review/ArchitecturesforCollabora/46313

Brazier, C. (2015). Great libraries? Good libraries? Digital collection development and what it means for our great research collections. In D. Baker & W. Evans (Eds.), *Digital information strategies: From applications and content to libraries people* (pp. 41–56). Oxford: Chandos.

Brindley, L. (2009). Foreword: Digital library economics: An introduction. In D. Baker & W. Evans (Eds.), *Digital library economics: An academic perspective* (pp. xiii–xxvi). Oxford: Chandos.

Brundy, C. (2015). Academic libraries and innovation: A literature review. *Journal of Library Innovation, 6*(1), 22–39. Retrieved from http://www.libraryinnovation.org/article/view/420/625

Buchanan, S. (2010). Planning strategically designing architecturally: A framework for digital library services. In A. Woodsworth (Ed.), *Advances in librarianship* (p. 32). Bingley, UK: Emerald Group Publishing Limited.

Carpenter, L., & Milloy, C. (Eds.). (2007). *Digital images in education: Realising the vision.* London: JISC Collections.

Carr, R. (2007). *The academic research library in a decade of change.* Oxford: Chandos.

Carr, R. (2009). A history of digital library economics. In D. Baker & W. Evans (Eds.), *Digital library economics: An academic perspective* (pp. 57–70). Oxford: Chandos.

Castelli, D. (2006). Digital libraries of the future – And the role of libraries. *Library Hi Tech*, *24*(4), 496–503.

Chakraborty, M., English, M., & Payne, S. (2013). Restructuring to promote collaboration and exceed user needs: The Blackwell library access services experience. *Journal of Access Services*, *10*(2), 90–101.

Chakravorti, B., Tunnard, C., & Chaturvedi, R. S. (2015). Where the digital economy is moving fastest. *Harvard Business Review*. Retrieved from https://hbr.org. Accessed on February 19.

Chan, D. L. H., & Spodick, E. (2014). Space development – A case study of HKUST library. *New Library World*, *115*(5/6), 250–262.

Chan, D. L. H., & Spodick, E. F. (2015). Transforming libraries from physical to virtual. In D. Baker & W. Evans (Eds.), *Digital information strategies: From applications and content to libraries people* (pp. 103–116). Oxford: Chandos.

Chowdhury, G. (2010). From digital libraries to digital preservation research: The importance of users and context. *Journal of Documentation*, *66*(2), 207–223.

Christensen, G., Steinmetz, A., Alcorn, B., Bennett, A., Woods, D., & Emanuel, E. J. (2013). *The MOOC phenomenon: Who takes massive open online courses and why?* Retrieved from http://papers.ssrn.com/sol3/papers.cfm?abstract_id=2350964

CILIP. (2007). Online information 2007. *Library and Information Update*, *6*(11).

Curtis, G. (2012). *Academic libraries of the future: Scenarios beyond 2020*. British Library. London/Bristol: British Library/Jisc. Retrieved from http://www.futurelibraries.info/content/system/files/Scenarios_beyond_2020_ReportWV.pdf

Deiss, K. J. (2004). Innovation and strategy: Risk and choice in shaping user-centered libraries. *Library Trends*, *Summer*, 17–32. Retrieved from http://liaisonprograms.pbworks.com/w/file/fetch/11033922/deiss.pdf

Dolphin, I., & Walk, P. (2008). *Towards a Strategic Approach to the Integrated Information Environment*. Unpublished JISC discussion document.

Duke, & Jordan Ltd. (2006). *Impact study of the JISC eLib programme*. Retrieved from http://www.jisc.ac.uk/publications/publications/elibimpactstudyreport.aspx

Eccles, T. (1996). *Succeeding with change: Implementing action-driven strategies*. Berkshire: McGraw-Hill.

Estelle, L. (2009). Cost-effective decision-making in collection building. In D. Baker & W. Evans (Eds.), *Digital library economics: An academic perspective* (pp. 211–227). Oxford: Chandos.

ESYS Consulting (2001). *Summative evaluation of phase 3 of the eLib initiative: Final report summary*. London: ESYS Consulting.

Feather, J. (2004). *The information society: A study of continuity and change* (4th ed.). London: Facet.

Follett, B. (1993). *Joint funding councils' libraries review group report*. London: The Funding Councils.

Greenaway, J. (1997). *The Coordinated Interlibrary Loan Administration Project [CILLA]: Final report & recommendations of the feasibility study*. Canberra: AVCC.

Greenstein, D. (2002). *Next generation digital libraries?* Proceedings of the second ACM/IEEE-CS joint conference in digital libraries, Portland, OR. July 14–18, 2002. New York: ACM.

Guthrie, K., Griffiths, R., & Maron, N. (2008). Sustainability and revenue models for online academic resources. Ithaca. Retrieved from http://sca.jiscinvolve.org/files/2008/06/sca_ithaka_sustainability_report-final.pdf

Hamilton, V. (2004). Sustainability for digital libraries. *Library Review, 53*(8), 392–395.

Henry, J., & Mayle, D. (Eds.). (2002). *Managing innovation and change* (2nd ed.). London: Open University Business School in association with Sage.

Higher Education Consultancy Group. (2006). *A feasibility study on the acquisition of e-books by HE libraries and the role of JISC.* Bristol: JISC.

Hyams, E. (2010). Where next for the serials crisis? *Library and Information Gazette, June,* 4.

Johannsen, C. G. (2015). From clients to participants – How information technology impacts relationships between professionals and users. In D. Baker & W. Evans (Eds.), *Digital information strategies: From applications and content to libraries people* (pp. 157–166). Oxford: Chandos.

Johnson, J. A., & Palmer, K. (2013). Organic, symbiotic, digital collection development. In D. Baker & W. Evans (Eds.), *A handbook of digital library economics* (pp. 59–66). Oxford: Chandos.

Joint Information Systems Committee [JISC]. (2008). Libraries unleashed. *Guardian supplement,* April 22.

Kingston, W. (2000). Antibiotics, invention and innovation. *Research Policy, 29,* 679–710.

Kirchhoff, A., & Wittenberg, K. (2013). Sustainable economic models: Portico. In D. Baker & W. Evans (Eds.), *A handbook of digital library economics* (pp. 143–154). Oxford: Chandos.

Law, D. (2013). The universal library: Realizing Panizzi's dream. In D. Baker & W. Evans (Eds.), *A handbook of digital library economics* (pp. 233–246). Oxford: Chandos.

Lee, S. (Ed.). (1997). *Economics of digital information: Collection, storage and delivery.* New York, NY: Haworth Press.

McGrath, M. (2009). To be or not to be: Prospects for document supply in the digital library. In D. Baker & W. Evans (Eds.), *Digital library economics* (pp. 193–210). Oxford: Chandos.

Minor, D., & Kozbial, A. (2013). The Chronopolis digital network: The economics of long-term preservation. In D. Baker & W. Evans (Eds.), *A handbook of digital library economics* (pp. 115–124). Oxford: Chandos.

Molaro, A., & White, L. L. (2015). *The library innovation toolkit.* American Library Association.

Noori, H. (1990). *Managing the dynamics of new technology: Issues in manufacturing management.* New Jersey, NJ: Prentice Hall.

Parry, J. (2008). Librarians do fly: Strategies for staying aloft. *Library Management, 29*(1/2), 41–50. Retrieved from http://dx.doi.org/10.1108/01435120810844630

Partridge, H., Lee, J., & Munro, C. (2010). Becoming "Librarian 2.0": The skills, knowledge, and attributes required by library and information science professionals in a web 2.0 world (and beyond). *Library Trends, 59,* 315–335. Retrieved from http://muse.jhu.edu/journals/lib/summary/v059/59.1-2.partridge.html

Peters, T., & Waterman, R. (1982). *In search of excellence.* New York, NY: Harper & Row.

Pinfield, S. (2004). eLib in retrospect: A national strategy for digital library development in the 1990s. In J. Andrews & D. Law (Eds.), *Digital libraries* (pp. 19–34). Aldershot: Ashgate.

Porter, S. (2015). *To MOOC or not to MOOC: How can online learning help to build the future of higher education?* Oxford: Chandos.

Rowley, J. (2011). Should your library have an innovation strategy? *Library Management, 32*(4/5), 251–265.

Rusbridge, C. (1998). Towards the hybrid library. *D-Lib Magazine,* 4(7/8).

Savenije, B. (2009). Digital library economics: International perspectives – The Dutch perspective. In D. Baker & W. Evans (Eds.), *Digital Library economics: An academic perspective* (pp. 145–160). Oxford: Chandos.

Smith, A. (2003). Issues in sustainability: Creating value for online users. *First Monday, 8*(5).

Smith, C. (2015). Presence, permeability and playfulness: Future library architecture in the digital era. In D. Baker & W. Evans (Eds.), *Digital information strategies: From applications and content to libraries and people* (pp. 227–244). Oxford: Chandos.

Smith, D. (2013). Project MUSE. In D. Baker & W. Evans (Eds.), *A handbook of digital library economics* (pp. 47–58). Oxford: Chandos.

Smyth, C. (2015). 'Where' matters: Keeping a pace with Geo-ubiquity in a digital world. In D. Baker & W. Evans (Eds.), *Digital information strategies: From applications and content to libraries and people* (pp. 167–184). Oxford: Chandos.

Starr, J. (2013). EZID: A digital library data management service. In D. Baker & W. Evans (Eds.), *A handbook of digital library economics* (pp.175–184). Oxford: Chandos.

Tanner, S. (2009). The economic future for digital libraries: A 2020 vision. In D. Baker & W. Evans (Eds.), *Digital library economics: An academic perspective* (pp. 291–310). Oxford: Chandos.

Tavistock Institute. (1998). *Electronic libraries programme: Synthesis of 1997 project annual reports.* Tavistock Institute, London.

Tavistock Institute. (2000). *Synthesis of eLib annual reports: Phase 2 and phase 3.* Tavistock Institute, London.

Townsend, A. (2013). *Smart cities. Big data, civic hackers and the quest for a new utopia.* New York, NY: W.W. Norton & Company.

Van de Pas, J., van Bussel, G.-J., Veenstra, M., & Jorna, F. (2015). Digital data and the city: An exploration of the building blocks of a smart city architecture. In D. Baker & W. Evans (Eds.), *Digital information strategies: From applications and content to libraries and people* (pp.185–198). Oxford: Chandos.

Vassilakaki, E. (2015). Knowing your users, discovering your library: An overview of the characteristics of user generations. In D. Baker & W. Evans (Eds.), *Digital information strategies: From applications and content to libraries and people* (pp. 215–224). Oxford: Chandos.

Veaner, A. B. (1982). Continuity or discontinuity – A persistent personnel issue in academic librarianship. *Advances In Library Administration and Organization, 1*, 1–20.

Wallace, L. (1989). From circulation control to information provision: Automation in the Brynmor Jones library, 1980–7. In B. Dyson (Ed.), *The modern academic library: Essays in honour of Philip Larkin* (pp. 81–93). London: The Library Association.

Walton, G. (2008). Theory, research and practice in library management 4: Creativity. *Library Management, 29*(1/2), 125–131.

Watson, L. (2011). From the passive library to the learning library – It's an emotional journey. In D. Baker & W. Evans (Eds.), *libraries and society: Role, responsibility and future in an age of change* (pp. 153–164). Oxford: Chandos Publishing.

Woodhouse, S. (2001). The people's network and the learning revolution. *Ariadne, 29.* Retrieved from http://www.ariadne.ac.uk/issue29/woodhouse/

FACING THE CHALLENGE OF DATA-INTENSIVE RESEARCH: RESEARCH DATA SERVICES AND DATA LITERACY IN ACADEMIC LIBRARIES

Tibor Koltay

ABSTRACT

Purpose — *This chapter describes challenges that academic libraries face in the era of data-intensive research.*

Methodology/approach — *A review of current literature about the topic was performed. The main features of the data-intensive paradigm of research are outlined and new tasks to be performed by academic libraries are explored.*

Findings — *To fulfil their mission in this environment, academic libraries have to be equipped with tools that can be epitomised as research data services and include research data-management and digital data curation. Issues of data quality, data citation and data literacy are also of prime importance for related academic library services that also need to employ*

Innovation in Libraries and Information Services
Advances in Library Administration and Organization, Volume 35, 45–61
Copyright © 2017 by Emerald Group Publishing Limited
All rights of reproduction in any form reserved
ISSN: 0732-0671/doi:10.1108/S0732-067120160000035008

'new' librarians, that is professionals, armed with novel and adequate skills.

Originality/value — *The chapter outlines both background and practice, associated with data-related opportunities and responsibilities.*

Keywords: Research data management; data curation; research data services; data quality; data citation; data literacy

INTRODUCTION

The key focus of service development in academic and research libraries (henceforth *academic libraries*) has been information literacy education, but it is now joined by research data management (RDM) (Corrall, 2014). Still, as we will demonstrate, information literacy is also present in data-related library activities materialising as data literacy.

Research data is data that is collected, observed, or created during the course of any research, in the domain of natural sciences, the social sciences and the humanities, taking the form of text, numbers, images and other types not yet identified (Erway, 2013). Resulting research data sets are unique in the sense that they have been produced and published at one institution, then trusted to another institution (usually a data archive) for curation and dissemination (Mooney, 2013).

Research data is often *big data* that can be defined by using some measures. The amount of data undoubtedly continues to increase at an unprecedented rate, so the first and most straightforward measure is volume, even though views on it also depend on the conceptions in the given field of research, and may be influenced by geographical factors. The second measure is variety, which is about managing the complexity of multiple data types. Data is in motion at an accelerated speed that causes difficulty in capturing and processing it, so velocity is also a measure. Last, but not least, the reliability of data comes into picture (Zikopoulos, deRoos, Bienko, Buglio, & Andrews, 2015).

Obviously, data has always been a fundamental resource of scholarly research, especially in most branches of the natural sciences and a number of other fields involved in quantitative approaches of the social sciences and the humanities. The difference between these and the role of data in today's research activities is in the availability and — perhaps, to a lesser extent — the awareness of the importance of data.

Research data became prominent first of all because research funders have increasingly begun to mandate the creation of RDM plans and the deposit of research data in recognised data centres. Many leading journals also require data sets underlying scholarly articles to be published or made accessible (University of Edinburgh, 2015). Notwithstanding, the awareness of these needs and the involvement of different stakeholders (research funders, data managers, research institutions and publishers, as identified by the RECODE (Policy RECommendations for Open access to research Data in Europe) project) are fairly different by regions and by countries. If there are requirements and mandates, they are also diverse and are enforced to varied degrees (RECODE, 2015). While there is uncertainty, how RDM support and services will be distributed among varied stakeholders, the library is well-situated to be a key player in these issues (Erway, 2013). The possible involvement of libraries has been identified early, for instance, in the form of data literacy courses (Hunt, 2004). Notwithstanding, we can see a revival of the RDM idea since the 2010s. This is one of the main reasons why this chapter will be based on publications that appeared in the latter period.

THE BACKGROUND: THE DATA-INTENSIVE PARADIGM OF RESEARCH

Alongside books and journal articles, research data becomes another mode of scholarly communication. Its complexity does not lend itself to neat, well-defined packaging, thus managing it will require very different technologies, policies and services. As yet, only a small number of disciplines have developed sophisticated infrastructure for managing research data. The majority of researchers, who make data available to others, do it in *ad hoc* ways (Smith, 2011).

The deeper involvement and changing behaviour of differing stakeholders was induced by the widespread availability of research data, resulting from the numerous technological innovations, including the abundance of social media. Full-scale data-intensive research promises new approaches in research methodologies, new modes of knowledge production and new patterns of development. A rapid build-out of this new cyber-infrastructure is forecasted to involve radical changes in the methodologies of numerous disciplines. There is, however, considerable divergence of opinions concerning the depth and pace of the changes. While the strong presence and popularity of social media may lead to transformations that will change the principles underlying research activities, there are several factors that hinder its wider uptake (Koltay, Špiranec, & Karvalics, 2015).

Nonetheless, the potential of data-intensive research has influenced not only the sciences and part of the social sciences. The example of the digital humanities clearly shows that this development has extended to the humanities, first in the form of humanities computing that began with introducing computational methods in literary, philological and philosophical fields in the 1950s, then the appearance of the digital humanities (Dalbello, 2011). As defined by Little (2011, p. 352) 'the digital humanities use information technologies like high-speed computing, textual analysis, digitisation, data visualisation, and geo-spatial mapping techniques in support of research and teaching in fields like literature, languages, history, art history, and philosophy'. At its core, the digital humanities is directed by the assumption that data can be interpreted as texts, and – conversely – texts can be interpreted as data. This thinking is exemplified by the idea of *distant reading*, conceived by Franco Moretti (2005), which – instead of deep reading – applies deliberate reduction and abstraction by using graphs, maps and trees instead of reading concrete, individual works.

The potential availability of research has prompted data-related activities such as data management, data citation and data sharing. The latter would seem self-evident in the natural sciences and other fields, where quantitative research has played a role. However, it is not, because there are numerous barriers to data sharing. For instance, while there is technology to ensure open access to data, technologies enabling data protection and data quality are still subject to discussion, thus we can speak about technological barriers to data sharing. The social, organisational and economical barriers are also numerous. Researchers argue that there are logistic barriers to data sharing, as costs are seriously hampering the sharing of research data. Data sharing requires considerable time and effort and data documentation is a labour-intensive process. It is seriously impeded by the lack of sufficient rewards and incentives for researchers. Unsatisfactory data quality and standardisation also present an obstacle (Sayogo & Pardo, 2013). The latter two have been also identified by the RECODE project, which concentrated on the situation in Europe, but also found legal and ethical barriers, including questions of intellectual property data protection also can inhibit data sharing (RECODE, 2015).

Under these conditions, the results of an international survey of researchers practices and perceptions regarding data sharing show that the majority of researchers from various disciplines have a positive attitude toward data sharing, while only a minority shares their data in the real world (Tenopir et al., 2011).

THE TASKS

Taking the complexity generated by data-intensive research into consideration, there is a need to explore first what tasks have to be undertaken in order to provide assistance for its development.

Research Data Management and Digital Data Curation

Data management is a crucial element in the publication of research data sets and one of the key determinants of open data publication and data curation services, perceived as a new information service, offered by academic libraries (Li, Xiaozhe, Wenming, & Weining, 2013). RDM means caring for research data, facilitating access to it, preserving and adding value to this data throughout its lifecycle. It enables the finding and understanding of data, helps in avoiding unnecessary duplication, validating results, ensuring the visibility and impact of research. Accordingly, it can be regarded to be a set of general activities not specifically attached, but potentially performed by the library (University of Edinburgh, 2015).

RDM requires both data management skills and organisational involvement (Sayogo & Pardo, 2013). It is not always differentiated from data curation, which involves maintaining, preserving and adding value to digital research data throughout its lifecycle (DCC, 2015; McLure, Level, Cranston, Oehlerts, & Culbertson, 2014). Therefore, data curation is broader than data management, but it is still a developing practice, and there are currently no effective ways to prepare people for this hybrid role. Digital curation is performed by individuals who have varied professional experience, many of whom have had no specialist training in the disciplines that they now serve. There is lack of conformity among the places of curation, as they have varied, sometimes idiosyncratic approaches, different attitudes, cultures and practices (Jahnke, Asher, & Keralis, 2012).

Data repositories provide not only one important means through which data may be curated and shared but strengthen the data connectedness of data curation with libraries (McLure, Level, Cranston, Oehlerts, & Culbertson, 2014). Education to data curation is often embedded in standard library and information science courses, and efforts to teach data curation as a discrete set of intelligible practices are both recent and few (Jahnke et al., 2012).

Compliance with the varied requirements of funding agencies has begun with the preparation of data-management plans (DMPs) that require discipline-specific interpretation (Molloy & Snow, 2012), so — as it will be demonstrated below — libraries can fill in this niche.

Data Quality and Data Citation

Paramount to achieve the goals of efficient data-intensive research is achieving and maintaining data quality. The problem is that evaluation of data requires deep disciplinary knowledge. In addition to this, manually appraising data sets is very time consuming and expensive, and automated approaches are in their infancy (Ramírez, 2011). Notwithstanding, the quality of data, determined by multiple factors, is one of the cornerstones in the data-intensive paradigm of scientific research. Its key element is trust (trustworthiness), about which there is extensive literature (Giarlo, 2013; Kowalczyk & Shankar, 2011; RECODE, 2015; Sayogo & Pardo, 2013). One basic component of trust can be approached by answering the question if the given dataset has been reviewed by anyone other than its creator, or not (Smith, 2011).

Standardised forms of data citation would be of utmost importance as they are a potential source of motivation for researchers to share and publish their data, because citation may become a source of reward and acknowledgement for them. There are contradictory views about how widespread are the principles and practice of data citation. Mooney and Newton (2012) asserted that full citation of data is not yet a normative behaviour in scholarly writing. Altman and Crosas (2013) stated that data citation is rapidly emerging as a key practice. Apparently, there is considerable development in this field. For instance, there are documents on data citation standards and practices. One of them was devised by the Committee on Data Science and Technology of the International Council for Science (CODATA, 2010). A citation guide was elaborated by the International Association for Social Science Information Services and Technology (IASSIST, 2012). Thomson Reuters, a major commercial information provider also sees the importance of data citation, so it provides Data Citation Index (Torres-Salinas, Martín-Martín, & Fuente-Gutiérrez, 2014). Supporting diverse initiatives for promoting data citation standards and operating in close collaboration with researchers in advancing reward and acknowledgement for data citation is paramount for academic libraries (Mooney & Newton, 2012).

Data Literacy

Data literacy is tied to the educational role, fulfilled by academic librarians. It pertains to the cluster of emerging literacies that can be found at the intersection between scholarly communication and information literacy (ACRL, 2013). It puts emphasis not only on the data consumer's viewpoint, but the data producers', that is its gives attention to the creation of data (Carlson, Fosmire, Miller, & Nelson, 2011; Schneider, 2013).

For its proliferation it would be beneficial if we could adopt unified terminology by calling this phenomenon *data literacy*, instead of using such diverse terms as *data information literacy* (Carlson et al., 2011), *science data literacy* (Qin & D'Ignazio, 2010) or *research data literacy* (Schneider, 2013).

The definition of data literacy by Johnson (2012) as the ability to process, sort and filter vast quantities of information, which requires knowing how to search, how to filter and process, to produce and synthesise shows that it is closely associated with information literacy.

Following the line of thought of Calzada Prado and Marzal (2013) and of Mandinach and Gummer (2013), data literacy can be defined from a slightly different point of view. As conceived by Koltay (2015), it is a specific skill set and knowledge base, which empowers individuals to transform data into information and into actionable knowledge by enabling them to access, interpret, critically assess, manage, and ethically use data.

THE TOOLS

There is a growing body of literature that reports on investigations of researchers' data-related needs from the viewpoint of the development of library services (McLure, Level, Cranston, Oehlerts, & Culbertson, 2014). Various writings address both the principles and the ways of practical delivery of these services. As to the theoretical underpinnings, Nielsen and Hjørland (2014) underline that the traditional role of the libraries, that is working with documents does not preclude them from providing data-related services, because data, when recorded and supplemented by metadata, should be considered as a type of document. Even though it is often difficult to differentiate them from the tasks themselves, related activities can be grouped under the name of *tools* for providing assistance to the researcher. These tools, named *research data services* (RDS), have two components: the services offered and library staff that offers them.

Research Data Services

While new roles in the scholarly communication of data are emerging, the strengths and interests of the traditional stakeholders remain. Libraries are forecasted to continue their role in stewarding the scholarly record and supporting local researchers (Smith, 2011). In accordance with this, in 2014, the Association of College and Research Libraries identified supporting research data as one of the current top trends for academic libraries. It is underlined that deeper involvement of libraries and different stakeholders would require the identification of a shared vocabulary and commonly understood definitions (ACRL, 2014). In 2016, RDS continues to be deemed highly important among academic librarians in the United States (ACRL, 2016).

An investigation of the impact of emerging technologies on academic libraries shows that libraries are in the unique position to become the managers and curators of data, first of all by digitally archiving the data sets from publications that contain research data and by supplying metadata (NMC, 2014).

RDS, as defined by Tenopir, Sandusky, Allard, and Birch (2014), are offered by libraries and librarians; and consist of informational services, like consulting with faculty, staff or students on data management plans and metadata standards; providing reference support for finding and citing data sets; or providing web guides and finding aids for data or data sets. They also include technical services in the form of providing technical support for data repositories, preparing data sets for a given repository and deselecting them from repositories, or creating metadata for data sets. A few academic libraries already offer RDS and the number of libraries that plan to introduce them is growing. As a rule, these services are extensions of traditional informational or consultative services, for example, librarians help faculty and students locate data sets or repositories. Beyond this, a number of libraries began to offer help in preparing data management plans and in preserving research data.

Lyon, Patel, and Takeda (2014) developed a model for assessing requirements for RDM support in academic libraries, according to which a key activity in developing RDM services in libraries is to understand the variety and state of legacy data and the range of disciplinary practices and norms, which underpin the research data lifecycle.

We see divergent opinions about the readiness of libraries in fulfilling a role in RDM and RDS. While the use of data resources is a key area, where libraries and librarians can take a leadership role and the model for the involvement of academic libraries is there, it is questionable whether libraries will have sufficient resources to meet demand (MacMillan, 2014; Smith, 2011). The RECODE findings suggest a lack of current practices among libraries, especially in digital preservation strategies, as well as in terms of meeting the demands of researchers and users in the provision of data management and support services (RECODE, 2015).

Data Literacy Education

RDS would be incomplete without data literacy education and the demand for data literacy programmes will increase, as RDM becomes a more normative part of scholarship (Carlson & Stowell Bracke, 2015; MacMillan, 2014; Merrill, 2011). As Haendel, Vasilevsky, and Wirz (2012) state, education in data literacy and information literacy should accompany the training of researchers to establish a new cultural standard, especially because researchers often do not realise that their own scholarly communications constitute a primary source of data.

Research on data management usually looks not only at researchers, but also at faculty and graduate students. The latter deserve distinguished attention in data literacy education, as they tend to gain greater autonomy to curate data sets for themselves and for research teams, while there is growing recognition of the fact that instruction in the use of data resources may be relevant at the undergraduate level, as well (Carlson et al., 2011; MacMillan, 2014; Shorish, 2015).

Besides the above audiences, data literacy is also vital for (potential) data librarians (who appear under different names, which will be addressed below) who intend to acquire skills and abilities that are required for fulfilling their role as researchers' effective and efficient supporters.

Even if the above multiplicity of target audiences exists, it is difficult and often unnecessary to separate the data literacy skills of the researcher and of the librarian from each other. Still, both are needed as they contribute to the development of two distinct and legitimate career paths (RECODE, 2015).

Data literacy education should incorporate both the social and technical aspects of data (Sharma & Qin, 2014). Partnerships with faculty are vital. Parts of education are better thought within a given discipline, thus by faculty, while librarians could capably address other competencies, such as issues of preservation (Shorish, 2015). The ways of providing education depend to a substantial degree on the roles that 'new' librarians will play.

The 'New' Librarian

If librarians want to remain relevant, they have to develop new expertise and much deeper understandings of the research lifecycle (Christensen-Dalsgaard et al., 2012; MacMillan, 2014; Ramírez, 2011; Tenopir et al., 2014). This expertise is not without antecedents. For instance, social science data services have long ago evolved from traditional reference positions. There are also traditional strengths of libraries, such as the provision and possible enrichment of metadata that involve adequate skills (Buckland, 2011).

Besides developing new expertise and making use of old one, libraries can also adjust and reallocate relevant positions in order to make the best use of their existing staff. Even though to a limited extent, they also can hire new employees after identifying necessary skills and knowledge (Xia & Wang, 2014).

The librarians who want to meet the requirements set by the appearance and growing role of data-intensive research, have to acquire knowledge and skills that enable them to answer significant questions, which are at the intersections of storage, retrieval, preservation, management, access and policy issues. They also have to be able to work on issues related to the education of users and data professionals competently or successfully (Kowalczyk & Shankar, 2011).

Scholarly communication is a moving target to a certain extent that does not easily fit into the administrative structure of academic libraries (Thomas, 2013). New librarians thus come under different names. The title *data librarian* has a long tradition (Maatta, 2013; Soehner, Steeves, & Ward, 2010). Another label, put to these functions is *scholarly communications librarian*, whose duties are closely tied to information literacy (Davis-Kahl & Hensley, 2014). Professionals are also often called *embedded librarian* (Auckland, 2012; McCluskey, 2013).

An analysis of job advertisements for librarians, who are 'fluent in the language of scholarly communication' by Bonn (2014) shows that the requirements include master's degree in library and information science and advanced disciplinary degrees, coupled with an understanding of data management and excellence in oral and written communication. Other content analysis efforts of job descriptions for scholarly communication librarians show that a new type of library position is emerging, and is called *data management librarian* (Xia & Li, 2015; Xia & Wang, 2014).

The need for better RDM has also given rise to another new role for librarians: the *research informationist*. Working with research teams at each step of the research process, among other duties, research informationists provide expert guidance on data management and preservation which is the duty of these professionals (Federer, 2013).

Through an investigation of job postings, Li et al. (2013) identified the primary duties, required and preferred qualifications of *scientific data specialists*. The most requested duties were

- Offering consultation and reference services for scientific research and data curation;
- Making inquiries on data curation requirements of researchers;
- Providing users with instruction and training on scientific data curation

Independent of their title, the new librarian's role goes beyond planning, curation and metadata creation and conversion (Tenopir, Sandusky, Allard & Birch, 2013). There may be a need for using technological competencies that range from database design and content management, as well as data mining and programming. Even though the level of required domain expertise and technical know-how needs further investigation, there is agreement that a breadth of skill sets is needed, including personal, interpersonal and managerial abilities (partly mentioned above; Cox & Corrall, 2013). Such a broad view allows the identification of potential roles and potential partner services. Libraries and academic departments can share the work of gathering requirements for RDM. Research support units can be partners in assessing the impact of research data. There can be cooperation with doctoral training centres (or other units with similar functions) in planning RDM, including advocacy and guidance to researchers and administering RDM training (Lyon, 2012).

EXAMPLES FROM THE PRACTICE

Focus group interviews, conducted by Colorado State University librarians among faculty members and researchers revealed both varied familiarity with data life cycles and data curation, and varying awareness of data-management plans. On the other hand, interviewees readily identified, where they need assistance and would easily accept related library services, provided that they are adequate (McLure, Level, Cranston, Oehlerts & Culbertson, 2014). Such enterprises open the road for practice.

Instruction in compiling DMPs is frequently offered in the form of training workshops as it is done at Purdue University Libraries (Witt, 2015) the

University of Minnesota Libraries (Johnston, Lafferty, & Petsan, 2012) and at Johns Hopkins University (Shen & Varvel, 2013b).

The findings of the JISC Data Management Skills Support Initiative (DaMSSI) described by Molloy and Snow (2012) show – among others – that, besides generic RDM principles applicable across all disciplines, there are discipline-specific definitions, examples and exercises. Courses that successfully balance the need for discipline-specific detail with relatively brief and concise training show better delegate retention. From the recommendations, drawn together by DaMSSI, it has to be underlined that working closely with disciplinary experts is beneficial as it ensures that terminology used within courses is accurate and clear. It is also useful to interlace generic examples with discipline-specific ones.

A case study at the John Cotton Dana Library, at Rutgers University, Newark campus led to the conclusion that the ways and spheres of RDS are utterly varied due to different institutional environments and unique user needs. For instance, some institutions might have multiple departments that also provide data-related support, while others might lack research support that library data services can fill naturally. Some users need hands-on tutoring to alleviate their technology anxiety, while other users need comprehensive support. Besides the changing institutional environments, the user's backgrounds and needs, the capacity of the library and the librarian determine the levels and extent of the data services that are delivered. At Rutgers, RDS was provided mainly at the level of assisting researcher's data computing processes in the form of data analysis and presentation that is a middle part of the research process, following the stage when researchers have gathered the data and before publication of their results (Wang, 2013).

There may be a need to develop new models of data management services, as the example of Johns Hopkins University Sheridan Libraries model shows. This model encompasses a continuum that begins with from storage and ends with curation, via archiving and preservation layers (Shen & Varvel, 2013a).

Lyon et al. (2014) provide an overview of existing RDM assessment methodologies, available in the United Kingdom and the United States. They also introduce their own community capability model framework that builds on maturity, capability and readiness. A case study is also presented on how this framework may inform planning for RDM support services in academic libraries. Even though the framework was elaborated by researchers from the United Kingdom and the United States, the case study was performed at Purdue University, similarly to the Data Curation

Profiles Toolkit that was developed at the same institution. This interview-based toolkit is a suite of instruments used to gather information about disciplinary data collections and practice (Carlson, Johnston, Westra, & Nichols, 2013).

The Purdue University Research Repository (PURR) goes beyond its role of storing data and even providing help in preparing DMPs. It offers a suite of services, designed to help researchers in managing their data throughout the research lifecycle:

- Fostering collaboration, among others by enabling collaborators to join a private project space (virtual research environments), where they can share and develop data.
- Publishing, including the provision of DOIs, usage statistics (Witt, 2015).

At the University of Edinburgh, there is also a complex RDS infrastructure. One of its parts, MANTRA (2014) is a free online course designed for researchers, which offers a series of interactive online units to learn about terminology, key concepts and best practices in RDM. It helps to understand the nature of research data in a variety of disciplinary settings, to create DMPs, to name and document data sets and to understand the benefits of sharing (just to name a few goals).

CONCLUSION

This chapter examined the service environment of academic libraries, defined by data-intensive research that changes not only scholarly communication, but requires academic libraries to change their endeavour. To fulfil their mission in this environment, academic libraries have to be equipped with tools that can be epitomised as RDS. They also need to employ new librarians, that is professionals, armed with novel and adequate skills.

As research has metamorphosed through the ubiquitous use of information and communications technologies, Research 2.0, the new paradigm that influences the scholarly record, goes beyond data-intensive science by making use of social media and of alternative metrics of scientific output. Future work of academic libraries will be undoubtedly determined also by these developments, and librarians have to be prepared for meeting these challenges.

REFERENCES

ACRL. (2013). *Intersections of scholarly communication and information literacy: Creating strategic collaborations for a changing academic environment*. Chicago, IL: Association of College and Research Libraries. Retrieved from http://acrl.ala.org/intersections/

ACRL. (2014). ACRL research planning and review committee. Top ten trends in academic libraries. A review of the trends and issues affecting academic libraries in higher education. *College and Research Libraries News, 75*(6), 294–302.

ACRL (2016). ACRL research planning and review committee. 2016 top trends in academic libraries. A review of the trends and issues affecting academic libraries in higher education. *College and Research Libraries News, 77*(6), 274–281.

Altman, M., & Crosas, M. (2013). The evolution of data citation: From principles to implementation. *IASSIST Quarterly, 37*, 62–70.

Auckland, M. (2012). *Re-skilling for research: An investigation into the role and skills of subject and liaison librarians required to effectively support the evolving information needs of researchers*. London: Research Libraries UK.

Bonn, M. (2014). Tooling up. Scholarly communication education and training. *College and Research Libraries News, 75*(3), 132–135.

Buckland, M. (2011). Data management as bibliography. *Bulletin of the American Society for Information Science and Technology, 37*(6), 34–37.

Calzada Prado, J., & Marzal, M. Á. (2013). Incorporating data literacy into information literacy programs: Core competencies and contents. *Libri, 63*(2), 123–134.

Carlson, J., Fosmire, M., Miller, C. C., & Nelson, M. S. (2011). Determining data information literacy needs: A study of students and research faculty. *Portal: Libraries and the Academy, 11*(2), 629–657.

Carlson, J., Johnston, L., Westra, B., & Nichols, M. (2013). Developing an approach for data management education: A report from the data information literacy project. *International Journal of Digital Curation, 8*(1), 204–217.

Carlson, J., & Stowell Bracke, M. (2015). Planting the seeds for data literacy: Lessons learned from a student-centered education program. *International Journal of Digital Curation, 10*(1), 95–110.

Christensen-Dalsgaard, B., van den Berg, M., Grim, R., Horstmann, W., Jansen, D., Pollard, T., & Roos, A. (2012). *Ten recommendations for libraries to get started with research data management*. The Hague: LIBER, Association of European Research Libraries. Retrieved from http://www.libereurope.eu/news/ten-recommendations-for-libraries-to-get-started-with-research-data-management

CODATA. (2010). *Data citation standards and practices*. Paris: International Council for Science: Committee on Data Science and Technology. Retrieved from http://www.codata.org/task-groups/data-citation-standards-and-practices

Corrall, S. (2014). Library service capital: The case for measuring and managing intangible assets. *Libraries in the Digital Age (LIDA) Proceedings, 13*, 21–32.

Cox, A. M., & Corrall, S. (2013). Evolving academic library specialties. *Journal of the American Society for Information Science and Technology, 64*(8), 1526–1542.

Dalbello, M. (2011). A genealogy of digital humanities. *Journal of Documentation, 67*(3), 480–506.

DCC. (2015). *What is digital curation?* Digital Curation Centre. Retrieved from http://www.dcc.ac.uk/digital-curation/what-digital-curation

Davis-Kahl, S., & Hensley, M. K. (Eds.). (2014). *Common ground at the nexus of information literacy and scholarly communication.* Chicago, IL: Association of College & Research Libraries.

Erway, R. (2013). Starting the conversation: University-wide research data management policy. *Educause Review Online.* Retrieved from http://www.educause.edu/ero/article/starting-conversation-university-wide-research-data-management-policy. Accessed on December 6.

Federer, L. (2013). The librarian as research informationist: A case study. *Journal of the Medical Library Association, 101*(4), 298–302.

Giarlo, M. (2013). Academic libraries as quality hubs. *Journal of Librarianship and Scholarly Communication, 1*(3), 1–10.

Haendel, M. A., Vasilevsky, N. A., & Wirz, J. A. (2012). Dealing with data: A case study on information and data management literacy. *PLoS Biology, 10*(5), e1001339.

Hunt, K. (2004). The challenges of integrating data literacy into the curriculum in an undergraduate institution. *IASSIST Quarterly, 28*(2), 12–15. Retrieved from http://iassistdata.org/content/challenges-integrating-data-literacy-curriculum-undergraduate-institution

IASSIST. (2012). *Quick guide to data citation.* International Association for Social Science Information Services and Technology, Special Interest Group on Data Citation.

Jahnke, L., Asher, A., & Keralis, S. D. (2012). *The problem of data.* Washington, DC: Council on Library and Information Resources.

Johnson, C. A. (2012). *The information diet: A case for conscious consumption.* Sebastopol, CA: OReilly Media.

Johnston, L., Lafferty, M., & Petsan, B. (2012). Training researchers on data management: A scalable, cross-disciplinary approach. *Journal of eScience Librarianship, 1*(2), 79–87.

Koltay, T. (2015). Data literacy: In search of a name and identity. *Journal of Documentation, 71*(2), 401–415.

Koltay, T., Špiranec, S., & Karvalics, Z. L. (2015). The shift of information literacy towards research 2.0. *Journal of Academic Librarianship, 41*(1), 87–93.

Kowalczyk, S., & Shankar, K. (2011). Data sharing in the sciences. *Annual Review of Information Science and Technology, 45*(1), 247–294.

Lagoze, C., Edwards, P., Sandvig, C., & Plantin, J. C. (2015). Should I stay or should I go? Alternative infrastructures in scholarly publishing. *International Journal of Communication, 9*(20), 1052–1071.

Li, S., Xiaozhe, Z., Wenming, X., & Weining, G. (2013). The cultivation of scientific data specialists: Development of LIS education oriented to e-science service requirements. *Library Hi Tech, 31*(4), 700–724.

Little, G. (2011). We are all digital humanists now. *The Journal of Academic Librarianship, 37*(4), 352–354.

Lyon, L. (2012). The informatics transform: Re-engineering libraries for the data decade. *International Journal of Digital Curation, 7*(1), 126–138.

Lyon, L., Patel, M., & Takeda, K. (2014). Assessing requirements for research data management support in academic libraries: Introducing a new multi-faceted capability tool. *Libraries in the Digital Age (LIDA) Proceedings, 13*, 131–134.

Maatta, S. L. (2013). Placements and salaries (2013). The emerging databrarian. *Library Journal, 138*(17), 26–33.

MacMillan, D. (2014). Data sharing and discovery: What librarians need to know. *Journal of Academic Librarianship*, *40*(5), 541−549.

MacMillan, D. (2015). Developing data literacy competencies to enhance faculty collaborations. *LIBER Quarterly*, *24*(3), 140−160.

Mandinach, E. B., & Gummer, E. S. (2013). A systemic view of implementing data literacy in educator preparation. *Educational Researcher*, *42*(1), 30−37.

MANTRA. (2014). *About MANTRA*. University of Edinburgh. Retrieved from http://datalib.edina.ac.uk/mantra/about.html

McCluskey, C. (2013). Being an embedded research librarian: Supporting research by being a researcher. *Journal of Information Literacy*, *7*(2), 4−14.

McLure, M., Level, A. V., Cranston, C. L., Oehlerts, B., & Culbertson, M. (2014). Data curation: A study of researcher practices and needs. *Portal: Libraries and the Academy*, *14*(2), 139−164.

Merrill, A. (2011). Library+. *Public Services Quarterly*, *7*(3−4), 144−148.

Molloy, L., & Snow, K. (2012). The data management skills support initiative: Synthesising postgraduate training in research data management. *International Journal of Digital Curation*, *7*(2), 101−109.

Mooney, H. (2013). A practical approach to data citation: The special interest group on data citation and development of the quick guide to data citation. *IASSIST Quarterly*, *37*, 71−77.

Mooney, H., & Newton, M. P. (2012). The anatomy of a data citation: Discovery, reuse, and credit. *Journal of Librarianship and Scholarly Communication*, *1*(1), 1−14.

Moretti, F. (2005). *Graphs, maps, trees: Abstract models for literary theory*. London: Verso.

Nielsen, H. J., & Hjørland, B. (2014). Curating research data: The potential roles of libraries and information professionals. *Journal of Documentation*, *70*(2), 221−240.

NMC. (2014). *NMC horizon report: 2014 library edition*. Austin, TX: The New Media Consortium. Retrieved from http://redarchive.nmc.org/publications/2014-horizon-report-library

Qin, J., & D'Ignazio, J. (2010). Lessons learned from a two-year experience in science data literacy education. In *Proceedings of the 31st annual IATUL conference*, 2. Retrieved from http://docs.lib.purdue.edu/iatul2010/conf/day2/5. Accessed on June, 20−24, 2010.

Ramírez, M. L. (2011). Opinion: Whose role is it anyway? A library practitioners appraisal of the digital data deluge. *Bulletin of the American Society for Information Science and Technology*, *37*(5), 21−23.

RECODE. (2015). *RECODE policy recommendations for open access to research data*. Retrieved from http://recodeproject.eu/

Sayogo, D. S., & Pardo, T. A. (2013). Exploring the determinants of scientific data sharing: Understanding the motivation to publish research data. *Government Information Quarterly*, *30*, S19−S31.

Schneider, R. (2013). Research data literacy. In S. Kurbanoğlu, E. Grassian, D. Mizrachi, R. Catts, & S. Špiranec (Eds.), *Worldwide commonalities and challenges in information literacy research and practice* (pp. 134−140). Cham: Springer International Publishing.

Sharma, S., & Qin, J. (2014). Data management: Graduate student's awareness of practices and policies. *Proceedings of the American Society for Information Science and Technology*, *51*(1), 1−3.

Shen, Y., & Varvel, V. E. (2013a). Developing data management services at the Johns Hopkins University. *The Journal of Academic Librarianship*, *39*(6), 552−557.

Shen, Y., & Varvel, V. E. (2013b). Data management consulting at the Johns Hopkins University. *New Review of Academic Librarianship, 19*(3), 224—245.

Shorish, Y. (2015). Data information literacy and undergraduates: A critical competency. *College and Undergraduate Libraries, 22*(1), 97—106.

Smith, M. (2011). Communicating with data: New roles for scientists, publishers and librarians. *Learned Publishing, 24*(3), 203—205.

Soehner, C., Steeves, C., & Ward, J. (2010). *E-science and data support services: A study of ARL member institutions.* Washington, DC: Association of Research Libraries.

Tenopir, C., Allard, S., Douglass, K., Aydinoglu, A. U., Wu, L., Read, E., & Frame, M. (2011). Data sharing by scientists: Practices and perceptions. *PloS One, 6*(6), e21101.

Tenopir, C., Sandusky, R. J., Allard, S., & Birch, B. (2013). Academic librarians and research data services: Preparation and attitudes. *IFLA Journal, 39*(1), 70—78.

Tenopir, C., Sandusky, R. J., Allard, S., & Birch, B. (2014). Research data management services in academic research libraries and perceptions of librarians. *Library and Information Science Research, 36*(2), 84—90.

Thomas, W. J. (2013). The structure of scholarly communications within academic libraries. *Serials Review, 39*(3), 167—171.

Torres-Salinas, D., Martín-Martín, A., & Fuente-Gutiérrez, E. (2014). Analysis of the coverage of the data citation index — Thomson Reuters: Disciplines, document types and repositories. *Revista Española de Documentación Científica, 37*(1), e036.

University of Edinburgh. (2015). *Why is data management important?* Retrieved from http://www.ed.ac.uk/schools-departments/information-services/research-support/data-management/why-manage-data

Wang, M. (2013). Supporting the research process through expanded library data services. *Program: Electronic Library and Information Systems, 47*(3), 282—303.

Witt, M. (2015). Research data services for compliance, collaboration and scholarship. *Library Connect, 13*(5). Retrieved from http://libraryconnect.elsevier.com/articles/2015-05/research-data-services-compliance-collaboration-and-scholarship

Xia, J., & Li, Y. (2015). Changed responsibilities in scholarly communication services: An analysis of job descriptions. *Serials Review, 41*(1), 15—22.

Xia, J., & Wang, M. (2014). Competencies and responsibilities of social science data librarians: An analysis of job descriptions. *College and Research Libraries, 75*(3), 362—388.

Zikopoulos, P., deRoos, D., Bienko, C. h., Buglio, R., & Andrews, M. (2015). *Big data beyond the hype. A guide to conversations for today's data center.* New York, NY: McGraw Hill Education.

THEORY OF MANAGEMENT STRATEGIES FOR LIBRARIES: TRIGGERS FOR INNOVATIVE AND FUNDAMENTAL CHANGES

Masanori Koizumi

ABSTRACT

Purpose — *The purpose of this research is to describe a theory of management strategy for libraries based on library core values. This research also determines the fundamental rules that cause libraries' innovative changes.*

Methodology/approach — *This research focuses on 16 detailed management cases involving US and Japanese academic and public libraries from the 1960s to the 2010s. It analyses documents related to strategic management, organisation and operations, collected through surveys and interviews with library directors and managers. Based on those case analyses, the researcher identified the strategic patterns of libraries; a strong relationship of services, organisations, core skills and knowledge and environments. Finally, a strategic management theory for libraries emerged as a result of this research.*

Innovation in Libraries and Information Services
Advances in Library Administration and Organization, Volume 35, 63–85
Copyright © 2017 by Emerald Group Publishing Limited
ISSN: 0732-0671/doi:10.1108/S0732-067120160000035009

Findings — *This research constructed a theory of management strategies for libraries. It consists of four general strategies and eight specific strategies. In addition, this research also determines fundamental elements that cause strategic and innovative changes of libraries, and describes a rule for those innovative changes that dictates that library services and organisational structures follow strategy, and strategy follows media format.*

Originality/value — *The originality of this research is in successfully constructing the theory of management strategy for libraries based on library core values. In the library world, most librarians and researchers tend to describe library strategies based on business management theories.*

Keywords: Strategy; library management; academic libraries; public libraries; case analysis; management theory

BACKGROUND

Strategically managing a library requires management skills similar to business management. This is especially the case in the 21st century. In fact, librarians and library researchers have been learning management theories from the business management field throughout the long history of libraries. In the 1960s and 1970s, Kittle (1961) and Evans (1976) revealed that library managers applied theories of business management to libraries several years after business theories were published. In conjunction with the economic depression at that time, some libraries had been facing rapid service changes as well as organisational consolidations. At the same time, librarians have always had a sense of incongruity when applying theories of business management to libraries.

Evans (1976) pointed out that as libraries will be required to provide services at cost, libraries will begin to shift closer to the profit-making sector. Usherwood (1996) also warned against the risk of applying business philosophy and management theories to the library world. Since the library world first utilised business management theories in the 1970s, librarians' concerns about management always centre around the radical changes caused by a business management economic perspective.

Throughout the library's long history, it is clear that libraries have a unique managerial combination of both mission and core functions that makes them unlike any other organisation. Libraries require a theory that is constructed based on their unique priorities as demonstrated by the library's long history. However, there are a few theories of library management that were constructed by researching management in the library field. Although Evans (1976) fairly successfully tried to describe library management techniques, he focused more on daily library work and did not provide a comprehensive theory of strategic management. There are no other researchers describing library management theory based on fundamental library research.

The purpose of this research is to describe a theory of library strategy based on library priority values. As Pfeffer (1993) mentioned, the library management field has long used the same paradigm as for-profit organisations, and researchers need to build a foundation for a new paradigm developed for library management. In order to construct a fundamental theory of library management, we need to formulate a strategy that encompasses all basic and common services from the librarians perspective into a strategic management theory for the library world. This will make libraries become more resilient to external environmental influences, and allow the library director to focus on obtaining a clear understanding of fundamental strategic management for libraries in order to explain it to stakeholders both inside and outside of the library.

Research Methods

If we look at only one moment in the history of libraries, we inevitably see an image of the librarian trying to manage changes without having any clear policies. However, if we look at comprehensive library services, operations and organisational structure throughout the history of the library, we see predictable changes in the areas of knowledge and information, and libraries have reacted soundly to these changes. Furthermore, while the form of knowledge and technical skills hereto fostered by libraries has changed, they have stood the test of time. Libraries could certainly not continue providing these long-standing services without having appropriate policies in place.

As such, we see that in recent years libraries are not without management strategies; rather, as identified by Porter (1980), it can be said that, even if only implicit, libraries have always had some form of management strategy. In other words, although libraries may not have had a written management strategy in the early 1960s and 1970s, a management strategy was implied and the components of potential management strategies most certainly existed.

Thus, we begin this research paper with an explanation of management strategies in business, and afterwards focus on libraries' management strategies. Following this, 16 detailed library case analyses were conducted; nine university libraries and four public libraries in the United States (US) are covered, as well as the National Diet (Governmental) Library, Tokyo Metropolitan Library and University of Tokyo Library in Japan. Most are large-scale libraries, but small- and medium-sized libraries are also included, primarily in the area of organisation and operations (see Table 1).

The advantage of case analysis is that it allows historical investigations, and provides strategic patterns throughout the long history of libraries. Moreover, drawing a causal relationship from descriptions related to cases is possible, although it relies on fewer numbers of research targets (Eisenhardt, 1989; Yin, 2008). Conducting case analyses is appropriate when only a few cases are available, as in current library management research. It is also suited to analysing changes in library organisations within an extended time frame.

Table 1.   Cases for Analysis.

No.	Library	Country	State/City	Type of Library
1	Harvard University Library	US	Massachusetts	Academic library
2	Princeton University Library	US	New Jersey	Academic library
3	Yale University Library	US	Connecticut	Academic library
4	Columbia University Library	US	New York	Academic library
5	Boston Public Library	US	Massachusetts	Public library
6	New York Public Library	US	New York	Public library
7	New York University Library	US	New York	Academic library
8	University of Massachusetts Amherst Library	US	Massachusetts	Academic library
9	Rutgers University Library	US	New Jersey	Academic library
10	University of Hawaii Library	US	Hawaii	Academic library
11	University of Arizona Library	US	Arizona	Academic library
12	Pima County Public Library	US	Arizona	Public library
13	Princeton Public Library	US	New Jersey	Public library
14	National Diet Library	Japan	Tokyo	National library
15	Tokyo Metropolitan Library	Japan	Tokyo	Public library
16	University of Tokyo Library	Japan	Tokyo	Academic library

Additionally, because libraries conducted their operations implicitly from the 1960s to the early 1990s, unlike operations from the late 1990s to the 2010s, management documents from that period are not sufficiently available, particularly in the area of management strategy. Therefore, this study interprets documents on organisational structure and operational areas, which are more explicit than library strategies, as an outcome of strategic decision-making for library management.

In this research, documents investigated consist of four types of data: (1) strategic planning documents; (2) organisational structures and position descriptions; (3) other related documents, such as annual reports, library bulletins, phone extension directories and library handbooks and (4) interviews with directors and managers. The researcher collected this data from each library. Based on those case analyses, the researcher identified the strategic patterns of libraries comprising a strong relationship between services, organisations, core skills and knowledge and environments. Finally, a strategic management theory for libraries emerged.

Moreover, this research paper also takes into account the various library types. Generally speaking, public and university libraries have their own individual principles and organisations, and many different types of management exist. However, management strategies are widely applied to different types of businesses. Regarding management studies, these theories are being investigated across industries. As such, in practical terms, numerous cases of similar management theories are being applied across different types of libraries. In addition, when an explanation on library management is needed by external parties prior to analysing the subtle differences in library types, we must first provide an explanation of the management strategies of these libraries. Consequently, this chapter unifies library types and redefines them in terms of a unified and explicit management strategy from the viewpoint of those affiliated with libraries, services, operations and those organisational structures felt to be ubiquitous. In other words, any discussion of library management must reposition operations ordinarily conducted by libraries as management strategies transcending the type of library involved.

What Is Management Strategy?

The concept of management strategy came from the idea of strategy originally used by military schools, later becoming a part of management studies, as described in Alfred D. Chandler's *Strategy and Structure* (1962). As identified by Drucker (1954), up until the 1950s, functions indispensable to management were often discussed separately. However, Chandler's writings posited the idea that utilising the notion of strategy would unify enlarged functions within the organisation. Management strategies can be compared to onions, where each part of the strategy is a layer. If you peel off each element of the strategy, there is nothing left in the centre. In other words, a management strategy is a concept, and the central concept of the strategy integrates and bands each of its elements (services, organisations and environments).

Through the 1970s, this concept of strategy as identified by Chandler was systematically theorised by the likes of Igor Ansoff, George A. Steiner, Kenneth R. Andrews, Charles W. Hofer and Dan Schendel. Dozens of management studies researchers and business leaders have defined management strategy. Amongst these, Hiroyuki Itami (2003) shared his concise view of management strategies, defining them as 'long-term general plans for organisational activities in the market'.

Management Strategies for Libraries

Management strategies reserved explicitly for libraries were considered in terms of long-term planning for American libraries beginning in the early 1970s. Management strategies at the time consisted of attempts to apply management theory (considered as included in the field of management studies) to libraries several years after these theories had first been introduced (Evans, 1976). Moreover, several of these theories handled demands for management plans from organisations affiliated with libraries; as a general rule, libraries did not proactively implement management strategies themselves. The opportunity to draft management strategies was limited to cases such as when large-scale improvements were initiated by organisations affiliated with libraries.

Thereafter, in the 1990s, a continuous stream of management strategies were required by American libraries. Around that time, with the US at the forefront, worldwide economic conditions were deteriorating, and libraries subject to the demands of stakeholders were being held accountable. Meanwhile, management strategies for Japanese libraries were first considered in earnest in the early 2000s. Many of these involved long-term management strategies.

The Importance of Management Strategies Regarding Library Core Values

Regardless of the library type involved or whether in the US or Japan, the majority of management strategies considered for libraries have rarely been implemented in an appropriate fashion. Instead, management strategy and the actual organisations were often treated separately, with management strategy planning operations and practical affairs of the library frequently not working in tandem. Thus, libraries had little experience when it came to considering management strategies. Moreover, designing management strategies differs greatly from traditional library duties. In a nutshell, librarians were inexperienced regarding the business of formulating management strategies, and implementation thus proved difficult.

Non-profits such as hospitals and educational institutions have recently been targeted, with distinctive management strategies considered for each organisation. This is because for non-profits with distinctly different principles and objectives, it is essential to have a management strategy specific to the organisation in question. In other words, when traditional methods are ineffective, specific management strategies that are consistent with the libraries' primary objectives and unique characteristics are needed, especially as libraries are non-profits.

RESULTS: THEORY OF MANAGEMENT STRATEGIES FOR LIBRARIES

Management strategies for libraries can be explained in terms of general strategies and specific strategies. General strategies transcend library type, and often comprise the services, operations, and operational structures common to most libraries; these management strategies are adopted by all libraries. Libraries continue to utilise these management strategies even as the economic and information environments continue to change, as does the information behaviour of users dependent on this information.

Specific libraries also adopt specific strategies based on their environment and library type. In addition to general strategies, libraries also adopt individual strategies matching their various environments and use these strategies in tandem.

General Management Strategies for Libraries

General management strategies for libraries consist of (1) *subject-based knowledge and information services by collections*; (2) *coping with new media and the increase in document formats*; (3) *effective collection distribution and archival*; and (4) *sharing collections and bilateral cooperation* (see Table 2).

Table 2. General Strategies for Libraries.

General Strategies	Summary	External and Internal Environment Impact on Strategies	Main Organisational Structure	Core Knowledge and Skills
Subject-based knowledge and information services by collections	Provides fundamental library services; libraries continuously provide public services and technical services to the users	Not dependent on any environment	Subject-based organisation, Functional organisation	Special knowledge about subjects and collections Skills for public services and technical services
Coping with new media and the increase in document formats	Deals with the ever-increasing amount of publications and new electronic resources	Outside environment of information technology Changes of user's information behaviour	Media format-based organisation	Knowledge about media format and information technology Skills of creating metadata and classifying both paper and electronic collections
Effective collection distribution, maintenance and archival	Consists of maintaining materials for the user and deploying them in a user-friendly fashion	Collection deterioration over time and changes of information technology	Functional organisation, media format-based organisation, subject-based organisation	Knowledge of media formats and information technology
Sharing collections and bilateral cooperation	Uses sharing systems like OCLC, thereby advancing the joint ownership of collections by which libraries continue to provide their information systems	Library systems' limitation of budgets from the organisations that libraries are affiliated with	Functional organisation	Skills of project management and coordination

The first type of basic strategy, *subject-based knowledge/information services by collections*, is based on public services and the technical services supporting it. Public services and technical services are unique characteristics of libraries and employed by all libraries in the world; these can be considered basic and fundamental library services.

Librarians need to develop, select, acquire, classify, catalogue and preserve collections based on subjects, and to develop the services based on these collections. For this strategy, libraries basically create a subject-based organisation. However, in the history of libraries, budgets have been decreasing while efficiency has been increasing. Technical services have gradually moved toward a functional organisation in search of efficiency, and subject-based organisations currently have an affinity with reference services.

The second type of general strategy is *coping with new media and the increase in document formats*. In an effort to deal with the ever-increasing amount of serial publications and new electronic resources, libraries have begun adopting organisational structures based on the media format they handle. Similarly, libraries are earnestly improving their procedures to manage changes in document formats. Coping with changes to the format of the books comprising the core of the library is an unavoidable part of these duties, which also serve as a general strategy of library management.

For example, from the late 1990s to the present, libraries have been developing E-resource-based divisions in order to cope with the new electronic documents. Librarians in the electronic documents division collected and learned new knowledge on new electronic documents, and developed their new systems and services to provide electronic documents to library users. In the 1970s and 1980s, the same management approach was utilised by librarians to deal with the increasing number of publishing journals and new types of media, such as microfilms, CDs and multimedia. Librarians developed special divisions for each format and learned how to deal with those new types of media format.

The third type of general strategy, *effective deployment of documents and archival*, is directly related to the book collection comprising the heart and soul of the library, and consists of maintaining materials for the user and deploying them in a user-friendly fashion. This strategy is strongly related to the first basic strategy, *subject-based knowledge and information services by collections*, and is often characterised by investigations of this deployment by the subject involved. At the very heart of the library is the book collection; its ongoing maintenance is the most important task faced by the library manager. This strategy is highly related to library buildings, facilities, and space planning in libraries.

Lastly, we have the strategy of *sharing collections and bilateral cooperation*. As with the previous three strategies, this one is also adopted by all libraries. There are limitations on library budgets, buildings and facilities, and one library simply cannot store every type of document. Therefore, all libraries cooperate using OCLC, ReCAP, NELINET, RLG and similar systems, thus advancing the joint ownership of collections by which libraries continue to provide their information systems. For example, in the 2000s and 2010s, Columbia University Libraries and Cornell University Library developed the cooperation project 2CUL, working and cooperating together in order to increase working efficiency. The joint ownership of materials and bilateral cooperation are conducted for both paper documents as well as electronic documents. In the business world, companies do not always cooperate with each other, but in the library sphere, this general strategy of *sharing collections and bilateral cooperation* has been continuously adopted over time.

Specific Management Strategies for Libraries

Specific management strategies are those adopted in response to library types and the administrative environment of individual libraries (see Table 3). Pursuant to adopting general strategies, individual libraries considered which specific management strategies take precedence as they formed their plans in response to environmental factors. The question of which specific management strategies these libraries would adopt depended on their surrounding environment; the adopted strategies were in response to the scale of the organisation, the budget and environmental factors. Accordingly, specific management strategies adopted by the libraries were not necessarily limited to a single strategy, as libraries needed to adapt to their current needs.

Multi-Directional Strategies
Multi-directional strategies are utilised to enhance a wide range of services for all types of users. An abundant workforce and budget are needed to implement these strategies, so it is often considered an appropriate plan for larger libraries. These multi-directional strategies were characteristic of public libraries in times of prosperity, when they were blessed with ample budgets. Examples of libraries utilising such strategies include the

Table 3. Specific Strategies for Libraries.

Specific Strategies	Summary	External and Internal Environment	Main Organisational Structure	Core Knowledge and Skills	Typical Examples
User-Based Strategies					
Multi-directional strategies	Strategies for placing an emphasis on enriching a broad range of services for all users	Prosperous with abundant finances	Subject-based organisation, media-based organisation	Knowledge of subjects Skills of public and technical services	Boston Public Library (until the 1990s), New York Public Library, National Diet Library, Tokyo Metropolitan Library (mainly in the 1970s)
Differentiated strategies for subject specialisation	Strategies for placing an emphasis on proactive fragmentation of the subject to provide specialty knowledge and information services	Prosperous and abundant finances	Subject-based organisations	Knowledge of subjects Skills of education and research supports for university students and researchers	Harvard University Library, Columbia University Library, Princeton University Library, Yale University Library, University of Tokyo Library System
				Knowledge of subjects Skills of library services for children, teens, adults and the physically challenged	Boston Public Library, New York Public Library, Tokyo Metropolitan Library (until the 1990s) (typical of public libraries)

Table 3. (Continued)

Specific Strategies	Summary	External and Internal Environment	Main Organisational Structure	Core Knowledge and Skills	Typical Examples
Strategies to expand remote user services	Strategies for emphasising providing a services for users to receive services without visiting the library	Changing social environment (regional population gains)	Subject-based organisation	Knowledge of marketing Skills of implementation of library construction projects, deployment of mobile libraries	Boston Public Library, New York Public Library, Tokyo Metropolitan Library (from the 1970s to 1980s)
		Advances in information technology and changes in user information behaviour	Functional organisation (particularly organisations based on IT)	Knowledge of marketing Specialty knowledge related to electronic data and information technology systems Skills of IT, remote access services, chart references	Columbia University Library (since the 1990s)

Librarian-Based Strategies

Consultation service strategies	Strategies for integrating provision of all types of library services based on thorough knowledge of user demands	Advances in information technology and changes in user information behaviour	Subject-based organisation	Specialty knowledge related to subjects and media, analytical methods Skills of research support services provided to library patrons	Harvard University Library, Columbia University Library, Princeton University Library, New York University Library, Pima County Public Library (since the 2000s)

				Specialty knowledge related to media and topics, analytical methods Skills of research support services for library user environments	Columbia University Library, University of Arizona Library (since the 1990s; e.g. liaisons, embedded librarians, etc.)
Sophisticated service strategies	Strategies for providing a high level of service supporting the detailed analysis demanded by research to satisfy user needs	Advances in information technology and changes in user's information behaviour	Subject-based organisation	Specialty knowledge related to media and subjects, analytical methods Skills of research support services	Harvard University Library, Columbia University Library, Princeton University Library, New York University Library (since the 2000s)
Strategies to expand editing and publishing functions	Strategies for gathering and editing information for publication or proactive transmission on websites	Market changes and changes in user's information behaviour	Functional organisation	Expertise related to the subjects, editing, publication features Skills of editing and publishing	New York University Library, Harvard University Library
Facility-based Strategies					
Visitor service strategies	Strategies for emphasising the improvement of library facilities in order to allow users to more efficiently conduct study and research activities	Changes in user's information behaviour through development of IT and improvements in small, outdated facilities	Functional organisation	Knowledge of marketing, public service, information technologySkills of managing facility-based services	New York University Library, University of Arizona Library, UMass Amherst Library (from the 1990s to the 2000s), University of Hawaii Library, Princeton University Library (since the 2000s)

Table 3. (*Continued*)

Specific Strategies	Summary	External and Internal Environment	Main Organisational Structure	Core Knowledge and Skills	Typical Examples
Operation-based Strategies					
Service and operational improvement strategies	Strategies aimed at improving service levels for patrons while at the same time decreasing costs	Recession, austere financial environment	Functional organisation, project team organisation	Knowledge of management, public services, technical services Skills of improving library operations and cost reduction	University of Arizona Library (from the 1990s to the 2000s), National Diet Library, Tokyo Metropolitan Library (since the 2000s), University of Tokyo Library

New York Public Library, Boston Public Library, National Diet Library and Tokyo Metropolitan Library. Public libraries adopting this management strategy created structures in response to user characteristics, providing each group of users with individualised services within subject-based organisations.

Differentiated Strategies for Subject Specialisation
Differentiated strategies for subject specialisation involve structural subdivision based on the media and users involved in providing specialty services related to specific subjects. When advancing this specific strategy, it is unrealistic to expect one librarian to become an expert on multiple subjects. As such, structures to be adopted within this strategy involve subject-dependent structure formats in which the structure is fragmented based on the subject at hand. At the same time, librarians must possess a deep understanding of a narrow range of subjects.

With the adoption of this specific strategy, the organisation becomes fragmented, making it necessary to retain several librarians. Thus, this strategy is difficult to implement for libraries other than those with large budgets. Typical libraries adopting this strategy include the Harvard University Library, Yale University Library, Princeton University Library, New York Public Library (up through the 2000s), Boston Public Library (up through the 2000s) and University of Tokyo Library System. This management strategy is characteristic of American libraries and some Japanese university libraries.

Furthermore, in response to budgetary conditions, libraries should consider fragmenting only those specialty subjects in high demand by users. For example, upon entering the 21st century, both the Harvard University Library and Boston Public Library decreased their numbers of subdivided subjects. This was one way of countering a difficult budgetary situation. In addition, when introducing this management strategy, the library administrator should simultaneously consider structural subdivision as well as arrangements for lateral coordination of the organisation. For example, in the 2000s, the Columbia University Library utilised information technology in the form of business-use software at the business level to implement job-related coordination transcending subdivided organisational structure.

Strategies to Expand Remote User Services
Strategies to expand remote user services are management strategies emphasising services for users that are unable to visit the library. These strategies can be considered in the context of increases in regional

populations, the spread of the Internet and electronic media and changes in the users' information behaviour. For example, from the 1970s through the 1980s, both Japanese and American libraries saw increases in the general population and number of local residents. In response, libraries deployed bookmobiles and expanded their outreach services for remote users who had difficulty visiting the library. This management strategy was characteristic of public libraries.

However, from the 1990s to the 2000s, changes in the format of media in library collections comprising the core of libraries' administrative efforts stimulated strategies designed to expand services to remote users. The spread of the Internet and electronic media and changes in users' information behaviour served as an impetus for this, as there was a sense that with traditional services, patrons would not visit the library. In response to this changing environment, libraries began providing electronic media via the Internet and chat reference services in an effort to capture potential users. Representative examples can be seen at the Columbia University Library, Princeton University Library and New York Public Library. In order to effectively manage this specific strategy, libraries need to develop systems which are able to intelligently route users' questions to a suitable subject librarian. If systems are not developed in this fashion, librarians who receive questions from users will be unable to answer them correctly.

Consultation Service Strategies
These strategies involve proactively providing all manner of library services based on user needs. This involves providing services transcending the scale of mere reference services; responding to user needs, it often involves the library providing users with information literacy training, research support and related services. One result has been the appearance – mainly in American university libraries – of what are referred to as liaison librarians and embedded librarians. This is part of consultation service strategies: in responding to changing users' information behaviour, librarians have begun following users closely, providing them with customised services. This can be considered as a step away from lending books and towards providing personal service with an attention to detail. Structures supporting this management strategy are often created for each subject. As librarians gain specialty knowledge in different fields, they create structural formats based on a particular subject. Accordingly, it is critical to boost their specialty knowledge. These consultation service strategies are particularly common at university libraries in the US, for example at Princeton University Library, Columbia University Library and similar university libraries.

Sophisticated Service Strategies

Sophisticated service strategies provide a high level of service supporting the detailed analysis demanded by research to satisfy user needs. An example can be seen in librarians providing detailed knowledge related to data analysis for surveys, research and statistical analysis tools. With this management strategy, structures for individual subjects are adopted, and procedures and structural formats are frequently redesigned. To be more precise, this strategy involves newly hiring and training librarians possessing expertise in these respective subject areas. This type of service optimisation strategy is especially evident in American university libraries, as witnessed by the Princeton University Library and Columbia University Library beginning in 2010. These libraries employ librarians with a PhD and can thus provide a high-level of specialised, subject-specific service.

Strategies to Expand Editing and Publishing Functions

Strategies to expand editing and publishing functions involve increasing the functions by which the librarian gathers information, edits this information and then transmits it to the user. By editing this gathered information, librarians can create new output and add value to existing information. When this management strategy has been employed, library administrators often establish a specialty structure related to editing/publishing directly below the management layer. This is because publishing and editing functions differ from the basic library services of public and technical services.

New York University Library provides a representative example of such a strategy to expand editing/publishing functions. It established these functions beginning in the 1970s, enabling it to proactively disseminate the library's scholarly information. Overall, in selecting, gathering, preserving and offering information, libraries have placed minimal importance on functions involving newly producing and disseminating information. However, similar to New York University Library, some libraries have quickly recognised the importance of producing and disseminating information and have begun to strategically establish specialty structures directly below the management layer.

Moreover, with advances in IT and electronic media in the early 21st century, the importance of these editing/publishing functions is only increasing. Similar to the way in which electronic journals are changing how libraries maintain their book collections, libraries providing their own collections online is a significant factor in this increase. To create unique collections, libraries now need to produce and disseminate their own information; regardless of type, libraries are now proactively adopting specific strategies for editing/publishing such information.

Visitor Service Strategies
Visitor service strategies involve improving the library building and facilities so patrons can effectively study and conduct research. This specific strategy tends to be used by university libraries with small budgets and numerous facilities restrictions. This is because the smaller the library building, the more important it is for existing facilities to be effectively utilised, as user information behaviour changes. Examples include the New York University Library located in the centre of New York City, and the UMass Amherst Library with its miniscule budget.

Adoption of this specific management strategy often centres on equipment installation, but there are cases utilising it along with other strategies. For example, the New York University Library has adopted both visitor service strategies and consultation service strategies. Consequently, users have increased dramatically, representing an example of success based on visitor service strategies.

Service and Operational Improvement Strategies
This specific strategy involves emphasising efficient administration and improving service and operations, which aims to elevate the quality of services provided to the user. For example, if individual services provided by general strategies and specific strategies are the same, service quality and operations can be improved by improving structure format and procedural content. Please note that the general procedural improvements made as part of everyday affairs are not included in this management strategy.

Because libraries as non-profits depend on external budgets, improving their profitability is extremely difficult. Thus, service and operations improvement strategies often aim primarily at cost reductions. Originally, service and operations improvement strategies sought to improve existing service quality. Budgets allowing for this cost reduction are preferentially set aside for other new services because if the budget arising from this strategy is not used for this new service, the library facilities will soon become dated. In this way, service and operations improvement strategies comprise an attempt to thoroughly rationalise existing library operations.

In addition, structures for individual functions are often employed as structural formats at the time when service and operations improvement strategies are provided. This is because by integrating the library structure into functional units, the proficiency level of librarians is increased, and it becomes possible to work at the library at lower costs. Representative examples of these strategies can be seen with the National Diet Library, Tokyo Metropolitan Library and University of Arizona Library. However, if a mistake is made with objectives and importance is placed only on business rationale, it is possible that the knowledge and skills gained so far regarding library operations will be lost. As cutting costs was not the original aim when introducing this management strategy, this situation is important, particularly regarding these harmful effects.

TRIGGERS FOR INNOVATIVE AND FUNDAMENTAL CHANGES IN LIBRARIES

As previously discussed, the method I used to construct the theory of strategy for libraries was successful and effective because it allowed me to construct a theory of strategy based on library priority value using concrete library case analysis. The theory of library strategies is more theory and research-oriented and better justified than those of previous studies.

In the strategy, I also determined the element most influential to the strategic change of libraries; a type of media format which is radically changed by information technology. The innovative change of media format became a trigger of strategic changes, and brought not only service innovation but also organisational innovation. Media format is the fundamental element of change in library strategies.

I would like to highlight a typical case where strategic change was caused by the transformation of media formats. This case is the Boston Public Library: in 2009, the library implemented large management reforms and simplified the organisation, which had become complex through specialisation and segmentation. Under the 2009 organisational reforms, the library pursued streamlining library management by reducing the number of management personnel and integrating overlapping organisations. At the same time, they created E-resource-based division and media-based organisation, emphasised information technologies and systems, and established the Resource Services and Information Technology Division (see Fig. 1). Organisations related to electronic documents were consolidated under this division, integrating entities that were previously separate (document digitisation and technical services).

Along with this development, function-based organisations related to technical services were merged, forming an electronic, media type based

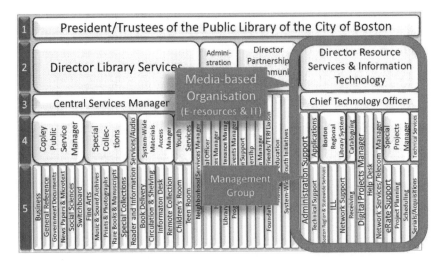

Fig. 1. The Boston Public Library Organisational Chart in 2009.

organisation. The expanded electronic media-related divisions absorbed the reduced technical service-related divisions. Subsequently, organisations based on electronic documents were created. There are some statements in the strategy that the Boston Public Library had been focusing on information technology and E-resources (Trustees of the Public Library of the City of Boston, 2007). In conclusion, I can determine the strategic rule that library services and organisational structures follow strategy, and strategy follows media format.

As evidenced by the strategic and innovative changes of the Boston Public Library in 2009, most academic and public libraries created the same type of strategy and organisational structure, and created E-resources media organisations (see Fig. 2). For example, a very similar strategic change at Harvard University Library is also evident. E-resources and information technology had a strong impact on the library's strategy; there is a trigger that caused this strategic and innovative change in the background of the library's management (see Fig. 3).

In the late 1990s and early 2000s, increases in the use of technology within the library led to confusion and difficulty as libraries had few specialists or skills to deal with these new technologies. Furthermore, the technology was scattered within the various divisions without a clear direction, so people in one division were unable to assist users in other divisions.

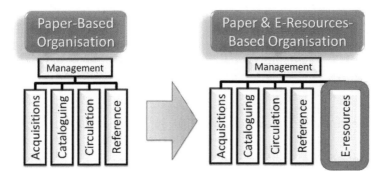

Fig. 2. Strategy Follows Media Format: Organisational Transitions to E-Resources Based Organisation.

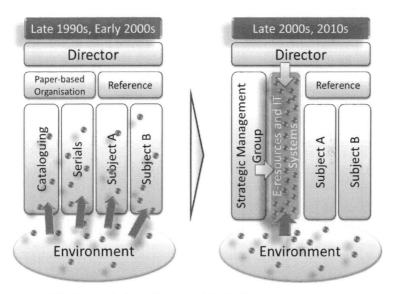

* The dots symbolise technology related to E-resources

* The figure shows only one part of the organisation.

Fig. 3. Gathered IT Works into a Unified E-Resource Division. *Notes:* The symbolise technology related to E-resources. The figure shows only one part of the organisation.

Without specialised skills or training, organisations became more and more confused when dealing with the ever-changing technological demands on their organisations. In the late 2000s and 2010s, library directors collected the technology and various resources into one division in order to better manage the use of technology within the library. This division reports directly to the library director. The strategic management group was formed to create new strategies and foster changes in the organisations in response to changing technologies. The introduction of E-resources and information technology is the trigger for innovative changes in strategic management of libraries.

SUMMARY

Library strategies transcend country and library type. They can be explained in terms of specific strategies adopted in response to shared general strategies or differences in library type and environment. Prior to facing the steady decrease of libraries' budgets due to the economic depression and the need of accountability for stakeholders in the late 1990s, the common belief was that libraries need not employ management strategies, and that management based on the idea of gradual improvement was sufficient. Nonetheless, libraries were pressured to transform themselves in response to the move towards online catalogues and other changes during the 1980s without explicit strategies. With the dawn of the 21st century, digitalisation expanded to library systems and media format. Related to this, libraries have been making strategic and innovative changes in their services, organisations and operations. Moreover, users' information behaviour is also changing, rendering it impossible to continue utilising past procedures if libraries expect to remain relevant. With libraries facing the necessity of responding to these environmental changes, management strategies providing explicit and external explanations became indispensable. However, while responding to external changes, libraries actually found potential new users, shifting from library collection services to human services, optimising traditional library services to highly sophisticated services, bringing publishing and editing functions into the library and undertaking similar management strategies. Therefore, these innovative changes could be described as a theory of library strategies.

Looking towards the future, the collections comprising the core of libraries will evolve, and the market environment will also continue to change greatly. To avoid being consumed by these changes, libraries must continuously reinvent themselves moving forward. However, it will become ever more difficult to permanently provide better services for users without continuing to expand based on core library services, procedures and organisational competencies. I hope this theory serves as a springboard for individual libraries to consider the management strategies explained herein.

REFERENCES

Chandler, A. D. (1962). *Strategy and structure: Chapters in the history of the industrial enterprise*. Cambridge, MA: MIT Press.

Drucker, P. F. (1954). *The practice of management*. New York, NY: Harper Collins Publishers.

Eisenhardt, K. M. (1989). Building theories from case study research. *Academy of Management Review*, *14*(4), 532–550.

Evans, G. (1976). *Management techniques for librarians*. New York, NY: Academic Press Inc.

Itami, H. (2003). *The logic of management strategies* (3rd ed.). Tokyo: Nihon Keizai Shimbun.

Kittle, A. T. (1961). *Management theories in public library administration in the United States, 1925–1955*. PhD thesis, Columbia University, New York, NY.

Pfeffer, J. (1993). Barriers to the advance of organizational science: Paradigm development as a dependent variable. *The Academy of Management Review*, *18*(4), 599–620.

Porter, M. E. (1980). *Competitive strategy: Techniques for analyzing industries and competitors*. New York, NY: Free Press.

Trustees of the Public Library of the City of Boston. (2007). *Boston public library/Metro Boston library network*. Retrieved from https://www.bpl.org/general/trustees/tech-plan0811.pdf

Usherwood, B. (1996). *Rediscovering public library management*. London: Library Association.

Yin, R. K. (2008). *Case study research: Design and methods*. London: Sage.

CAPACITY AND CAPABILITY: HOW CAN LIBRARY AND INFORMATION SERVICES MAKE SURE THEY SUCCEED?

Derek Law

ABSTRACT

Purpose — *The chapter is a personal opinion piece designed to provoke thought and discussion.*

Methodology/approach — *It reviews the ways in which libraries have responded to technological change over the last 50 years.*

Practical implications — *The focus is very much on higher education libraries, however the conclusions also have general applicability. The chapter concludes that libraries have to rethink their approach to services and accept a cultural change which embeds them as part of an information flow rather than a filter for the organisation and encourages them to focus much more on integration with corporate mission. There are real implications for the practice of libraries and for a rethinking of their social value and nature.*

Innovation in Libraries and Information Services
Advances in Library Administration and Organization, Volume 35, 87–101
ISSN: 0732-0671/doi:10.1108/S0732-067120160000035012

Originality/value — The chapter synthesises many strands of thought and the practical recommendations for change are of undoubted value to the reader.

Keywords: Library; information services; higher education libraries

INTRODUCTION

From the mid-twentieth century onwards, libraries prided themselves on being early adopters of the new technology and celebrated in a somewhat self-congratulatory way their ability to transform ancient practices incrementally. In parallel there was a growing tendency to see publishers, especially journal publishers as the price-gouging enemy, rather than another element in the information chain. By the end of the century it slowly became clear that what had actually arrived was a period of disruptive technology heralded first by the World Wide Web and then by the Cloud. The question then arises of whether libraries and librarians have the capacity and the capability to change and adapt.

The metaphor to be used here is that of gardening. Prior to the industrial revolution, English stately homes had spent the time following the restoration of Charles II creating gardens in the style of the French royal gardener André Le Notre. He famously built the royal gardens at Versailles where formal neat box like spaces formed beautiful patterns but in which the carefully delineated spaces did not interact and where his formal title for at least some of his life was 'Draughtsman of Plants and Terraces'.

This approach changed in the late seventeenth century when the hugely imaginative Lancelot 'Capability' Brown literally transformed the landscape and used the disruptive new tools and power of the industrial revolution to create a new concept of gardens. His style produced vistas of smooth undulating grass, running from the horizon to the country house or stately home, filled with clumps, belts and scattering of trees and pleasingly shaped lakes which were formed by invisibly damming small rivers, and with small neat bridges crossing them. The landscape was peppered with the herds of animals which provided for the great house. Some of this was achieved by his adoption of the sunk fence or ha ha which confused the eye into believing that the individual features offered a single connected, coherent and elegant view from house to horizon rather than being the product of sophisticated use of technology.

Creating such effortless coherence is then the challenge facing libraries today. It requires us to move out of our formal boxes to work with all those in the information chain to provide elegant access to an [apparently] seamless but connected world of information.

This chapter is based on the author's personal experience in UK Higher education, but it is hoped that the views expressed will be seen as having a wider sectorial and geographic application.

BACKGROUND

From ancient times to almost the end of the last millennium, libraries remained largely unchanged. They built collections of material presumed to be of use to users, selecting, cataloguing and storing items to be used by readers. The role of the librarian was to collect, preserve and help users exploit what was in the collections. Almost without exception the entire university passed through the doors of the library. No serious researcher, scholar or undergraduate could work without the collections of the library and, later, the inter-library loan service. There was as yet no national library service and very little co-operation with other libraries beyond the local. According to the Dempsey Paradox (Dempsey, 2010), this was the time when researchers were time rich and information poor, so that local collections had to be mined exhaustively and librarians who knew the collections in detail were integral to research. International co-operation and travel existed, but remained unusual, and in any case there was no record of what other library collections might contain until some libraries began to publish their library catalogue in book form.

This began to change from the mid-twentieth century with the arrival of computers. Libraries were early adopters of this technology, and so-called library automation began. In truth what was undertaken was library mechanisation, since the technology was simply applied to existing practices to make them more efficient. Thus it was library catalogues, not library collections which were put online. Book circulation was put online not content delivery and reference services involved e-mailing the reference librarian who looked things up in books, rather than providing access to content. With hindsight, we can see that what seemed to be the perceptive and incremental use of technology to enhance library services was actually a dead-end, retreating into Le Notre style boxed terraces surrounded by impenetrable but neat hedges (Carr, 2007).

DISRUPTIVE TECHNOLOGY

That the library world had begun to suffer disruptive change by the mid-1980s was not evident to librarians, but was evident to others. As the novelist David Lodge presciently noted in his 1984 novel of academic life *Small World*:

> ... information is much more portable in the modern world than it used to be. So are people. Ergo, it's no longer necessary to hoard your information in one building, or keep your top scholars corralled in one campus. There are three things which have revolutionized academic life in the last twenty years, though very few people have woken up to the fact: jet travel, direct-dialling telephones and the Xerox machine. Scholars don't have to work in the same institution to interact, nowadays: they call each other up, or they meet at international conferences. And they don't have to grub about in library stacks for data: any book or article that sounds interesting they have Xeroxed and read it at home. Or on the plane going to the next conference. I work mostly at home or on planes these days. I seldom go into the university except to teach my courses.

> ... As long as you have access to a telephone, a Xerox machine and a conference grant fund, you're OK, you're plugged into the only university that really matters – the global campus. A young man in a hurry can see the world by conference-hopping. (Lodge, 1984)

Of course, such disruption is not unique to libraries. From the Luddites protesting over the new labour-saving technology of power textile looms to the taxi drivers currently protesting about Uber's use of new technology, the pattern is all too predictable. The protesters are not inherently against the technology but like the Luddites afraid of losing their livelihood. And so libraries and librarians continued to mechanise their operations but began to wage war on both publishers and library users as they defended their position.

Publishers were beginning to move their output to digital format, notably in the area of scientific journals. At the same time the industry was being concentrated into a smaller number of publishers who were seen as heartless profit-driven fat cats. Libraries responded first with the use of their collective purchasing power to gain better deals, then later with the push towards open access in an effort to undermine the commercial publishers.

There was also a confused approach to library users. On the one hand libraries were at the forefront of providing user access to computers, offering ready access to desktop computers when these were rare and laptops unknown. At the same time barriers were placed in the way of users.

Initially Internet database searching was mediated, carried out by library staff, since the formulation of search strategies was considered beyond the grasp of users. Then when CDs arrived, there was a grudging acceptance that users could undertake such searches – but only after undertaking a training course. And there was a widely expressed view that such technologies were a transient flash in the pan which caused rather than solved problems. (Law, 1990). Library collections were still being built and user preferences were either ignored or dealt with through conventional inter-library loan channels.

LIBRARY DODOS

A recent light-hearted book entitled *21st Century Dodos* (Stack, 2014) drew attention to rapid changes in technology and society between about 1950 and 2000 and listed and described a whole series of artefacts and events which would be familiar to the reader, but after a brief flourish were already extinct and would never be known by the reader's children and grandchildren except in museums. The list was long and varied and included: the fax machine, cassette players, Net Cord judges in tennis matches, rotary dial phones, holiday postcards, milk bottle deliveries, Concorde, handwritten letters, typewriters, countries that no longer exist (such as Yugoslavia), 80 column punch cards, etc. The list was never intended to be exhaustive but is sadly accurate. Ironically, libraries have bought and shelved the book in their collections, apparently without considering whether they themselves, or at least part of their traditional functions are not also dodos.

Libraries appear to remain besotted with formats rather than content. And yet many of those formats have disappeared or are in the process of disappearing, mainly as a result of digitisation. The large printed catalogue, such as the National Union Catalogue, which used to fill up dozens of metres of shelving has gone. The printed bibliography has almost entirely disappeared[1] the printed scientific journal – or at least expensively bound backfiles – has almost entirely gone – or at least is wholly unnecessary; newspapers and newspaper reading rooms have disappeared. Even the British Library Newspaper Reading Room at Colindale closed in 2013. Although some reference works are still published, encyclopaedias are a format of the past as users have largely migrated to the web and Wikipedia. Even the computer printout is in steep decline as apps such as

Dropbox allow the sharing of documents and papers in electronic formats (Crothers, 2012).

The future of the academic book itself is in serious doubt. Typically the average academic monograph sells around 250 copies priced at £80 with an average discount to booksellers of 30%. This brings in a gross £14,000. After paying for the direct costs of printing, paper, marketing, copy editing and typesetting, around £7,000 is left to go towards the editor's salary and other overheads. Like shaving a pig it is a lot of work for a little wool (Gasson, 2004). In addition print scholarly book sales have been and are in decline. Recent research published in the *Journal of Electronic Publishing* finds that sales now average 200 for each title, as opposed to 2,000 in 1980 (Willinsky, 2009). And even when the books are purchased to build library collections there is strong evidence of limited use. The common estimate is that 40% of all books in academic libraries never circulate (Esposito, 2012).

It is then all too easy to make the case that the decline of so-called dead tree format is inexorable and that the Canute like stance of all too many libraries is not sustainable.

Many library services also look like relics of the past. Libraries still cling to legacy services which are capable of being moved to the web and in some libraries have been. In-house binderies have almost all disappeared; cataloguing can be outsourced; the issue desk can be replaced by self-service loans and even reference can be made an interactive IT-led activity.

COLLECTION BUILDING AND
COLLECTION MANAGEMENT

Collection management and collection building have often been treated as synonyms but are in truth quite different and increasingly separate activities (Law, 1991). Librarians have traditionally seen it as part of their distinctive role to select books and journals and to build specialised collections for tomorrow's as well as today's use. The specialised collection was and is still seen as defining the library's role and relevance to the community. The library's services and values then centred around these collections. This traditional academic library has been elegantly and eloquently described by Rick Anderson in a paper describing the views of young librarians taking part in an essay competition looking at library futures:

> A librarian-built, just-in-case collection is at the core of the traditional library's service model and of the value proposition it makes to its sponsoring institution. Historically,

virtually all of the library's practices and service offerings have centered on that kind of collecting and that kind of collection: reference services and bibliographic instruction focused largely (though not exclusively) on helping patrons use the collection; catalogers cataloged the collection; collection-development staff selected materials for the collection, and acquisitions and serials staff ordered and processed those materials. Interlibrary loan, special collections, even IT services were all focused either significantly or exclusively on management of the collection itself and access to it. If the young librarians who wrote these essays are correct, then library employees like me are basically feeding on a carcass. (Anderson, 2015)

USERS

Users too are changing. Prensky's hotly debated model of digital natives and digital immigrants has been much cited and much maligned but as with climate change denial, the weight of evidence seems overwhelming. The model has itself been refined, using the less divisive terminology of digital residents and digital visitors (White & Le Cornu, 2011).

The amount of time 8- to 15-year-olds spend on the Internet has more than doubled over the last decade, Ofcom's most recent report (Ofcom, 2015) in to media attitudes among children and parents found both a steadily growing use of Internet resources, but also a growing inability to filter 'good' information from 'bad' information, to separate the true and impartial from the special pleading or the plain wrong. Some 8% of children who use the Internet believe that information from social media websites or apps is 'all true' — doubling from 4% last year — and most 12- to 15-year-olds are unaware that 'vloggers', or video bloggers, can be paid to endorse products. Almost a fifth of online 12- to 15-year-olds (19%) believe information returned by a search engine such as Google or Bing must be true, but only a third (31%) are able to identify paid-for adverts.

The study also found that children are increasingly turning to YouTube for 'true and accurate' information. Some 8% of the children studied named the site as their preferred choice for current information — up from 3% last year. But just half of 12- to 15-year-olds who watch YouTube (52%) are aware that advertising is the main source of funding on the site, and less than half (47%) are aware that vloggers are often paid to favourably mention products or services.

Sites such as Buzzfeed, YouTube, TED lectures and even podcasts as well as social media in general have transformed the way in which digital natives gather information. In turn there is an emerging skills gap in assessing the quality of this information. The problem is not information overload but filter failure (Shirky, 2008).

The number of devices connected to the Internet is increasing dramatically. It has been estimated that by 2020 there will be 50 billion networked devices connected, up from 500 million in 2003. In other words there will be seven networked devices for every individual on the planet. This influences equally dramatically how users interact with information (Alleyne, 2015).

THE LIBRARY OF THE FUTURE

Institutional Mission

As is so often the case Lorcan Dempsey has encapsulated the dilemma facing libraries in his blog:

> As regular readers know, 'network level' is a favourite expression of mine. This question is interesting because of the transition we are working our way through. Libraries tend to be institution-scale in reach as they were organized as a pre-network response to information management. In that context, institutionally based services make sense. For example, information materials were acquired and made available to the local population on a just-in-case basis. The institution remains the appropriate scale for many activities. However, researchers may now be drawn to newer network level approaches which aggregate supply and/or attention across the network, or across a discipline. Think for example of initiatives like ICPSR, SSRN, Repec, Arxiv or more generally of Google Scholar or Twitter. At what scale will researchers look for applications to do their work – institution, collaborative group, discipline, network? Where does it make sense to let services be provided by external network level providers and where should the library provide services? There is no right answer of course, and practices are shifting. (Dempsey, 2011)

New Forms of Content

Although the majority of libraries will have to manage their legacy content and in some cases retain much of it, the need to distinguish the medium from the message will become increasingly important. Vast quantities of information are available to the user, either online, through the cloud or even in paper form faster and cheaper than off-site delivery or inter-library loan. Immediate and global access is available 24×7 through Internet search, e-commerce; book digitisation; one penny books on Amazon, Abebooks, print on demand, kindle instant delivery and massive digitisation projects, such as the Europeana Newspapers project offering twenty million pages of newsprint. As the references to this chapter demonstrate, the range of material used in a scholarly article has changed out of all recognition in the last decade or so. No longer do citations list only monographs and journal articles. They may include blogs, online articles, papers in repositories, powerpoint presentations on Slideshare, raw data and so on. A significant element in this new content is the ability to add a Digital Object Identifier (DOI) which identifies content uniquely. Originally developed by and for publishers and treated with great suspicion by libraries when first introduced, the DOI now allows individuals or organisations to provide a unique identifier to all forms of output, thereby making it more reliably accessible.

As most libraries move from collection building to collection management, demand-driven acquisition using subscription models to deliver e-books and content will increasingly have an impact as the normal method of information delivery. This new approach to meeting reader needs has become commonplace remarkably quickly, with a rapid and continuing growth in take-up (Zeoli, 2015). Although such new content is wholly disruptive to old models of working and thinking it can be used as a challenge to relocate the library's role to the centre of the community served (Schmidt, 2015).

Cloud-based content will have to be managed rather than collected. Huge new categories of content have become available electronically and are required by readers. Short term loan e-books and demand-driven acquisition will require libraries to focus on defining and meeting readers needs through subscriptions to such services. To this rapidly growing area of content we can now add streamed content of all sorts. Again usage is subscription based and aimed at meeting current user needs. This requires a quite different set of skills from the traditional library collection building. There are significant budget-management issues as well as a much greater focus on the needs of current users.

Dempsey again neatly encapsulates the problem and its consequences. 'One downside of this fragmented systems and collections environment is that it becomes more difficult to build services out on top of the collections. Too much effort is going into maintaining and integrating a fragmented systems infrastructure. This becomes more of an issue as the pressure on the library to be seen to be "making a difference" grows. Increasingly, the library needs to bring its services to the users within their work- or learnflow, and be seen to be adding value to the collection of resources' (Dempsey, 2014).

Change in the Library's Local Role

Despite this shift to web-based content, the future of the physical library remains a matter of debate. Even the need for a physical space called the library has been called into question in recent decades. In a seminal paper in 1978 Lancaster stated 'We are already very close to the day in which a great science Library could exist in a space less than ten feet square' (Lancaster, 1978). President Ronald Reagan made the same point in a speech to the English Speaking Union where he pointed out that the United States had the technology to put the entire information of the Library of Congress into a space the size of a telephone booth (Reagan, 1989).

This debate remains alive. At the extreme end of the spectrum are those who believe that the library as a space is dead (Stachokas, 2014). The future library will exist as 'an organizational unit, not a building or physical facility'. Technological determinism decrees that resistance to this change is futile. But most organisations still see the library as a necessary shop window for the representation of institutional mission. New libraries continue to be built at a remarkable rate in a time of economic problems. And it is clear that users wish to have and value that space, including the presence of physical books if not the use of books (Smith, 2014). But the function of space in the library has to change to meet user needs. A study at the University of Manchester (Wilkinson, 2013) found that students want spacious group areas to support new ways of learning and social spaces such as cafes and relaxation areas that allow them to spend extended periods of time in the building. And so the concept of 'rightsizing' (Ward, 2015) has emerged. Libraries need to scale back dramatically the size of their legacy collections, move to digital acquisition and be seen as places for knowledge creation, collaboration and interactive learning.

Institutional Role

But the library also has the opportunity to move much further in its local role in delivering the institutional mission. It can become the collector and authoritative source for institutional output (Lynch et al., 2015). Institutional repositories have moved in this direction, but there is a clear space to become the collector, manager and disseminator of research output, of institutional papers and publications and their data, recording and preserving everything from lectures, to podcasts, to graduations or even local events and to take on a long-term preservation role for this material. But this can be taken much further through the use of social media. Everything from managing Wikipedia entries about the institution and its staff to ensuring publications are posted on Researchgate or Academia.edu and even using social media such as Twitter or LinkedIn to promote institutional output all help to meet institutional mission (Thomson, 2016). The allocation of DOIs will help to make non-traditional output more accessible. And if the information managers do not take on this role at an institutional level, who will? Universities have become obsessed with their position on league tables both for research and for student recruitment. Libraries can help to ensure that institutional output is given prominence and by extension is more read and more cited through the use of social media.

As users' habits change it is also becoming clear that the unfortunately named activity of user instruction can become a central focus. The ability to select, evaluate, use and cite reliable information is not innate and it is clear that academic skills training will be crucial in supporting users to as they try to navigate the increasingly complex world of information, make judgements about relevance and most importantly quality, and correctly to cite their sources.

Staffing

All of this poses huge challenges for library staff and the skills they require. Amongst those who recognise the need for a significant reappraisal of the role and function of library staff, the phrase 'New Era Librarian' has emerged (Hashim & Mokhtar, 2012). It is also the case that these are generic professional issues relevant to all sectors of the profession and not just to universities or the public sector. For example, the LAC Group, self-described as a 'boutique agency for temporary personnel serving the law library community in Los Angeles' makes it clear that this development and refashioning of the skills of the librarian is not unique to universities and public sector bodies. Their Chief Operating Officer (COO) identifies the five critical skills as: information curation; in-depth, high value research; digital preservation; mobile environment; collaboration, coaching and facilitation (Corrao, 2013).

A similar list can be developed for public sector organisations, but a list which will be valid for all libraries, albeit with emphases being varied by local circumstances. Collection management requires new budgetary approaches and much closer interaction with users. Quality assurance of sources becomes a much greater issue. Offering training to users on how to navigate the jumbled web of information becomes a central role. Constantly refreshing physical space to match it to changing user expectations is essential. Staff must be technically proficient both in the support of technology from apps to tablets and in quality assurance of sources from Buzzfeed to Twitter — as well as the output of publishers and public sector bodies. They need to manage and preserve local output, often in repositories (Simons & Richardson, 2012). They need increasingly to see their role as part of a globalised information chain and not the destination for those who seek information.

There is perhaps a certain irony in the fact that much of the burden of making this change and in developing staff will fall on the present generation of library managers. Universities (and by extension library schools) tend to have detailed, arcane and slow procedures for changing curricula. And yet it is in the nature of disruptive technology that change is rapid and abrupt. Quite apart from the detailed skills required to do everything from create and manage a website or implement changing digital preservation standards, there is a need to change the philosophical approach to the nature and role of the library within the organisation. Staff training whether on formal courses or conference attendance should be a key and expensive element of the annual budget.

CONCLUSION

Capability Brown developed his skills at a time of disruptive technologies and changing aspirations. Libraries have the capacity and the capability to do the same. Many of the activities mentioned in this chapter already happen in the best and most progressive libraries. The library itself remains an iconic element in the thinking of most organisations. The challenge then facing the profession is to develop the capacity to make such thinking universal and then to implement change, creating and supporting broad global vistas of information, while ensuring the relevance of information skills to supporting institutional mission.

Perhaps the most challenging element is to create the Capability Brown-like sweeping vistas towards information horizons. This involves working much more closely with everything from publishers to archivists, from ICT staff to organisational PR departments. It means recognising that all of these are components of the same broad picture and not antithetical elements to be avoided as we occupy our own little box gardens and requires both a change in our understanding and a leap of faith.

NOTE

1. The author has personal experience of this. His exemplary and authoritative (sic) bibliography *The Royal Navy in World War II* (Scarecrow Press, 2002) went through two editions. No publisher would contemplate publishing a third edition of a book which would sell only a few hundred copies. The bibliography is now online at the Centre for Maritime Historical Studies at the University of Essex, where it is widely used and much more current than a printed volume published every decade. https://humanities.exeter.ac.uk/history/research/centres/maritime/resources/dlaw/

REFERENCES

Alleyne, A. (2015). *Cloud city and the internet of things.* Blog post of September 9, 2015. Retrieved from https://www.microsoft.com/en-gb/enterprise/it-trends/cloud-computing/articles/cloud-city-and-the-internet-of-things.aspx#fbid = hSO6UmhZYP_

Anderson, R. (2015). The death of the collection and the necessity of library—publisher collaboration: Young Librarians on the Future of Libraries. *The Scholarly Kitchen.* Retrieved from http://scholarlykitchen.sspnet.org/2015/11/17/the-death-of-the-collection-and-the-necessity-of-library-publisher-collaboration-young-librarians-on-the-future-of-libraries/. Accessed on November 17, 2015.

Carr, R. (2007). *The academic research library in a decade of change.* Oxford: Chandos.

Corrao, R. (2013). *Top five skills required for librarians today & tomorrow.* Retrieved from http://lac-group.com/top-five-skills-required-for-librarians-today-tomorrow/. Accessed on January 10, 2015.

Crothers, B. (2012). *Dead-tree format's demise is slow, steady.* CNET. Retrieved from http://www.cnet.com/uk/news/dead-tree-formats-demise-is-slow-steady/. Accessed on August 6, 2012.

Dempsey, L. (2010). *3 Switches.* Lorcan Dempsey's Weblog. June 13, 2010. Retrieved from http://orweblog.oclc.org/archives/002104.html. Accessed on November 21, 2015.

Dempsey, L. (2011). *The institution and the network ... a question of scale.* Retrieved from http://orweblog.oclc.org/archives/002157.html

Dempsey, L. (2014). *The network reshapes the library.* Chicago, IL: American Library Association.

Esposito, J. (2012). Hawking radiation: Figuring out how many books are sold to libraries. *The Scholarly Kitchen.* Retrieved from http://scholarlykitchen.sspnet.org/2012/02/22/hawking-radiation-figuring-out-how-many-books-are-sold-to-libraries-2/. Accessed on February 22, 2012.

Gasson, C. (2004). The Economics of Academic Publishing. *Royal Economic Society Newsletter Online*. No. 125. Retrieved from http://www.res.org.uk/view/art2Apr04 Features2.html. Accessed on April 2004.

Hashim, L. B., & Mokhtar, W. N. H. W. (2012). Preparing new era librarians and information professionals: Trends and issues. *International Journal of Humanities and Social Science*, *2*(7), 151–156. Retrieved from http://www.ijhssnet.com/journals/Vol_2_No_7_April_2012/16.pdf

Lancaster, F. W. (1978). *Toward paperless information systems*. New York, NY: Academic Press.

Law, D. (1990). *CD-ROM: A young technology with a great future behind it?* Papers presented at 13th annual UKSG conference. Serials 3(3).

Law, D. (1991). The organization of collection in academic libraries. In C. Jenkins & M. Morley (Eds.), *Collection management in academic libraries*. London: Gower.

Law, D. (2002). *The royal navy in world war two: An annotated bibliography*. Metuchen, NJ: Scarecrow Press.

Lodge, D. (1984). *Small world*. London: Secker & Warburg.

Lynch, C. A., Almes, G. T., Anderson, C., Hillegas, C. W., Lance, T., Wetzel, K. A. et al. (2015). Curation. Big data in the campus landscape (series). *EDUCAUSE Center for Analysis and Research Campus Cyberinfrastructure (ECAR-CCI) Working Group*. November 20, 2015.

Ofcom. (2015). *Children and parents: Media use and attitudes report 2015*. Retrieved from http://stakeholders.ofcom.org.uk/market-data-research/other/research-publications/childrens/children-parents-nov-15/. Accessed on November 20, 2015.

Reagan, R. (1989, July 13). *The Churchill lecture to the English speaking union*. London: English Speaking Union.

Schmidt, J. (2015). *Demand-driven acquisitions: The hegemony of the canon interrupted*. Retrieved from http://www.ala.org/acrl/sites/ala.org.acrl/files/content/conferences/confsandpreconfs/2015/Schmidt.pdf

Shirky, C. (2008). *Keynote address at web 2.0 expo New York*. Retrieved from https://www.youtube.com/watch?v = LabqeJEOQyI

Simons, N., & Richardson, J. (2012). New roles, new responsibilities: Examining training needs of repository staff. *Journal of Librarianship and Scholarly Communication*, *1*(2), 16. Retrieved from http://jlsc-pub.org/articles/abstract/10.7710/2162-3309.1051/

Smith, C. (2014). Future of the book and library creatively explored. *New Library World*, *115*(5–6), 211–224.

Stachokas, G. (2014). *After the book: Information services for the 21st century*. Oxford: Chandos.

Stack, S. (2014). *21st century dodos: A collection of endangered objects (and other stuff)*. London: The Friday Project.

Thomson, S. D. (2016). *Preserving Social Media*, DPC Technology Watch Report 16-01, February 2016.

Ward, S. M. (2015). *Rightsizing the academic library collection*. Chicago, IL: American Library Association.

White, D. S., & Le Cornu, A. (2011). Visitors and residents: A new typology for online engagement. *First Monday*, *16*(9). Retrieved from http://firstmonday.org/article/view/3171/3049#author. Accessed on September 5, 2011.

Wilkinson, J. (2013). Library futures: Manchester University. *The Guardian*. Retrieved from www.theguardian.com/higher-education-network/2013/aug/07/library-futures-university-of-manchester. Accessed on August 7, 2013.

Willinsky, J. (2009). Toward the design of an open monograph press. *Journal of Electronic Publishing*, *12*(1). doi:10.3998/3336451.0012.103. Retrieved from http://quod.lib.umich.edu/j/jep/3336451.0012.103?rgn = main;view = fulltext

Zeoli, M. (2015). Academic libraries and the scholarly book marketplace: Death by 1,000 [paper] cuts? *Against the Grain*, *27*(5), 14−16.

THE DEVELOPMENT OF DOCUMENT SUPPLY[1]: NAVIGATING IN STORMY WATERS

Mike McGrath

ABSTRACT

Purpose — *This chapter aims to describe the development of the interlending and document supply (DS) service over the past 30 years and to show that this service still has much to offer.*

Methodology/approach — *After a historical introduction, the current environment for researchers is assessed and analysed in the current context of the rapidly changing access to information.*

Findings — *The interlending and DS service has declined in the last 10 years owing to the dual impact of the 'Big Deals' and the growth in open access. However the service retains its value for providing access to the vast amounts of material that is still not freely available or is hidden behind expensive pay walls.*

Innovation in Libraries and Information Services
Advances in Library Administration and Organization, Volume 35, 103–119
Copyright © 2017 by Emerald Group Publishing Limited
All rights of reproduction in any form reserved
ISSN: 0732-0671/doi:10.1108/S0732-067120160000035013

Originality/value — *This is the only study that analyses the current global situation regarding the interlending and DS service.*

Keywords: Document supply; interlending; non-digitised material; big deals; open access

INTRODUCTION

Interlibrary lending (ILL) and document supply (DS) will always be with us. Serious researchers will never be able to access all that they need from their own institution or from accessing free-to-use material directly or indirectly on the web. There are two reasons: firstly, much material remains and will remain undigitised and hence only accessible from a printed copy — whether a book, a report or a journal article. Secondly so long as commercial publishing exists there will be pay walls, often very high pay walls, which will restrict access to those who can afford to pay. In these circumstances fair use provision for interlibrary loan will usually be used — today more often for articles but also for books but with constraints on the increasing number of ebooks that libraries wish to share with others. There is also a further underlying factor — many articles are read by very few,[2] so that subscribing to a particular title may not be cost effective; for example research by CIBER in 2009 demonstrated that over 90% of title use derived from 50% of journals in a number of research universities in the United Kingdom (UK) (CIBER, 2009).

HOW IT WAS THEN

It all kicked off seriously with the Russians. In 1957 they launched Sputnik the first satellite and the West panicked. One response was a sharp increase in scientific research- needless to say focused on the military but also in other areas. In the UK — a documentation centre was established in Boston Spa, North Yorkshire at the site of what had been the largest ammunition production facility in the world — a relic of World War 2. The place was chosen because it was best placed to supply published and non-published (e.g. theses and reports, conference proceeding) data to research establishments throughout Britain — this was long before electronic delivery made physical location irrelevant. The centre included in its staff a married couple from the Ukraine who translated from Russian scientific literature. From this beginning grew the world's largest supplier of documents in all languages and disciplines. By 1999 it was satisfying four million requests a year from over 30,000 organisations worldwide – large research universities in the UK were requesting up to 80,000 items a year. Its central position in DS developments over the past 50 years makes it a useful exemplar in the study of Document Delivery (DD). Major changes whether organisational or service driven have been marked by name changes. Created in 1962 as the National Lending Library for Science and Technology it has undergone a number of major transformations most recently into British Library On Demand. Clearly DS is not a conservative backwater. It has always been a minor part in a library's budget – no higher than 5% at its peak in the 1990s – but it provides a vital support for researchers wanting material not held in their own institution's library. At Boston Spa in the 1960s and 1970s requests for documents were sent by post or telex. Article requests were then photocopied from printed journals and delivered by post. The introduction of facsimile reproduction (fax) in the early 1970s speeded up delivery of articles but the quality or reproduction was never very good. This was followed by Ariel (Landes, 1997). Then e-journals were developed in the 1990s which gave rise to scan, print and deliver in the 2000s. And now, in the UK at least, direct transmission to the end user was enabled by new legislation in 2014. The delivery of books has been a different story – sent by post in the 1960s – still posted in the 2010s; but ebooks are beginning to have a limited presence in ILL, limited mainly by publishers' fears of losing revenue such that even public libraries have found it difficult to use the new development to the benefit of their customers – see for example Zhu and Shen (2014).

GROWTH OF DOCUMENT SUPPLY

The driver of the developments described above and the consequent increase in DS of both returnables and non-returnables is simple and has often been noted: no library could or can hold collections comprehensive enough to satisfy all the needs of all their users. Arguably this has always been the case but by the 1960s the issue became sufficiently important for the development of systematic solutions; either via centralised document centres (France and the UK); cooperation and resource sharing

(US, Germany, Scandinavia). Most other countries continued with inefficient systems such that it was often said in the 1970s and 1980s and even into the 1990s that it was cheaper and certainly quicker to request material from the UK DS centre at Boston Spa in North Yorkshire. The demand at Boston Spa expresses this most clearly rising, to four million requests a year in 1999 from articles to books to reports, conferences and theses of which over a million were international – it was often said to this author that 'Boston Spa is quicker than using our own service'. However by the late 1990s domestic growth developed in France with INIST, another centralised DS centre (for the latest radical developments see Bérard et al., 2015), Germany within an effective consortial system (Rosemann & Brammer, 2010) and even in Italy with its very complex system of local and national government structures – where today there are 94 hubs covering nearly 6,000 libraries [1] and until recently there were eight national libraries now effectively two – Rome and Florence. (Mangiaracina, Cocever, Chiandoni, & Arabito, 2014). In the United States (US) the cooperative model of DS grew, strongly facilitated by the increasingly dominant OCLC which began in 1967 as the Ohio College Library Center which created a cooperative, computerised network for Ohio libraries. This has grown to a vast global network linking 70,000 libraries with nearly 17,000 full members in 113 countries (OCLC Annual Report, 2013–2014). It is important to stress that OCLC does not itself supply documents – it is rather a facilitator for libraries to share records and documents between themselves. See Mak (2011) for an overview of research library DD in the US and virtually any issue of the *Journal of Interlibrary Loan, Document Delivery & Electronic Reserve* [2]. Geographical proximity and rapid economic development have encouraged resource sharing in Scandinavia (Denmark, Sweden, Finland, Norway and Iceland). Also in Belgium and the Netherlands sharing occurs with the very effective PICA system bought by OCLC in 2007. Germany, Austria and Switzerland are served by Subito, the German document supplier.

The late 1990s saw a number of developments that have had a very significant impact on DS. This impact has varied from country to country and generalisations are difficult. In the UK demand had dropped from four million in 2000 to less than a million in 2015 via the British Library Document Supply Centre (BLDSC). A similar fall has occurred in France and Germany. However the US has remained relatively robust and peaked only in 2010 and in 2012 still stood at about 10 million requests per annum.[3,4]

FACTORS AFFECTING THE DECLINE IN DOCUMENT SUPPLY

One powerful way of grasping the scale of the decline in DS is to look at the demand changes experienced by the BLDSC. The decline is most severe because of the growth of resource sharing between institutions but it is a useful exemplar as noted above. From its origin in 1961 it climbed to four million requests in the late 1990s and declined to below one million in 2014 − lower than 1970 (Fig. 1). Nonetheless owing to dramatic and focussed process and technological improvements it remains a viable service (Appleyard, 2015).

No one factor is responsible for the decline − but the key ones are described briefly below.

Big Deals

E-journals were well established by the mid-1990s. In 1996 the UK Higher Education Funding Council for England (HEFCE) initiated a process 'The result (of which) was a three-year experiment involving four publishers − Academic Press, Blackwell Science, Blackwell Publishing and the Institute of Physics Publishing. These publishers offered access to their entire journal collection for between 60% and 70% of the normal price. A number of regional site licence agreements had been set up in the USA but nothing on the geographic scale of the HEFCE initiative' (White, 2012).

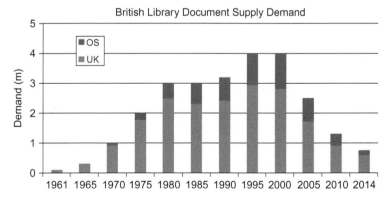

Fig. 1.   Trend in Demand for BLDSS, since it started in 1961 (Appleyard, 2015).

These deals became popular with users and hence with librarians very quickly, this had two consequences for DS. Firstly, users had access to material immediately that previously had to be obtained via DS. Secondly a culture developed rapidly of an expectation of receiving free and immediate access. This has had an enormous impact on DS. These deals remain controversial because of the very high price charged for them – much ink has been used over the years to criticise these tenacious deals, a good example being given by Ball (2004). Of course not everyone has access to a Big Deal – Elsevier's alone costs over £1 million for a UK research university; universities and institutions that cannot justify the cost, public libraries and therefore non-affiliated researchers of which there are many. All these can obtain copies of articles but usually at exorbitant prices – typically between £20 and £40 per article direct from the publisher. The price of a fair use DS article will be much less – often free if you are affiliated to a university – variable if via a public library but typically in the UK about £7.00.

Retrospective Files

If Big Deals weren't enough back files followed. A British Library report concluded that 'All in all, it is fair to say that journal back files are a commercial success' (Wijnen, 2007). This process had been substantially completed for at least the big commercial and many society publishers by the early 2000s. Just as for the Big Deals the price charged is enormous but the impact on DS has also been severe as those endless shelves of old journals become immediately accessible (to some) electronically (Davis, 2014).

Open Access

As the phenomenon of Open Access (OA) grows so does its effect on DS. But this development is complex and we are likely to live in a 'mixed economy' for very many years. In essence the reason is simple – the laudable vision of 'free information for all' is clashing with the commercial imperative to maximise profits for shareholders as well as the understandable fear by many librarians that dismantling the current system is too risky. The publishers, at least in the UK, have wrestled victory from the jaws of defeat when the Finch Committee recommended that the Gold[5] route should be taken whilst allowing Green to be used as an alternative. The UK government agreed and very quickly publishers have put in place systems that allow them to charge similarly high prices as they charge for subscriptions, but, and it is a big but, most other countries so far have opted for the Green route whilst allowing Gold OA. The UK accounts for only 7% of the world's published research output and the burden of Article Processing Charge (APC) payments are already being felt by funders (Estelle, 2014). So it is likely that we will move to a publishing context in which an increasing number of Gold published articles will be freely available to everyone immediately (and hence not required via remote document supply (RDS)) but this will take place over a number of years. Many authors in this category will be limited to those funded to publish, Elsevier for example currently charges between US$500 and US$5,000 depending on the title (taken from the Elsevier pricing section of their website, August 2015). Then again many non-commercial OA journals do not charge a fee. There will also be a greater number of Green published articles where the author/ editor agreed version or post print — but rarely the publisher's Version of Record (VoR) — is available via repositories but often only after an embargo period of up to two years. However most demand for articles occurs within the first two years so accessibility will grow slowly as will the commensurate decline in the need for DS. The overall implications of OA for DS are difficult to quantify — as the authors of a recent paper state — '... the open access article processing fee approach is a model in an early and still highly volatile phase', (Morrison, Jihane, Calvé-Genest, & Hora, 2015). All one can safely say is that Gold OA will cause a decline in DS requests. Similarly Green OA will impact DS requests to the extent that researchers are prepared to accept an editor agreed version and can find it — not often an easy task. In addition the extent to which authors can allow immediate access to their post print is controversial although at least one respected authority states 'authors retain the rights to all earlier versions of their work, certainly under UK and EU law. As such, they are free to post earlier versions of their papers on the Web' (Oppenheim, 2014).

Perhaps one of the most remarkable changes to have taken place in the last 10 years is access to theses. Previously obtaining copies of theses was laborious and expensive involving the copying of a print from microfilm or from an original paper copy. The advent of electronic theses and dissertations (ETD) has changed all that. 'In 2014, the international directory OpenDOAR listed more than 1,200 institutional repositories with ETDs, representing roughly half of all registered open archives' (Schöpfel et al., 2014). Many if not most currently produced theses are now available freely and immediately — an extraordinary transformation of the information landscape.

So long as we live in a society in which the drive for profit is paramount no institution will be able to satisfy all the demands of its users from resources that it makes available either from paid for access or freely on the web. The academic publishing industry – worth US$10 billion annually in scientific publishing alone – will fight to retain these massive revenues and sky high profits until the very last page. In practice only those authors with access to substantial research funds will be able to publish immediately OA articles in commercially produced journals. Material in repositories will grow quickly with the impact of more closely managed mandates from funders but access will continue to be patchy for many years to come and the preference for the publisher's VoR will likely mean a modest increase in use. There will clearly be a negative impact of paid for DS but staff involved in the process of DS will increasingly act as support navigators to content available via multiple free channels.

CULTURAL SHIFTS – WANT IT NOW BUT NOT TOO MUCH

As noted above an extraordinary cultural shift in the last 20 years has been driven by the immediate access offered by electronic journals – at least for those fortunate enough to belong to institutions that can afford to pay for them. This has been reinforced by the growth of OA which combined with the development of simple but powerful search tools such as Google and Google Scholar is providing immediate access to an increasing proportion of research material. This cornucopia available at the click of a button has had unforeseen consequences. One example being the decline in 'must have' items; if I have 100 items for my research immediately available do I really need that 101st? Research has shown that increasingly the answer is no. In an earlier period when perhaps only 50 items were found the 51st may have seemed more important and would have been obtained via DS. A more drastic variant on this effect is the perception of new generations of students that if it is not immediately available on the web then it doesn't exist – a very worrying trend.

RESOURCE SHARING CONSORTIA

In the 1980s and 1990s the growth of document suppliers that relied on access to their own massive collections was paralleled by the growth of resource sharing between institutions, particularly in the United States. It is worth noting that the US government twice considered constructing a library along the lines of the BLDSC but rejected on both occasions on cost grounds. It is perhaps needless to say that the possibility of this happening today is inconceivable. Resource sharing consortia have exploited developments in technology that facilitate fast and efficient access to their shared collections initially via the library but increasingly direct to the end user — with or without payment of copyright fees. The most visible expression of this phenomenon is the explosive development of OCLC which via services such as WorldShare Interlibrary Loan, now facilitates the sharing of resources between 16,857 members in 113 countries giving access to over two billion holdings (OCLC Annual Report, 2013—2014). Just under nine million ILL requests were facilitated in 2014.[6] Because the collection strategies of consortia members can, to an extent, be coordinated the growth of DS has been more robust although establishing an overall pattern is difficult and would require an extensive research project to shed light on this activity. However it would be reasonable to assume that the impact of Big Deals — tightly controlled for access by the publishers and the growth of OA should lead to an overall reduction in the scale of resource sharing.

TIGHTER PUBLISHER CONTROLS

Publishers are fearful of their bottom line being eroded by the unauthorised sharing of their e-content between libraries — although surveys have shown this to be unjustified. However it is certainly the case that prior to the electronic era there was widespread informal sharing of photocopies of journal articles between end users independent of libraries. Publishers have invested very considerable sums in developing digital rights management (DRM) software that effectively prevents access to their published content without payment. DRM is combined with strict contracts for usage that usually prevent the direct transmission of articles from one library to another. This leads to the bizarre process of 'print scan and transmit' in order to comply with this restriction which is both laborious and expensive — as intended by the publishers. The only country so far that has overcome this constraint is the UK where legislation was passed in 2014 which prevented contract trumping copyright law (Cornish, 2014). This now allows UK libraries to share their e-content between each other so long as they comply with the fair use provisions of UK law. This is an immense improvement in terms of speed, simplicity and costs and may well lead to greater use of DS at least in the UK.

PATRON DRIVEN DEMAND FOR BOOKS

Patron Driven Demand (PDA) sometimes referred to as Purchase on Demand has become popular in recent years even though the full costs are often not taken fully into account (van Dyck, 2011). There are two main reasons – firstly most purchasing programmes at universities are poor at predicting reader usage, a large proportion of stock sits on the shelf and is never or rarely used; books purchased via PDA programmes consistently achieve greater circulation than those conventionally purchased. Secondly the advent of online bookstores such as Amazon, Abebooks (purchased by Amazon in 2008) and Alibris enables libraries to purchase books cheaply and quickly – some even give the book to the reader having purchased it for a penny thus avoiding the costs of ingestion – for an extensive review of the subject see Tyler (2011).

PAY PER VIEW (PPV) FOR ARTICLES

Publishers have for many years offered a PPV alternative to subscribing. However the price is high – often US$40 and more – reflecting the high costs of subscription, if they price PPV too low subscription income will fall. However publishers have experimented with individual libraries in the past few years by offering discounted PPV – Elsevier's ArticleChoice [3] being one such for which prices are negotiable and Elsevier asserts that 'it is a sensible and competitively priced alternative to Document Delivery'.

BUT THERE ARE UPS AND DOWNS ...

It may seem from the above jeremiad that DD is doomed but there are a number of factors that suggest this not to be the case. Consider first the case of the USA.

The USA

Until recently the United States had bucked the general decline in both DS and ILL in the developed world – demand continued to increase through the 2000s albeit at a slower rate than previously. However even the US has begun to decline. The broadest indicator of this is the OCLC

figures for the US —total interlibrary loan requests were 8.7 million in 2012/
2013 which declined to 8.1 million in 2013/2014 and to 7.6 million in 2014/
2015 (OCLC, 2015). No single factor explains this anomalous growth and
decline but a highly effective and efficient decentralised system combined
with the well-known 'can do-ism' of US workers are key factors. A more
detailed analysis is made by Mak (2011) – 'It was found that the effectiveness of resource sharing facilitated by intra- and inter-state cooperatives
using OCLC as a framework is a major factor, others being the improvement
in discovery tools, requesting processes and the more recent improvements
in the delivery process. Finally, the widespread subsidising of access and
delivery enables cheap or even free use of document supply'. Just to take two
examples – Borrow Direct is a superb resource sharing system for books
amongst major research libraries and is described by Collins (2015).
Demand currently is 250,000 loans a year and is still rising robustly. And
OhioLink – which 'is a consortium of 90 Ohio college and university
libraries, plus the State Library of Ohio, that work together to provide Ohio
students, faculty and researchers with the information they need for teaching
and research. Serving more than 600,000 students, faculty, and staff,
OhioLink's membership includes 16 public/research universities, 23 commu-
nity/technical colleges, 51 independent colleges and the State Library of
Ohio'. A detailed analysis is given by the former Director (Sanville, 2007).
Even a cursory look at the contents pages of *Interlending and Document
Supply* and the *Journal of Interlibrary Loan, Document Delivery & Electronic
Reserve* especially will illustrate the constant innovation that goes on in US
libraries to provide users with better and cheaper DD services.

Retrospective Digitisation Exposes more References

The retrospective digitisation programmes have exposed a vast number of
references to material that may not be available to the researcher. This is
an argument often used by US librarians but is not convincing – after all
the same phenomenon exists in other countries, perhaps it is a contemporary example of 'American exceptionalism'. However it has likely to have
had some positive effect on DS globally.

Growth in Researchers

The number of researchers has grown dramatically in the past 50 years.
For example the World Bank estimates 8.9 million in 2014 with a growth

rate of 4–5% per annum (Ware & Mabe, 2015. pp. 37–38). Researchers generate papers that they hope will be published as a record of their work and these may be read by other researchers; this leads to more journals and more articles being published. With limited resources libraries will need to continue using ILL to satisfy their users' demand. The growth in researchers is driven by the massive expansion in higher education; this in turn had led to many governments and universities imposing fees, often very high fees (the UK currently charges £27,000 for a three-year undergraduate course). As a result students are becoming more demanding and are likely to be dissatisfied if they have to pay for material not held locally. When DD fees are dropped demand increases significantly.

Systems Are Smarter

We have come a long way from users filling in a request form by hand – sending or taking it to the library – the library checking a union catalogue then sending the request by post to a library that held the item or send it to a document supplier such as BLDSC – the time to satisfy was at least five or six working days for an article – weeks for a book. Now a user finds a reference in some sort of bibliographical form and with one click populates a request form using Open URL technology – created by Herbert Van de Sompel, a librarian at the University of Ghent, in the late 1990s – (The impact of using OpenURL for DD requests is analysed in a useful article Munson & Otto, 2013). Another click and it is sent to the library which can then send directly to a document supplier or into an automated rota. Articles can be delivered instantaneously if a copyright fee is paid or within hours or even minutes by fair use provision depending on the country. Books still take a few days but are more easily accessible via consortia-based catalogues such as Borrow Direct in the US or centralised catalogues such as the British Library; processing systems are faster and simpler to use with very little human intervention until the book is physically handled. And of course ebooks are increasingly available for ILL although as has been pointed out, 'A 19th-century scholar would have had to travel to a library to access a book. A 20th-century scholar could acquire the book through ILL and not have to travel. But a 21st-century scholar might well have to travel to access a book from a different library if that book was available only as an ebook' (Bivens-Tatum, 2014). The author goes on to describe the difficulties of negotiating ILL from ebooks in the US where copyright law actively discourages access to material and protects the interests of commercial publishers. In the UK the situation is somewhat easier with a more sympathetic copyright regime as noted above. The overall impact in service improvements is difficult to gauge. Some studies have shown increases in ILL when systems have been radically improved – especially when these involve unmediated request and delivery – but it is difficult to generalise.

Not Everything Is Digital

The amount of material that remains undigitised and likely to remain so is vastly underestimated. The legal lock down on the Google Books project has slowed the rate of book digitisation dramatically. There are various estimates of the number of books ever published – Google estimates 130 million although this is a minimum as there will be many that even Google cannot trace – the real figure is probably nearer 150 million. In addition about two million are published every year and being in copyright are mostly only available for purchase, for informal sharing or available via ILL if the reader's library does not hold a copy. Google estimates that it has digitised about 30 million books but only those in the public domain are accessible freely on the web and 'Of the seven million books that Google reportedly had digitised by November 2008, one million are works in the public domain; one million are in copyright and in print; and five million are in copyright but out of print' (Darnton, 2009). A more up-to-date figure is difficult to source but given that Google did not distinguish between books in and out of copyright that number to date would be about four million in the public domain, *no more than 3% of the total books ever published.* Other bodies have digitised perhaps as many as two million. Thus the large majority of books can only be obtained via ILL unless they are held in the reader's library or they are able to physically visit – a very long tail indeed! Perhaps not surprising then that the ILL of returnables is declining far less than the decline in non-returnables. Nobody knows how many journals remain undigitised – most are now defunct but many are not. It is generally acknowledged that there are about 28,000 current English language peer reviewed journals most of which exist in digital form – at least the recent issues (Ware & Mabe, 2015, p. 27). However according to Ulrich there are currently over 300,000 journals and the British Library records 858,414 in their annual report for 2013/2014 which includes title changes which is an overestimate but on the other hand they would not presume to hold every journal ever published so let us assume 700,000 journals both current and defunct and that a researcher may wish to read. Let us assume that all 28,000 current journals have been digitised back to Vol 1 No 1 — even then *which is only 4% of all journals ever published*. Most of these will never be digitised as the demand would be insufficient to justify the cost. Most researchers will not have access to more than a small proportion of these journals and hence will need to use a slower but cheaper DS service. The effect of this long tail of books and journals — popularised in the book of the same name (Anderson, 2008) is likely to remain significant for levels of DS requests.

Not Everyone Has Access to Material

There are many millions of independent researchers who have very limited access to most research publications. Realistically most of them must use DD via their public libraries — although some universities in some countries have agreements to allow local tax payers access to their collections. The same goes for the many SMEs (Small and Medium sized companies) who engage in research and development and who cannot afford to subscribe to very high-priced scientific journals. Both these large groups are poorly served by the publishing industry — and their dependence on DD will continue if not grow although access to freely available material will benefit them considerably.

CHANGES FOR STAFF

So what impact do all these changes have for staff working in DD and resource sharing generally? The most obvious change is the reduction in staffing — brought about by a reduction in demand and technical changes to the DD process removing the need for much manual intervention; examples of which are the widespread acceptance of copyright signatures, the use of link resolvers to populate requests forms, electronic searching including Google, automatic searching of the library's own catalogue for material already held. On the other hand there is great demand for skilled searching in an increasingly complex environment particularly for the growing amount of material that is freely available but often 'hidden' in repositories. These skills are of course bread and butter for DD librarians and they have taken to the demands with enthusiasm — see an example from the US (Baich, 2015).

CONCLUSION

The radical changes in the production and access to the research literature will have a complex impact on the service that provides access to material not available via the resources of the researcher's institution or easily available on the web. The key factors have been briefly adumbrated in this chapter. The *raison d'etre* of DS remains throughout all the current changes. Librarians can neither justify nor afford to buy all that their users want. Some will be little used journals and books but some will be more heavily used but simply too expensive — the so-called 'Serials crisis'. This will not go away so long as the publishing industry is driven by the need to maximise its profits and thus neither will DS or resource sharing ...

NOTES

1. Nomenclature is a difficult issue for this aspect of information access and provision. I will use 'Document Supply' (DS) when referring to non returnables (article copies etc) and ILL when referring to returnables (printed books etc). When referring to both I will use Document Delivery (DD) – clumsy but nobody has come up with a good solution.
2. Download figures are enormous — so enormous that it is difficult to believe that many are looked at let alone read; research in this area would be useful if difficult to carry out.
3. http://www.arl.org/storage/documents/service-trends.pdf
4. http://nces.ed.gov/pubs2014/2014038.pdf
5. OA terminology can be elaborate and off putting for the newcomer to the subject. Essentially Gold OA delivers articles via conventional journals for payment by or on behalf of the author or in fully open access journals which may charge a fee; Green OA delivers via repositories with publication for free in a conventional journal.
6. https://www.oclc.org/worldshare-ill/statistics.en.html.

REFERENCES

Anderson, C. (2008). *The long tail: Why the future of business is selling less of more.* New York, NY: Hyperion.

Appleyard, A. (2015). British library document supply: An information service fit for the future. *Interlending and Document Supply*, *43*(1), 9–13.

Baich, T. (2015). Open access: Help or hindrance to resource sharing? *Interlending and Document Supply*, *43*(2), 68–75.

Ball, D. (2004). What's the "big deal", and why is it a bad deal for universities? *Interlending and Document Supply*, *32*(2), 117–125.

Bérard, R., Fleuret, E., Gillet, J., & Mougel, J.-Y. (2015). Academia and document supply: Unsustainable contradictions at INIST? *Interlending and Document Supply*, *43*(3), 131–137.

Bivens-Tatum, W. (2014). Ebooks and the demise of ILL. *Library Journal*. Retrieved from http://lj.libraryjournal.com/2014/04/opinion/peer-to-peer-review/ebooks-and-the-demise-of-ill-peer-to-peer-review/#_

CIBER. (2009). *E-journals: Their use, value and impact*. Research Information Network. Figures are taken from CIBER Working Paper 4, Information usage and seeking behaviour. Table 18. Retrieved from http://www.rin.ac.uk/our-work/communicating-and-disseminating-research/e-journals-theiruse-value-and-impact

Collins, P. (2015). User analysis in the borrow direct marketplace. *Interlending and Document Supply*, *43*(4).

Cornish, G. (2014). Reform of UK copyright law and its benefits for libraries. *Interlending and Document Supply*, *43*(1), 14–17.

Darnton, R. (2009). Google & the future of books. New York Review of Books. Retrieved from http://www.nybooks.com/articles/archives/2009/feb/12/google-the-future-of-books/. Accessed on Feb 12.

Davis, P. (2014). Growing Impact of Older Articles. *The Scholarly Kitchen*. Retrieved from http://scholarlykitchen.sspnet.org/2014/11/10/growing-impact-of-older-articles/

Estelle, L. (2014). What price open access? *Research Information*. Retrieved from http://www.researchinformation.info/news/news_story.php?news_id=1804. Accessed on December 2014.

Landes, S. (1997). ARIEL document delivery: A cost-effective alternative to fax. *Interlending and Document Supply*, *25*(3), 113–117.

Mak, C. (2011). Resource sharing among ARL libraries in the US: 35 years of growth. *Interlending and Document Supply*, *39*(1), 26–31.

Mangiaracina, S., Cocever, C., Chiandoni, M., & Arabito, S. (2014). Assessing the effectiveness of a national resource sharing system. *Interlending and Document Supply*, *42*(2–3), 98–104.

Morrison, H., Jihane, S., Calvé-Genest, A., & Hora, T. (2015). Open access article processing charges: DOAJ survey May 2014. *Open Access Scholarly Publishing Journal*, *3*(1), 1–16.

Munson, D. M., & Otto, J. L. (2013). Have link resolvers helped or hurt? The relationship between ILL and OpenURL at a non-SFX library. *OCLC Systems and Services: International Digital Library Perspectives*, *29*(2), 78–86.

OCLC. (2015). Personal communication with OCLC.

OCLC Annual Report. (2013–2014). Retrieved from https://www.oclc.org/en-US/annual-report/2014/home.html

Oppenheim, C. (2014). *Guest Post: Charles Oppenheim on who owns the rights to scholarly articles*. Retrieved from Richard Poynder's blog 'Open and Shut'. Retrieved from http://poynder.blogspot.co.uk/2014/02/guest-post-charles-oppenheim-on-who.html

Rosemann, U., & Brammer, M. (2010). Development of document delivery by libraries in Germany since 2003. *Interlending and Document Supply*, *38*(1), 26–30.

Sanville, T. (2007). OhioLINK: A US resource sharing facility – Issues and developments. *Interlending and Document Supply*, *35*(1), 31–37.

Schöpfel, J., Chaudiron, S., Jacquemin, B., Prost, H., Severo, M., & Thiault, F. (2014). Open access to research data in electronic theses and dissertations: An overview. *Library Hi Tech, 32*(4), 612−627.

Tyler, D. (2011). Patron-driven purchase on demand programs for printed books and similar materials: A chronological review and summary of findings. *Library Philosophy and Practice*. Retrieved from http://unllib.unl.edu/LPP/tyler.htm

van Dyck, G. (2011). Interlibrary loan purchase-on-demand: A misleading literature. *Library Collections, Acquisitions, and Technical Services, 35*(2−3), 83−89.

Ware, M., & Mabe, M. (2015). *The STM report: An overview of scientific and scholarly journal publishing* (4th ed., p. 27). Netherlands: Association of Scientific Technical and Medical Publishers. Retrieved from http://www.stm-assoc.org/2015_02_20_STM_Report_2015.pdf

White, M. (2012). Mining the archive: The development of electronic journals. *Ariadne*, 70. Retrieved from http://www.ariadne.ac.uk/issue70/white

Wijnen, J. W. (2007). *Journal backfiles in scientific publishing: A marketing white paper.* London: British Library. Retrieved from http://www.bl.uk/reshelp/atyourdesk/docsupply/productsservices/digitisation/journalbackfileswhitepaper.pdf

Zhu, X., & Shen, L. (2014). A survey of e-book interlibrary loan policy in US academic libraries. *Interlending and Document Supply, 42*(2−3), 57−63.

WEB REFERENCES

[1] Retrieved from http://www.iccu.sbn.it/opencms/opencms/en/main/sbn/poli_biblioteche/

[2] Retrieved from http://www.tandfonline.com/action/journalInformation?show = aimsScope& journalCode = wild20#.Ve6j-mKFO70

[3] Retrieved from http://www.elsevier.com/solutions/sciencedirect/content/articlechoice

THE LIBRARIANSHIP PORTFOLIO, PART TWO: A RUBRIC FOR EVALUATION

Chloe Persian Mills

ABSTRACT

Purpose — *The author proposes the broad use of a Librarianship Portfolio in performance evaluation of librarian work performance and promotion decisions, and a rubric is formulated to guide managers in its use.*

Findings — *The librarianship portfolio and rubric offer a flexible and significant alternative to many performance evaluation techniques. Tailored to a broader array of institutional types and employment situations these tools can provide both management and employees with collaborative and substantive information about professional performance and appraisal.*

Practical implications — *The librarianship portfolio itself and the proposed rubric offer the library world a structured, summative and collaborative process for performance evaluation of work performance. They offer employees a means of 'looking their best' to the management, and the management a calibrated and clear method of feedback.*

Innovation in Libraries and Information Services
Advances in Library Administration and Organization, Volume 35, 121–133
Copyright © 2017 by Emerald Group Publishing Limited
All rights of reproduction in any form reserved
ISSN: 0732-0671/doi:10.1108/S0732-067120160000035014

Originality/value – *The librarianship portfolio discussed as well as the rubric proposed are original formulations and tools, based on well-established and effective evaluative techniques.*

Keywords: Assessment; work performance; professional portfolios; higher education; faculty evaluation; summative assessment

DEVELOPMENT OF THE LIBRARIANSHIP PORTFOLIO, AND CONSIDERATIONS FOR ITS BROADER USE

In her 2015 article, 'The Librarianship Portfolio', this chapter's author discusses the development of a new instrument for the evaluation of library faculty in their specific roles as librarians, as a part of a promotion dossier (Mills, 2015). The portfolio provides a rich, evidence-based summative portrait of an individual library faculty member's professional work distinct from the scholarship and service that is required for rank promotion for all faculty, both library and teaching. This evaluative instrument emerged directly as a part of the negotiations for the Robert Morris University (RMU) Faculty Federation Collective Bargaining Agreement (CBA). Use of an evaluative portfolio was proposed initially by the administrative negotiations team. That portfolio was based upon evaluation language in the previous CBA, which, by the time of negotiation was over seven years old (Mills, 2015, p. 531). The library faculty member on the union team deemed this proposal outdated and inappropriate, and created the Librarianship Portfolio as it now exists in the 2014 CBA (Robert Morris University and Robert Morris University Faculty Federation, 2014, pp. 97–98). The RMU CBA is a legal contract, and, as such, both library faculty members and administration are required to use it for evaluation purposes. At the time, however, no consideration by either the union or the administration was given as to how the portfolio might be evaluated. The rubric proposed here is not part of the legal contract, but rather, the rubric was created only after the experience of the author in creating a portfolio to be used for her own continuation of probationary employment evaluation.[1] Herein lies the motivation for the rubric discussed in this chapter.

Necessity was the mother of the Librarianship Portfolio, but it did not lack for other ancestors. It was based on the construction of teaching portfolios long in use by educators at the K-12 level, job searching port-folios and evaluative instruments described in the library professional literature or published online. In addition, it takes portions of its structure from the specific teaching portfolio being developed at RMU for the eva-luation of the teaching portion of teaching faculty performance and promo-tion dossiers; the teaching portfolio had been developed by a joint task force of faculty members and departments heads without input from any library faculty. The use of a portfolio to document and provide evidence of superior performance of librarianship appears to be novel (Mills, 2015, p. 531). The author offers the portfolio and this rubric as the basis for eva-luative instruments at other institutions out of a belief that rich, documen-ted evidence of work performance is a superior tool for institutional decision-making in general. In her study of 1,904 unionized colleges and universities, Applegate noted that only three percent are private and have unionized faculty librarians (Applegate, 2009, p. 452). Keeping these powerful instruments only to unionized institutions is unnecessarily restric-tive. The broader application of these tools provides others with the oppor-tunity to use, enhance and tailor the concepts of the portfolio and rubric in ways that move toward important administrative goals of documentation, accountability and equity of treatment, while also allowing employees to provide a full and attractive picture of their individual contributions to institutional initiatives.

As mentioned above, the original proposition to include a Librarianship Portfolio originated from the administrative side of the table, but was col-lectively shaped by librarians and union members in its final version (Mills, 2015, pp. 530−531). This constructive collaboration is unusual but is a technique that can be used by non-unionized institutions to create mutual appreciation of the evaluative process, and to enhance communication and interactivity between employees and administrators. Thus, the portfolio can help to make the evaluation into a performance appraisal that serves as a 'conduit for mutual feedback … [and] can be an effective motivational tool' (Edwards & Williams, 1998, p. 16). Using similar, but not identical, portfolios to that of teaching faculty for promotion and tenure decisions serves to highlight how both teaching and library faculty work to attain educational goals met in similar but not identical ways by the teaching faculty. The Librarianship Portfolio is 'an educational opportunity and an educational tool' (Mills, 2015, p. 534). The rubric proposed below could easily be adapted to the evaluation of teaching faculty. As such, these tools serve to support and enhance the value of academic librarianship in the wider higher educational institution.

THE EVALUATION OF ONE
LIBRARIANSHIP PORTFOLIO

In the particular instance in which the portfolio shown in the appendix was submitted, the timeline for the submission and administrative response was detailed in the CBA; the format of the administrative evaluation of the portfolio was left unspecified. One meeting was held between the library faculty member and the library director to review the submitted portfolio. This review focused on the portfolio's structure and demonstrated that the two people did interpret the requirements of the portfolio somewhat differently. These differences were mostly structural or related to formatting. It was noted in this meeting that the portfolio was an entirely new thing for both the director and the faculty member, and that some interpretive differences were to be expected in a new process. The director deemed the portfolio and the evidence it presented as clear enough and acceptable for submission. This meeting did not include any analysis or evaluation of the faculty member's job performance. The library director later responded to the portfolio in a briefly written memo. It concluded that the portfolio submitted was 'satisfactory for purposes of meeting the requirements set forth' by the CBA, and, two minor points were appended suggesting possible improvements for the portfolio itself (T. Schlak, personal communication, September 28, 2015). This response was adequate to the situation, but its simplicity and lack of elaboration motivated the thought-processes that created the rubric proposed in this chapter.

A PROPOSED RUBRIC

The evaluation rubric presented in Table 1 is proposed as a structured means to an administrative response to the employee's portfolio that is helpful to both parties. This scale has not been a part of the evaluation of promotion or retention decisions at RMU to date, and there is no mention of specific evaluation criteria for the portfolio of the RMU CBA. The CBA indicates minimum requirements for promotion and retention and delineates the procedures that determine how faculty are considered for these. There is some considerable leeway in the process for administration to build its own practices for how evaluation is done (Robert Morris University and Robert Morris University Faculty Federation, 2014). It is intended to apply to a multitude of different institutional contexts and to

Table 1. Evaluation Rubric for Librarianship Portfolio.

Evaluation Scale	Explanation of Details
SEE – substantially exceeded expectations Clearly and consistently exceeded many expectations	Substantial evidence of librarianship achievement a level beyond basic job requirements in all indicated librarianship competencies, in particular, likely to indicate achievement in more than one competency; evidence of achievement in librarianship as initiated by the librarian, not merely achievement in management-assigned projects; likely to achieve levels appropriate to promotion to next higher rank, if other promotion requirements are met (if faculty member); retention of employment is not in question
EE – exceeded expectations Clearly exceeded some, and met all other expectations	Evidence of librarianship achievement in at least one competency at a level beyond basic job requirements; evidence of beyond – basic achievement in all assigned duties/projects; likely to achieve levels appropriate to promotion to next higher rank, if other promotion requirements are met (if faculty member); retention of employment is not in question
ME – met expectations Clearly met all expectations	Evidence of librarianship achievement in at least one competency at basic job requirements, above basic job requirements in some cases; likely will achieve levels appropriate to promotion at next higher rank, if some improvement is documented and other promotion requirements are met (if faculty member); likely to be retained in employment
MSE – met some expectations Met some expectations, but clearly needs to improve to meet expectations	Evidence of librarianship achievement in chosen competency(ies) is spotty and not beyond basic job requirements; may achieve levels appropriate to promotion at next higher rank, if improvement is well-documented and all other promotion requirements are met (if faculty); retention of employment is in question – remediation activities will be discussed, documented and agreed upon by employee and management
NME – did not meet expectations Clearly needs significant improvement to meet expectations	Evidence of librarianship achievement in chosen competency(ies) is insufficient or not up to basic job requirements; unlikely to achieve levels appropriate to promotion at next higher rank, unless improvement is well-documented and all other promotion requirements are met (if faculty); retention of employment is unlikely but not impossible – remediation activities will be discussed, documented and agreed upon by employee and management

provide a model. The rubric represents an attempt to minimize confusion and also to streamline the work of evaluation for the manager.

ADMINISTERING AND RESPONDING TO THE LIBRARIANSHIP PORTFOLIO: MANAGEMENT PERSPECTIVES

The librarianship portfolio offers both management and the employee or faculty member a structured document that will have important aspects in common across employees. But, by design, it will vary somewhat in its contents according to individual interpretations of its requirements and the nature of the provided evidence. It is strongly recommended that the rubric (or an institution-specific variant) be shared with the employee *prior to the submission of the portfolio* because, in this way, the rubric establishes a mutually-known basis for evaluation. In addition, the explanations provide a platform from which a conversation about the evidence and the evaluator's conclusions can proceed. The wealth of documentation options available to the employee helps to dispel some difficulties inherent in the evaluation process. Since the employee has considerable control over which aspects of her librarianship are considered for evaluation, she has an opportunity to highlight the best parts of her job performance, and this may alleviate some of the fearfulness of the performance assessment process (Aluri & Reichel, 1994, p. 147). It is good practice for administrators to be aware of how the individuals who work for them may vary in their ability to construct the portfolio and respond to its requirements. In some cases, employees may need guidance on how best to present themselves.

The structured aspect of the portfolio combined with the rubric for evaluation provides both the manager and the employee with a common baseline of knowledge, which can be helpful in preventing disagreements and differences in interpretation. Naturally, no evaluative instrument or rubric can completely remove differences of perspective. This reality should be specified and known to all parties involved in the evaluation. Management may wish to add commentary to the final evaluation, and, in fact, further explication will be required for a conclusion of 'MSE − Met Some Expectations' or 'NME − Did Not Meet Expectations'. This requirement is good for management in that it helps to document reasons if non-appointment or firing becomes necessary later; it is good for the employee because it encourages improvement, indicates the severity of the need and makes explicit the requirements for remediation. Because of its connection to the collective bargaining process the procedures and timelines for producing and evaluating the portfolio discussed here are carefully described within the CBA itself. Other institutions who elect to use or adapt the portfolio and rubric for their purposes will want to develop these procedural matters or fit them into already existing policies. The portfolio could be used for yearly assessments or as a part of rank promotion applications. There is also potential for use in the profession more widely; certainly, the portfolio could be used in the way that it was traditionally developed for the K-12 context, as a way of highlighting the teaching/educational practices and successes of job applicants and new employees. Library science students could develop similarly structured documentation during their education and internships prior to the beginning of their careers, as a way of supplementing their job applications with substantive and job-relevant information.

This rubric is only a proposal, one based upon the specific situation in which the RMU Librarianship Portfolio was developed. The evaluation scale is also based on the specific institution and uses the summarized evaluation terminology for non-academic staff and administration. The particular language for the scale is probably the most flexible aspect of this rubric and can be adapted to other institutions with slightly different means of or scales for evaluating. The explanations are similarly adaptable, but are intended as a foundation on which other institutions may wish to build. As mentioned above, since the librarianship portfolio and this rubric are specific to the duties of academic librarians in their library positions, these evaluative tools should be able to be used in academic institutions of numerous types, whether librarians have faculty status or not. The use of the rubric may help justify decisions about rank promotion in cases where the librarians are faculty because it helps to eliminate surprises and standardize the process.

Administrators and employees may have concerns that a rubric such as this one could be connected to numerical values and used in predetermined formula(e) to provide a 'grade' or value for the employee's librarianship, or as part of an overall formula for evaluating librarianship alongside scholarship and service activities. Naturally, a one to five numerical scale would be trivial to map onto this particular evaluation scheme. Indeed, such practices have been used for faculty and/or employee performance evaluation in libraries before (Pan & Li, 2006; Wallace, 1986). Evidence from the professional literature suggests that this kind of formulaic assessment of employee performance can lead to problematic, possibly invalid and unfair conclusions about work performance (Pan & Li, 2006, pp. 463–467; Aluri & Reichel, 1994, p. 150), and, in some cases even when employees were generally given high rankings, 'leniency error' can contribute to invalidity in the results (Martey, 2002, p. 413). The university at which the Librarianship Portfolio was developed does not rely on formulaic or even inter-departmentally consistent means of assessment of the portfolios of library or teaching faculty. Thus, administrators who may wish to use the librarianship portfolio or a modification of it are strongly encouraged not to attach the rubric to a numerical scale for ultimate evaluations of tenure, merit pay or annual performance raises. These documents are offered as tools for more consistent and robust evaluation, but not intended to replace the good judgement of knowledgeable and engaged managers employing a range of mechanisms for assessing the whole employee and his or her professional contribution to institutional objectives.

NOTE

1. Long-time practice at this institution divides full-time faculty employment into periods of 'probationary' and 'non-probationary' status; this status corresponds, more or less, with 'non-tenured' and 'tenured' at other United States institutions. When a faculty member is probationary she is required to create a portfolio on a yearly basis to advocate for her continued employment retention. Once non-probationary status is achieved a portfolio is necessary only if the faculty member is applying for rank promotion. For the purposes of this chapter, the institution-specific terms and the more usual concept of tenure are used interchangeably. At RMU, if an application for rank promotion is accepted for promotion from Assistant to Associate Professor, non-probationary status is automatically granted.

ACKNOWLEDGMENT

The author wishes to thank Christopher Devine and the anonymous reviewers for helpful and significant advice for improvements to this work.

REFERENCES

Aluri, R., & Reichel, M. (1994). Performance evaluation: A deadly disease? *Journal of Academic Librarianship*, *20*(3), 145−155.
Applegate, R. (2009). Who benefits? Unionization and academic libraries and librarians. *Library Quarterly*, *79*(4), 443−463.

Edwards, R. G., & Williams, C. J. (1998). Performance appraisal in academic libraries: Minor changes or major renovation? *Library Review, 47*(1), 14−19.

Martey, A. K. (2002). Appraising the performance of library staff in a Ghanaian academic library. *Library Management, 23*(9), 403−416.

Mills, C. (2015). The librarianship portfolio: A case study of innovation in faculty evaluation at Robert Morris university. *New Library World, 116*(9−10), 527−539.

Pan, J., & Li, G. (2006). What can we learn from performance assessment? The system and practice in an academic library. *Library Management, 27*(6−7), 460−469.

Robert Morris University and Robert Morris University Faculty Federation, Local 3412, AFT, AFL-CIO. (2014). *Collective bargaining agreement.* Retrieved from https://sentry. rmu.edu/OnTheMove/findoutmore.open_page?ipage = 993092&iattr = ssl. Accessed on July 19, 2014−May 19, 2017.

Wallace, P. M. (1986). Performance evaluation: The use of a single instrument for university librarians and teaching faculty. *Journal of Academic Librarianship, 12*(5), 284−290.

APPENDIX: THE LIBRARIANSHIP PORTFOLIO, A COMPLETED EXAMPLE

Required Components:

i. *Librarianship Philosophy – Personal Statement*

My life as a librarian at Robert Morris University has been character-ized overall by a strong service orientation, analytical acuity and an eagerness for and ability to succeed in new tasks. I have made it a per-sonal working philosophy never to say no to opportunities to broaden my horizons as a librarian or to carry the basic service attitude inherent in my work to the larger university community. Librarians can and should be fully immersed in faculty life, even while their specific job duties may differ significantly from teaching faculty. Librarianship is, in its essentials, a service profession, and that basic principle informs my willingness to adapt to the changing demands of this institution as well as my desire to participate in university and profession-wide service.

While my official job title is that of Distance Learning Librarian, I have multiple roles at the library, which have varied somewhat in the seven years I have worked here. I work multiple hours each week on the reference desk, perform library instruction, act as the university's archi-vist and develop outreach and services for our online students. Additionally, I am an active member of several committees, both library and university-wide and was elected as a RMU Faculty Federation Executive Committee member. I also stay abreast of the intellectual and cultural life of the university through attendance at events such as the Rooney Scholar programs, Women's Luncheons and presentations hosted by Multicultural Student Services and the Honors Program. I participate in the region's library and archives communities by attend-ing and presenting at conferences.

University and faculty service has consistently been one of the most engaging aspects of my work at RMU. Active service in university-wide committees has allowed me greater contact with other faculty and staff and has helped me more fully understand their information and service needs. Committee work has frequently informed how I approach refer-ence work, instruction and library outreach, as I have gained a fuller understanding of the broader picture of not only our institution but also the national higher education context. These commitments have also helped me to fulfil an educational purpose for our community, as I have no doubt that my input has helped other faculty and staff to understand more fully what the library can do for them and how it serves as a cornerstone of the educational experience. Working with students of history and library science as a supervisor of internships has been a personally and professionally gratifying opportunity to enhance the library's position within the institution and the greater Pittsburgh library community.

The principles of service and integration of the library into university life have strongly influenced my scholarly interests. In 2010, I presented at a library conference my efforts to improve and enhance faculty participation in library scholarship among our librarians through collegial support and collaboration, and in 2011 spoke to economics faculty about supporting student learning in economics through alternative resources. This work in teaching economics through popular literatures resulted in a 2014 peer-reviewed publication. I have explored the particulars of outreach to special populations through a research study looking into how our library might best serve RMU's growing student veteran population. My work with the RMU Faculty Federation both on the Executive Council and Negotiations team led to a publication about faculty evaluation, which demonstrates my commitment to service to the profession. In sum, through my professionalism and service, as well as my scholarly interests I have become one of RMU's most visible librarians, seeking constantly to broaden the reach of the library and integrate our services fully into university life.

ii. *Primary Librarianship Responsibilities*

I serve as the RMU Library's principal instruction and research assistance contact for all our distance learning students, at undergraduate and graduate levels. I create most online instruction modules and coordinate the creation of others with other library faculty. I manage the RMU Library YouTube channel. I am a member of the library instruction team with multiple class visits each semester. I manage the archives collections, answer archives research questions, create archives policies and initiate outreach among the university population for the archives. Along with [a colleague], I coordinate a feminist book club with the Women's Leadership and Mentorship Program, which meets at least twice each year for discussion. I also serve as a consultant for the collections acquisitions of our Henrietta Angus Popular reading collection.

In sum, I am a public services librarian who goes where she is needed most on any given day for any given project.

iii. *Primary Librarianship Competencies as defined in current RMU FF CBA*

Education and Communication
Information Access and Support (Archives)
Professional Development and continuing education
Collection development

iv. *Index of supporting materials:* (see also below, 'Optional Requirements')

(a) Curriculum Vitae
(b) Complete list of instructional videos, with hyperlinks
(c) List of professional literature regularly consulted
(d) Service on librarianship committees
(e) Copies of library policies/internal documents, authored or co-authored
(f) Copies of collegial recommendations

v. *Professional development and continuing education*

(a) Webinar − ALA, 'Teaching Information Literacy with Discovery Tools' 15 May 2014
(b) WPWVC-ACRL Fall Meeting, 'Under Construction: Building Community Among Students, Faculty, and Library Staff' 24 October 2014
(c) Webinar − ALA 'Reinventing the Library for Online Education' 8 January 2015
(d) RMU CITADEL seminar, 'Blackboard Collaborate − Basic' 27 January 2015
(e) Girls and Women in Sport Conference, 4 February 2015
(f) Webinar − ACRL, 'Putting the Framework for Information Literacy into Action' 4 March 2015

Optional Requirements: (As indicated in Index, above.)

(a) *Curriculum Vitae*

(b) *Complete list of instructional video created for library instruction at a distance: (including hyperlinks)*
(1) Introduction to library website: https://youtu.be/XN09ElE2sI8
(2) Getting to RMU databases: https://youtu.be/Si8lIXsP9FI

(3) Getting in touch with an RMU Librarian: https://youtu.be/UuH8l-y7mf4

(4) Introduction to Credo Reference database: https://www.youtube.com/watch?v = pasvau-cBkU

(5) Introduction to Project Muse database: https://www.youtube.com/watch?v = SGFQ06dHWVc

(6) Finding RMU dissertations online: https://youtu.be/mPfFdXTTbj0

(7) Introduction to the Proquest database platform: https://www.youtube.com/watch?v = hv9Hixn7nfA

(c) *List of professional literature regularly consulted:*
   (1) Library Journal
   (2) College and Research Libraries
   (3) College and Research Library News
   (4) Booklist
   (5) Publisher's Weekly
   (6) Choices for Academic Libraries
   (7) New York Review of Books

(d) *Service on librarianship committees:*
   (1) Co-lead, Online and Distance Education Librarianship Practice Group, 2010–2015
   (2) This Practice Group changed composition, title and direction somewhat in the 2014–2015 year, but the focus of the work has persisted from its earlier instantiation.
   (3) Co-Lead, External Services Work Group
   (4) Co-Lead, Information Literacy Practice Group
   (5) Chair, Scholarly Activities Committee, 2009–present
   (6) Strategic Planning Leadership Team, Member
   (7) IL, Instruction, and Research Planning Group, Member
   (8) Outreach and PR Planning Group, Member

(e) *Copies of library policies/internal documents, authored or co-authored:*
   (1) Co-wrote Online and Distance Education Librarianship Practice Group document
   (2) Co-wrote External Services Work Group document
   (3) Co-wrote Information Literacy Practice Group document
   (4) Annual Report of Archives and Distance Learning Activities, 2014–2015

(f) *Copies of collegial recommendations*

OPEN SOURCE SYSTEMS AND SHARED SERVICES: THE BLMS EXPERIENCE – A CASE STUDY

John Robinson

ABSTRACT

Purpose – *This is a case study on the opportunities provided by Open Source library systems and the experience of delivering these systems through a shared service.*

Methodology/approach – *This chapter derives from desk research, interviews, and direct involvement in the project. The format is a case study, setting out a detailed timeline of events with information that can be applied in other settings.*

Findings – *This chapter presents reflections on the value and limitations of collaboration amongst libraries and librarians on an innovative approach to library systems and technologies. It also presents reflections on lessons learned from the processes and detailed discussion of the success factors for shared services and the reasons why such initiatives may not result in the outcomes predicted at the start.*

Practical implications – *Libraries and IT services considering Open Source and shared service approaches to provision will find material in this study useful when planning their projects.*

Innovation in Libraries and Information Services
Advances in Library Administration and Organization, Volume 35, 135–225
Copyright © 2017 by Emerald Group Publishing Limited
All rights of reproduction in any form reserved
ISSN: 0732-0671/doi:10.1108/S0732-067120160000035015

Social implications – *The nature of collaboration and collaborative working is studied and observations made about the way that outcomes cannot always be predicted or controlled. In a genuine collaboration, the outcome is determined by the interactions between the partners and is unique to the specifics of that collaboration.*

Originality/value – *The case study derives from interviews, written material and direct observation not generally in the public domain, providing a strong insider's view of the activity.*

Keywords: Open Source library systems; case study; project planning; collaboration

ACKNOWLEDGEMENTS

The author acknowledges the following key contributors to this work: Jisc (for funding the case-study); the BLMS Partners (http://www.kualiole.org. uk); the OLE Partners (https://www.openlibraryenvironment.org); Sharon Penfold, the BLMS Project Manager 2012-2015 (for the original documents); Deborah Benady, Journalist (for the interviews). In particular, the author acknowledges the interviewees: Ade Aderemi (AA) SOAS Library; Rob Atkinson (RA) Birkbeck Library; Simon Barron (SB) Imperial College London Library; Frances McNamara (FM) University of Chicago Library; Claudia Mendias (CM) SOAS Library; Carlen Ruschoff (CR) University of Maryland Library; Sharon Wiles-Young (SW-Y) Lehigh University Library; Mike Winkler (MW) OLE Partnership Managing Director as well as many other Library staff too numerous to name (you know who you are).

The goal of the Open Library Environment Project (OLE Project) was to design a next-generation library system that breaks away from print-based workflows, reflects the changing nature of library materials and new approaches to scholarly work, integrates well with other enterprise systems and can be easily modified to suit the needs of different institutions.

The project planners went beyond designing for incremental improvement of current Integrated Library Systems (ILS's). They also viewed the role of library business technology systems to be more than purchasing and providing access to collected materials. The project planners chose to define a system that supports libraries as a central player in the research process. (p. 1)

[...]

Although this report accurately describes the facts, it does not convey the energy and enthusiasm that characterized the OLE Project this past year. Project planners engaged in lively debate, wrote and re-wrote documents, shared and discussed readings, responded to dozens of requests for phone calls and presentations by interested groups and individuals and faced challenging questions at public events, all with good humor. They wrestled with technology and phone systems to figure out how to collaborate across thousands of miles and a 14 hour time spread. They learned to say "June" instead of "summer," in recognition that there are two hemispheres in this world.

The response from the library community exceeded all expectations. Workshops quickly filled with participants from libraries large and small, near and far. Webcasts drew interest from around the world; project members began recording and posting the recordings for those who could not attend "live" in the middle of the night. Throughout all of these activities, individuals with deep respect and concern for libraries wrestled with difficult issues and diverse points of view.

The OLE Project completed its official goals, but beyond that, it launched a world-wide conversation about the desired future of libraries and what is needed to move libraries toward that future. (p. 12)

Open Library Environment Project Final Report – October 20 2009
http://www.kuali.org/sites/default/files/old/OLE_FINAL_Report.pdf
Accessed on December 2015

One of the elements that make up the total cash releasing savings of £490.1 million a year by 2010-11 is shared services. While the development of shared services is not mandatory in higher education there is an expectation that universities and colleges will wish to take advantage of such opportunities, as this would generate benefits to them and produce savings to further support teaching and research.

HEFCE: Efficiencies and shared services 2008-09, p. 2
http://www.hefce.ac.uk/media/hefce/content/about/Staff,and,structure/Board/2009/129/B75.pdf
Accessed on December 2015

Collaboration: "the unpredictability of the outcome of such practices can prevent it from being commodified or reproduced".

unpublished essay quoting Schneider
https://web.archive.org/web/20141224141111/http://summit.kein.org/node/190
Accessed on December 2015

INTRODUCTION

The idea of the Bloomsbury Library Management System (BLMS) was quite simple. As with all simple ideas, the complexity came later. Whilst the outcome was different from what had been envisaged, it was at the same time still in keeping with the original impulse.

Some background. In 2009 the Bloomsbury Colleges (BC group) was a formal alliance of six: Birkbeck (BBK), Institute of Education (IoE),

London School of Hygiene and Tropical Medicine (LSHTM), School of Oriental and African Studies (SOAS), School of Pharmacy (SoP) and Royal Veterinary College (RVC). These six colleges were a subset of the 18 colleges that – along with the Schools of Advanced Studies (SAS) and a number of institutes – made up the Federal University of London. The BC group had a number of successful examples of shared service to draw upon, of which the most notable (in this context) was the Bloomsbury Learning Environment (BLE), a shared Virtual Library Environment (VLE).

The Bloomsbury Librarians met regularly and had reviewed a number of options for developing library-oriented shared services. Each library had a history of working with the central library of the University of London (Senate House Library or SHL) in a number of different contexts. The situation in 2009 was defined by the SHL subscription model (each of the constituent colleges of the University paid a fee for use of SHL) and the University of London Access Agreement[1] (a framework defining the terms on which members of any of the University of London colleges could make use of each other's libraries). At the time of writing (May 2016), the interaction between the colleges and the Central Library continues via the Federal Libraries Group (FLG) and the SHL Board, which includes two college librarians and a nominee from the FLG.

The University Librarians had been organised since the 1950s, initially as the Standing Conference of the Librarians of the Libraries of the University of London (SCOLLUL). The University Senate set up a Committee on Library Resources in 1967 to investigate the possibilities of increasing cooperation in the rationalisation of resources. This led to the reform of SCOLLUL in 1974 as the Library Resources Co-ordinating Committee (LRCC).

In the 1980s and 1990s, a number of initiatives to develop Library Automation Systems resulted in shared service arrangements such as SWALCAP (South Western Academic Libraries Co-operative Automation Project), which developed a system called LIBERTAS and BLCMP (Birmingham Libraries Co-operative Mechanisation Project), which developed a system called Talis. A number of the University of London colleges used LIBERTAS, operated by the central library as part of the extensive range of services it offered to the colleges, with oversight by the LRCC. LIBERTAS was purchased by Innovative Interfaces Inc (III) in 1997 and deprecated in favour of its own INNOPAC system (later re-named Millennium). Once it was determined that LIBERTAS would not pass the 'year 2000 test' (a major software flaw arising from the use of two-digit year codes that made 2000 and subsequent years indistinguishable from 1900 onwards), all LIBERTAS libraries had to look elsewhere for their systems. Some but not all chose INNOPAC and the central library ceased to be the provider of a shared library management system.[2]

Another notable shared service operated by the central library is the University of London book depository (located on the campus of Royal Holloway at Egham), and a number of initiatives continue in the areas of shared print and shared access to e-resources. At the point when the Bloomsbury Librarians agreed to work together on the idea of the BLMS (modelled on the successful BLE), it became logical for SHL to become involved as it was also looking for a new system, and could see how a shared system might evolve into a University of London system, with significant benefits to all its subscribing colleges. From this point of view, it would be tempting to say that the shared library system pendulum that swung away from the central library when the colleges using LIBERTAS went their own ways was swinging back; the reality (as this study shows) was rather less simple. Whilst there are fascinating lessons to learn about the evolution of library automation technologies in the era of Open Source (and some of those lessons are documented here), there are also lessons about the success factors for a shared service initiative. Not least of the lessons are about the many ways in which institutional turbulence such as the departure of senior project sponsors, institutional mergers or restructuring can derail or deflect even the best-laid plans. To give two examples: of the six Bloomsbury College Librarians who were meeting regularly in 2009, only one remains in post; the BC Group has reduced to four as two of its members (SoP and IoE) are now part of University College London (UCL). SHL meanwhile has been restructured with a completely new management team and has decided on a completely different approach to its library systems.

The underlying theme, however, is that the urge to collaborate − evident amongst academic libraries almost as far back as one cares to look − is as strong in the 21st century as it has ever been, and the outcomes of that collaboration are sometimes surprising; but outcomes there are nonetheless and there is plenty of evidence from the librarians who have followed this project through, of the operational and cultural benefits arising from the initiative.

Where We Started

Two threads converged to produce the idea: an interest in the opportunities provided by Open Source library systems; the prospect of delivering these systems through a shared service.

The discussion about library systems had started in 2010. Librarians across the six libraries − and many of their staff − expressed a general sense of dissatisfaction with their current systems (two different suppliers and three different types of system were in use, most of which had been in place, little-changed for more than 10 years and in some cases as many as 20), and had started to look closely at Open Source alternatives.

Staffordshire University Library[3] had a successful implementation of the
Koha[4] system and was happy to talk about it; the Evergreen[5] system was
also attracting some attention. The development of library automation systems is well-documented elsewhere and this document does not propose to
study that in detail as the specific focus is on the opportunities offered by
the move towards Open Source.

The interest in Open Source was not primarily about saving money
(although the fees charged by current suppliers seemed in many cases like
money for old rope, given the paucity of improvements delivered in
return): there was a sense that Open Source − which was proving very
effective in other contexts such as virtual learning environments, repositories and research data management, not to mention forming the basis
of many web and systems implementations − could provide the opportunities to embed library systems into information and enterprise environments which the traditional 'black box' or 'turnkey' systems could not.
Not least of the opportunities, which seemed to be missed by the main
suppliers, was the dramatic rise in the late-20th and early-21st centuries
of the hybrid library delivering a mixture of print and electronic material
to users both on- and off-site. When they compared notes, the
Bloomsbury Librarians discovered that they had to rely upon patchwork
quilts of systems and procedures − with rather haphazard levels of support from their IT services − to manage their resources and deliver them
to their users. Surely there was a better way?

The hype-cycle around 'shared services' was approaching its peak, with
'Bloomsbury' seen by HEFCE as an exemplar of shared service initiatives.
This provided a good prospect for a Bloomsbury approach. Another key
factor was that the BC Librarians discovered that they were each approaching the need for a new library system at around the same time. In IT
jargon, this 'alignment of procurement cycles' was important.

The shared-service impulse was informed by a comprehensive understanding of the 'Bloomsbury' environment so admired by HEFCE: successful examples of shared services ranged from the Bloomsbury Heat and
Power Consortium (shared CHP boilers pumping hot water into a number
of buildings and shipping power back into the National Grid); the London
International Development Centre (shared buildings and facilities); the
Senate House Libraries (shared access for all University of London Colleges
as well as the Schools of Advanced Study); the Bloomsbury Learning
Environment (a Virtual Learning Environment (VLE) shared between five
of the six Bloomsbury Colleges); the University of London Computing
Centre (once *the* computing centre for the University, now a provider of
shared facilities and hosted services on a semi-commercial basis).

Fundamental to the Bloomsbury approach was the recognition that the smaller colleges could achieve service outcomes – on a variety of fronts – that they would find difficult to achieve acting alone. For the librarians, this manifested as a recognition that each library would struggle to achieve much more than a basic library system upgrade, if it had to work through a conventional 'reprocurement' exercise, whereas collectively, it was possible to imagine a truly game-changing 'next generation' system delivered as another flagship 'Bloomsbury' shared service.

From these initial thoughts, the idea of the BLMS arose.

Where We Ended Up

A large part of this document deals with the detail of how we got from an idea in 2011/2012 of 'the BLMS' to the present day (early-2016). The outcome, as it currently stands – and this could change, as we operate in a dynamic environment – is that SOAS, one of the original six Bloomsbury libraries, has adopted the Kuali Open Library Environment (OLE) to replace its legacy system and is working as a member of the OLE Partnership, a collaboration between 11 libraries and several suppliers which designs and commissions the OLE software on an Open Source basis, with governance provided by the Kuali Foundation, based in the United States.

This outcome aligns with the original vision to the extent that SOAS has a next-generation, Open Source library system supported as part of a flagship shared service. Everything else is different, and another part of this document will focus on the lessons which can be learned from the journey from vision to outcome for Open Source, for shared services, and for the relationships between libraries and their IT services.

Structure of the Document

The study is structured roughly along the lines of the chronology of the BLMS project, starting with its origins in 2010/2011 through to the present time (January 2016) with some references back to work started by the Open Library Environment initiative, Jisc and others in 2008. The metaphor of a journey recurs.

Alongside the narrative will be sample documents and summaries of lessons learned. Weaving through the narrative will be reflections from key actors in the project and associated initiatives (identified by their initials: see "Acknowledgements" for the key).

TIMELINE

Dates	Events
2008/2009	Jisc E Framework published as a result of collaboration between NL, UK, NZ and AUS – subsequently quoted in the OLE Project Final Report
June 2008–June 2009	Mellon-funded OLE project investigation
2008	Duke University hosts the first training and project planning meeting
July 2009	Final report of the investigation published, recommends joining the Kuali Foundation
2009	Formation of the OLE Build Partnership, which joined the Kuali Foundation in December 2009; the estimated cost to build OLE was $5.2m for release to early adopters in 2012
16th December 2009	Initial board meeting of Kuali OLE Partnership in Washington DC elects Deborah Jakubs (Duke) and Brad Wheeler (Indiana) as co-chairs
2008–2009	SCONUL studies the library systems environment and defines three major components: Electronic Resource Licensing Management; Discovery to Delivery Services; Local Library Management – it refers to Kuali OLE as a 'reference implementation' of an open system
Late 2009	SCONUL bid for circa £8m from HEFCE Universities Modernisation Fund (UMF) for comprehensive national programme is rejected but in 2010 £650k is put into ERLM (becomes KB+)
2010	OLE build phase funded by Mellon Foundation and the Kuali OLE Partnership for a 2-year software build phase
January 2011	OLE hires HTC to write its system
2010–2011	Birkbeck Librarian leads on several seminars looking at Open Source options for library systems; drafts his 'COILS' (Collaborative Options for Integrated Library Systems) paper
2012	OLE Partnership receives Mellon funding for 3rd and final year of development
2012–2013	Jisc 'LMS Change' project to address the 'squeezed middle'
January 2012	SOAS and Birkbeck Librarians attend a 2-day Jisc/ SCONUL workshop
2012	The COILS proposal is updated and becomes the BLMS proposal to Jisc for funds as a 'pathfinder' project to establish a shared service LMS – bid is not funded

(*Continued*)

Dates	Events
June 2012	BLMS partners (four active, contributing) employ a project manager as a shared resource with the clear intention to move forward with a shared service approach to delivering new library systems for the partners, and form themselves as BLMS Executive
June–October 2012	Project manager leads weekly meetings of systems librarians from the participating libraries to formulate a functional requirements document for the service
June–October 2012	Modelling of different shared service options
August–September 2012	Horizon scanning sessions involving vendors and Open Source providers
October 2012	BLMS makes 'decision in principle' to adopt Kuali OLE
October–December 2012	Further modelling of how a shared service based on Open Source can be developed, configured and supported
December 2012	Birkbeck librarian retires; replaced by deputy
January–April 2013	Detailed planning for how the shared approach will work, based on a joint venture vehicle
1st May 2013	BLMS joins the Kuali Foundation and OLE Partnership for two years in first instance
May–December 2013	Due diligence on procurement and planning for the joint venture vehicle (company limited by guarantee having no share capital) to deliver the shared service
July 2013	Shadow board for BLMS joint venture vehicle formed
October 2013	SHL librarian departs suddenly, interim librarian (ex-Goldsmiths) is appointed and joins shadow board
October 2013	Birkbeck decides to delay its implementation whilst studying the software in more detail; SHL and SOAS continue planning implementations; Shadow Board agrees that timings of the individual implementations are a local, not BLMS decision
November 2013	HTC, having cleared procurement hurdles, offers a contract to commission the library systems (one partner having stepped back and two others remaining on fence)
December 2013	SOAS Executive Board approves recommendation for SOAS to proceed whilst other libraries are considering their positions – SOAS becomes de facto lead partner in 'Joint Activity Not an Enterprise' (JANE) approach
January 2014	Project manager transfers to SOAS, work commences on OLE version 1.0 with plan to go live in July 2014 with 1.5

(*Continued*)

Dates	Events
January 2014	Other BLMS libraries decide to 'wait and see', at least until OLE version 2.0 is available for evaluation and testing, putting HTC arrangements under considerable pressure
April 2014	Shadow board agrees to postpone the formation of the Joint Venture company, pending further a review of the status of the system and the collaboration in July 2014; SHL Interim Librarian expresses hope that SHL will sign the contracts 'by the end of April'
May 2014	Interim Librarian at SHL fails to get agreement for SHL to proceed; departs and replaced by another Interim; SHL Assoc Director (major supporter) departs for Imperial and his assistant transfers to SOAS
July 2014	Shadow board meets for the final time, takes reports from SHL that it is not ready to implement and from Birkbeck that it is struggling to get a test system installed
July–August 2014	Lehigh then Chicago go live on OLE 1.5, SOAS delays implementation until December 2014
September–October 2014	SOAS launches new VuFind service based on the collaborative work by five Bloomsbury libraries since 2013
October 2014	Kuali Foundation launches KualiCo, a spin-out software company; OLE decides to carry on its existing path with HTC
December 2014	SOAS launches OLE 1.6 in shadow mode (full bibliographic data set loaded) and delays go-live until Easter 2015 whilst Circulation module (Deliver) configuration is completed
May 2015	SOAS accepted as single Library member of OLE Partnership as SHL and Birkbeck decline the invitation to extend consortial membership (but honour commitment to shared Business Analyst post through July 2015)
Easter 2015	SOAS launches full service based on OLE 1.6.0, shortly followed by 1.6.1 and 1.6.2 upgrades
July 2015	SOAS contract for its old system expires; OLE Partnership defined as 'supplier' of the new system
Q3 2015	SHL issues ITT for a managed-service library system, confirming it won't be joining a BLMS shared service; Birkbeck still 'evaluating' its position, waiting to see OLE 2.0
August 2015	OLE Functional Council reaffirms the values of OLE and recommends a streamlined management structure for the Partnership – accepted by a board meeting in late-August
August 2015	German Library Systems Consortia join OLE

(*Continued*)

Dates	Events
November 2015	OLE Partnership appoints a managing director and approves Agile approach to its work
December 2015	Mellon Foundation approves a further $1.1M tranche of funding
December 2015	Cornell and Texas A&M universities join the partnership
December 2015	SOAS confirms funding for the library to proceed with Phase 2 of its OLE implementation (version 2 and 3 upgrades, finance system integration)

PHASE ONE: GETTING STARTED

Why were the Bloomsbury Librarians so interested in the potential for an Open Source library system to replace their legacy, vendor systems? To explain this, a short detour is required.

Ethos

The notion of ethos is an important part of this narrative. It is often said that academics owe their first loyalty to their discipline and their loyalty to their institution is at best second, and at worst, non-existent, making the institution not much more than a temporary landing place. Of course, the same might be said of many professions, with their chartered institutions or worshipful companies taking first place but Academia has a second quality which sets it apart from the trades and professions: the dedication to the project of Enlightenment which aspires to promote reason and freedom of thought as core values. Libraries are critical to this project, bringing to its 18th century origins the much longer tradition of collecting, holding and preserving the knowledge of the saints, the sages and – latterly – the academics which forms so much of the content underpinning the Enlightenment.

Thus librarians and their libraries are bound together by a common ethos, which extends above and beyond their institutional homes. They have a common project – the collection, preservation and dissemination of knowledge – and are regularly reminded that they have more in common with other libraries than they do with other parts of their institutions.

This is not to say that libraries stand apart from their institutions; nor that they do not serve the missions of their institutions, which are themselves bound with other institutions in a common purpose. What it does say is that the glue which binds libraries together is one of the strong threads − alongside academic disciplines − which create an ethical education environment larger than any single institution, however wealthy, specialised, or famous.

Collaboration

> I think we've had a really good partnership and everyone understood. One thing people have realised over the last few years is they thought they would get everything they wanted and they realise in a shared environment we need to make things work in a broader way. Or it works, but it works differently from how individuals thought it would work. It works, but the procedures are different from what they do now and the way in which they wanted it to work − it's different to that. We have always called it a community Open Source which conveys the concept of the collaborative nature of it. Whereas a lot of people think Open Source, they think 'I pick it up I take it home I do whatever I want with it'. In our situation our value was that we wanted to have a project that was useable by a broad community. **CR**

Collaboration is in the DNA of libraries in a manner that is quite distinctive. From their earliest days, libraries collaborated with other libraries to ensure that more than one copy was made of important texts. In the modern era, the notion of 'holding libraries' and 'circulating libraries' pointed to the fact that libraries which did not hold a local copy of a book requested by a reader could get it on 'inter-library-loan' from the larger − or more specialised − library up the road. 'National Libraries', 'Research Libraries', 'Union Catalogues' and other initiatives point to a rich field of collaboration. The rise of the digital age and the move from collecting to subscribing has given rise to any number of attempts at coordination of effort and collective bargaining with publishers to ensure that resources are produced efficiently and managed in such a way as not to give complete control over to the publishers.

As the importance of open access publishing and research data management has emerged, the notion of the 'holding library' has taken on a new meaning (as the repository of its institution's intellectual property) and the pendulum which swung away from university presses to commercial publishers has started to swing back, to libraries as publishers of their institutions' outputs.

University Libraries are bound together by any number of national and international organisations: SCONUL,[6] RLUK,[7] M25 Consortium,[8] LIBER,[9] CILIP,[10] ARL,[11] ALA,[12] to name but a few. Librarians spend a lot of time with other librarians and this is important (as evidenced by the start of this story with the Bloomsbury Librarians). When there is a problem to solve, often the natural instinct is to look to other libraries and librarians for collaborative approaches to the solution.

Within universities, libraries have a special collaborative relationship with each other that is a longstanding relationship. Libraries have long recognised that our resources get extended by working together and that the sum is greater than the parts. Extending that into the core software that we all rely on to do our business makes sense to lots of libraries. When we go and talk to them that's the pitch we make to them. The value of the foundation is built on something we have been doing for a long time in libraries, this deep collaboration is more about that a lot of our needs are common, and our differences are where we want to concentrate our local specific resources.   **MW**

Even though the partnership is small we have included a larger number of people and everyone has adopted the same values and proceeded down the road from the same path as much as possible. Beyond that I have met some longtime colleagues and friends who will know each forever. The dedication of every individual I have worked with, the skill sets have been phenomenal. That mutual regard has helped us move forward.   **CR**

Technology

In the modern era, the Jisc initiatives in the 'Integrated Electronic Information Environment' have led to a rich tapestry of digital resources, discovery systems, collective bargaining, advice and support.

Meanwhile IT (in the sense of computers and data networks) has been following its own track. The Main frame era of the 1970s gave way to the mini-computer era of the 1980s and then the micro-computer eras of the late-1980s and 1990s. Mainframes had served librarians very well, as they held all the information in once place, were well-organised and well-managed (just like libraries) and a number of library systems had developed, based on these technologies. The move to mini- and then micro-computers fragmented the provision, giving rise to the 'personal computer' and the 'client-server' model, which replaced the centralised model, with the computing power pushed to the desktop.

Library systems during this era went in one direction (mini-computers serving individual libraries) and information provision − once the World Wide Web (WWW) took hold − in another (clients picking up content from almost anywhere where a server had an internet connection).

IT professionals had to run merely to keep pace with the changes in the computing environments. Networks of 'dumb terminals' connected to the 1980s mainframes or 1990s mini-computers were easy to manage compared with the hundreds or thousands of PCs and Macs, which, by the turn of the century, had landed on almost everyone's desk. Delivery of 'enterprise applications' (the classic 'big three' of HR, Finance and − in universities − Student Records) had likewise fragmented. Instead of computer scientists tending well-managed databases on their beloved PDP11 and Vax and ICL machines, there were 'vendors' offering 'best of breed' applications for specific purposes, on the new, relatively affordable (provided you didn't blanche at the prospect of spending £100,000 on a single machine) mini-computers from Sun and Alpha and HP and IBM. These new 'clusters' required new job titles such as 'database administrator', 'systems administrator' and 'analyst programmer' to work out not only how to get them to run but more importantly, how to exchange information with each other (not always an issue in the mainframe era).

Library system vendors followed a similar path but for reasons that remain unclear to the present day − maybe because the library requirements were so particular or because procurements were managed by librarians − they became a niche product. 'Turnkey' systems were common through the 1990s and into the 2000s: a system supplied by a vendor, plugged into the institutional network, possibly (but not always) sitting in the institutional machine room, managed by the vendor through remote access, sometimes using a dedicated dial-in modem to avoid firewall problems. All the local IT staff had to do was turn the key, make sure the lights were on, check that the terminals or client software on the library

PCs could get to the machine, and walk away. The vendor, working with the library, did the rest.

In the second decade of the 21st Century, the Bloomsbury Librarians – along with colleagues in other academic libraries across the world – got together and looked at this scenario and said, 'there must be something better than this'.

The biggest benefit, not from a technical perspective but as a wide-eyed library systems idealist, was the ethical imperative behind it, the ethical drive to move towards Open Source technology. I believe it is the role of libraries to resist the commodification of public commons and therefore we should move towards public funds for ownership, community-led structures for software design and maintaining control of own data rather that giving it to private sector companies. I have talked about this in presentations that Open Source requires balancing convenience and control – what you gain in control and freedom over the software and your own data is balanced by a loss of convenience because it is often harder to implement and harder to understand and requires a greater level of skills to implement. In the library it meant a steep learning curve for myself, the other technical people on the project and the library staff who were being exposed to the library management system. It was a big culture change to move from an 'easy' vendor-led solution to a more difficult community-led solution. It required a lot of engagement from SOAS library staff who had to attend meetings, think about software design, suggest new features, file book reports, test drive the system, perform UAT testing – there was a lot of work that doesn't come with a vendor system. Library staff used to cataloguing, circulation and shelving, suddenly had to perform tasks like logging books, user acceptance testing, the formal software developing stuff that they had no reason to be exposed to. It's stuff that you are not exposed to if you just buy a proprietary system. Some library staff accepted it wholeheartedly, accepted they were on an adventure moving toward a new library system, contributing to it and having a positive engagement with the community. Some staff were more reticent at first and that's where the community collaboration with them was important. Digital information is becoming more prevalent in the entire library information sector and I think for continued survival and relevance library staff will need to upskill, become hybrid library/IT people. **SB**

Defining a 'pathfinder' approach

The Jisc call
Jisc issued a funding call in 2012:

> Based on a 3-phase work plan, the LMS Change project will develop and disseminate a
> vision for the future of library systems and a delivery 'roadmap'.
>
> Working with the companion Pathfinder projects, the project will explore the potential
> for new approaches to library systems infrastructure, taking account of considerations
> beyond the traditional LMS to include other business critical and curatorial systems,
> both within and above campus.[13]

Building upon an earlier initiative called 'COILS' (Collaborative
Approach to Integrated Library Systems), which was the brainchild of the
(since-retired) Birkbeck Librarian, the Bloomsbury Librarians wrote a bid
to this call, which was not successful. The Jisc explanation for this was that
the 'funding pot was cut' otherwise 'the BLMS bid would have been
successful'. The Bloomsbury Librarians decided to spin this by saying 'Jisc
said we were big enough and ugly enough to manage without Jisc funding'.
Take your pick. Certainly, the process of writing the bid and thinking
through the aspiration was a strong factor in the decision to carry on.

Proceeding without Jisc Funding
The BLMS partners decided to get on with it as they all (at that point)
wanted a new system. Although not a funded project, they were invited to
attend Jisc Programme Management events (with a small travel budget),
were featured in the LMS Change Programme's web site[14] and referenced
in a number of other archives about the work (e.g. SCONUL[15]). The
Bloomsbury project communicated its method and findings widely within
this group and beyond, in particular sharing its more 'enterprise IT
approach' to the library systems world.

As a 'pathfinder' project, an output of the BLMS was to provide a repea-
table set of processes that could be applied to any institution migrating to a
new library system. Key elements in the Bloomsbury Approach were:

- Horizon scanning,
- Options appraisal,
- Scoping of a suitable shared-service model.

Looking back on this in 2016, a number of the Jisc-funded pathfinder
projects have produced results. The most common outcome was a consortial approach to procurement of systems from mainstream Vendors.[16] The

BLMS approach was based on a determination to realise its original goal of a 'next generation Library system delivered as a Shared Service'.

The BLMS Project Executive

At the same time as preparing the Jisc bid, the BLMS partners advertised for a project manager. A key part of the bid was the clear intention to proceed with a project to replace the library systems at the partner libraries with, or without Jisc support. The partners had secured sufficient internal funding to employ a project manager at least through to December 2012. An advertisement was placed and the project manager started in June 2012, employed by Birkbeck on behalf of the four contributing members at that time (Birkbeck, RVC, SHL and SOAS).

One of the first actions of the project manager was to propose that the project should have a formal project executive and that rather than this being a single person, it should be the librarians from the contributing partners, convened by the project manager. This was agreed and a schedule of meetings was set up. For most of 2012 and well into 2013, the librarians met regularly, generally for an hour on a Wednesday afternoon, as often as weekly, supplemented by several 'Away Days'. This regular meeting became an important driver for the project and was an essential part of the decision-making process, which was undertaken using a Horizon Scanning method followed by an Options Appraisal.

[In order to convince senior management, you need to]

Look at exactly how much you're spending now and how that compares to what you are going to be doing and projecting what the costs might be in the future for what you're doing now.

If you are in a vended system now, how long is that system going to last, are you going to have to move to another system anyway, how much is that going to cost you?

If you are going to go to a cloud-based one, how much is that going to cost you?

What if you don't like what they are doing or they go under or something: do you have a plan of how you are going to move it off? **FM**

DECISION-MAKING PROCESSES:
HORIZON SCANNING

What does 'next generation' actually mean in the library technology space? Some contextualisation is appropriate: the situation in 2011/2012 was one in which there was a narrowing of choices in vendor systems (most going for major off-site provision with large consolidated databases) and varying levels of systems integration. Against this backdrop, the Bloomsbury libraries (in common with many others) had aspirations for flexibility and extensibility, particularly to deal with the rapid transformation of their libraries from print-based services to hybrid services covering print, digital holdings and subscriptions to electronic information services.

The Horizon Scanning method which the BLMS adopted has a lot to do with how we arrived at our current place but it is also important as we look ahead.

Jisc was very keen on Horizon Scanning. Indeed, it still is, and even has a post called 'Futurist in Residence'. The principle is simple enough: try to get a feel for where a particular sector or set of technologies — almost anything really — will be in about five years' time and set a strategy based on those observations. Sometimes the horizons are much further away: the joint Jisc/SCONUL 'Libraries of the Future' study used a scenario planning method which postulated a number of different environments in 25–50 years' time and asked groups of respondents to brain-storm how Libraries might adapt. (The trouble with that study was that the environment has changed so radically in the five years following its report that the outcomes, whilst interesting, don't really provide a useful basis for action.)

Existing Systems

In order to develop an approach to system requirements, the current systems environment was studied and mapped. A starting point was to capture the reasons why all of the libraries engaged in the process were frustrated with their existing systems. A typical vended system model looked a bit like this:

Classic LMS model

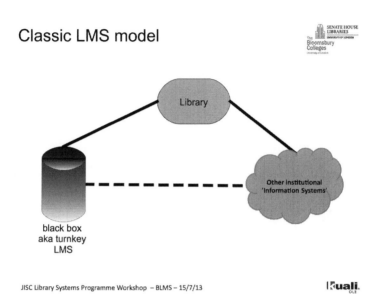

In this model, the library staff have access to the system via whatever interface the vendor has provided (generally a client application that has to be installed on staff PCs), with a web Online Public Access Catalogue (OPAC) for users and sometimes still with the text-mode option via telnet or SSH. Maintenance of the system is typically provided by the vendor using remote access, and in many cases access to the system by any means other than the vendor interfaces (e.g. by direct SQL calls) is severely limited. Application Programming Interfaces (APIs) might or might not be available for systems integration, and if available, are often subject to additional license and support fees.

One of the drivers for looking at Open Source alongside other options (apart from the obvious need for a system capable of supporting the 21st Century Hybrid Library) was an aspiration for much greater access to the Library's own data held in the Library System. The experience of most of the Bloomsbury Libraries was great difficulty in gaining access to the data for import or export other than via the proprietary interfaces.

In the long run, having control at the level of strategic planning is important for the libraries. A lot of library systems have gone to cloud-based systems and I have a real problem with that because in that case you have really lost control of what is going on and how do you get your data back out. What happens if they keep increasing the costs of subscriptions all the time, which is what happened with scientific and technical information where the information was created in the universities but then it went to profit-making groups to sell it back to the university libraries and the costs just were not controllable so I would be concerned with a cloud-based system, along with providing the kind of support that we need.   **FM**

Most of the libraries in the project had some form or other of a systems cluster rather than a single LMS. These were captured in diagrams like the one below:

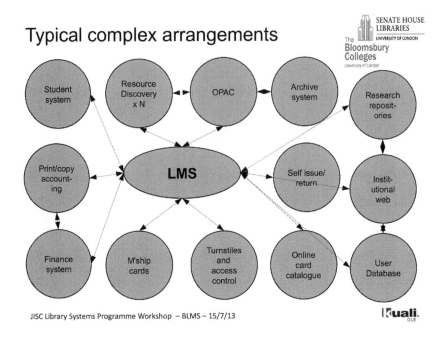

JISC Library Systems Programme Workshop – BLMS – 15/7/13

Functional Requirements

It is clear from the diagram above that one of the key requirements at all libraries was for a system which could integrate with a variety of other systems, ideally in an 'enterprise architecture' (meaning, a capacity to exchange data with other systems in an automated or semi-automated fashion).[17] This became one of the building blocks of the functional requirements document that was used in the horizon scanning process.

Another driver at the time was an aspiration for the development of a shared-systems model in which the libraries – operating in the University of London Federal Libraries context – would have options to share bibliographic data, patron and circulation data and access controls to facilitate the access of their users to other libraries within the system.

An early task in the project – led by the project manager – was the development of a shared Functional Specification document. The systems librarians from each of the participating libraries met weekly and prepared a 66-page document that captured their requirements. This document was designed as an early deliverable from the project. If any library chose to walk away from the project, it could take the Functional Specification as a project output (e.g. to use in a conventional procurement exercise). The document itself built upon work done by Ken Chad on a 'UK Core Specification'.[18] The specification captured core library and information processes as well the more sophisticated functionality that would make the BLMS a truly next generation system.

Technology Principles

Alongside the Functional Specification, the partners also agreed a number of underlying principles for the technology of their preferred system.

1. A vision of a library system which could sit within a modular enterprise suite of software (Finance, HR, Student Records, Research), enabling reuse of data across business processes.
2. Genuinely open APIs, without such tight control over the codebase that the only option for technical changes was to go to the original vendor.
3. Next-generation capability, vision and roadmap with clear visibility of where tailored requirements/fixes/changes sit in that technology roadmap.

4. Flexibility to request, commission or build changes or developments to the system, and to know they could happen in a timely fashion (including visibility of cost, schedule and resource implications).

As Open Source principles were not reason enough on their own to choose Open over Closed, it was recognised that Open Source options would need to have particular benefits to justify their selection. However, there was a clear bias towards Open Source as can be seen in the scoring sheets which were used in the presentation sessions by suppliers and representatives of Open Source systems.

Vendor Lock-In and Risk

It is common to hear the criticism of Open Source that it is more risky than commercial systems because there is no supplier to hold to account if things go wrong. Indeed, some of the conversations with senior managers about this question had arrived at a point where the conversation came down to

Q: what do I do if the supplier does not deliver according to the contract?

A: we will get our solicitors to sue them.

As a risk-mitigation action, this approach has a number of flaws, including the costs of going to law and the lack of service in the meantime.

One underlying hazard with proprietary systems is vendor lock-in. With a few notable exceptions in the corporate systems environment, the selection of a proprietary system locks the customer in to a licensing regime and a single source of support. Thus, if the relationship with the supplier breaks down (as in the example above) or if the quality of the support deteriorates, or the supplier decides to stop supporting the system, the customer can take its business elsewhere but at the cost of having to migrate to a different system. As anyone who has migrated a major system will tell you, this (in IT jargon) is 'non-trivial', time-consuming and potentially very expensive. (Even the tactic of withholding payment in order to get service improvements can be backfire if the system relies on a licence key, meaning that the supplier can turn the system off by allowing the key to expire or − worse in the case of an outsourced service − simply turn it off.)

I've worked for vendors so I know a lot of negative things about going that way to weigh against doing an Open Source thing. You really don't have control; you cannot get at the source codes so you cannot fix things you just need to fix. There were times when we had vended software and I had a programmer who knew exactly what was going wrong but it couldn't be fixed without them fixing it, you can't fix that.

With Kuali, if you don't like the way the systems are operating you can go right in and talk directly to a database or something so that's a flexibility that I think is useful. I have more hesitancy about some of the vended systems and what you are getting yourself into with those. **FM**

Anyone who has worked with corporate systems will be aware of scenarios in which the failure of a supplier to deliver an acceptable level of service or the decision by a supplier to declare a system 'end of life' has had expensive consequences, some leading to legal action.

The selection of an Open Source system (assuming the software is fit for purpose) can be a viable risk mitigation strategy to avoid vendor lock-in. Open Source gives options and choices for hosting and support. Hosting can be in-house, or with a supplier through several different managed-service models. Support, likewise, can be in-house or contracted out. If a hosting or support arrangement proves unsatisfactory, the arrangement can be changed without having to migrate to a different system. Thus the investment in adopting the system is protected.

The choice of Open Source therefore extends to an Open hosting and support model. Within the Bloomsbury group and the wider sector, sufficient examples of this model were available to demonstrate its viability (generally, at that time, more so in the electronic information services environment than the corporate systems environment) and this was another factor in the bias of the BLMS towards an Open Source system, provided that the functional requirements were met.

Vendor and Supplier Engagement

The Bloomsbury Librarians decided to ask each of the main vendors with whom at least one Library had a relationship, to present its road-map to a group of staff drawn from all six libraries. The exercise was repeated with a selection of Open Source providers. The road-maps were compared with the functional requirements which the Libraries had prepared – collaboratively – and scored methodically. The workshops were held in July 2012, typically attended by up to 20 staff from across the six libraries collaborating at that time. Vendors and suppliers were given time to make a presentation (categorically not a sales pitch) and then subjected to a question and answer session. Attendees used scoring sheets to ensure that each Q&A session covered the same ground. Each library was able to add extra questions to the sample sheet (below), drilling into its specialised requirements on topics ranging from Unicode, through complicated classification schemes to federated access management.

BLMS Project   *MASTER SCORING SPREADSHEET*

Supplier Horizon Day: Sample Scoring Sheet

SUPPLIER (enter name below)

YOUR NAME (enter name below)

*** Weight = importance of item*

No.	Question	Score (1-5)	Weight (1-3)**
1	Do you think there is a future for traditional siloed LMSes, archives, repository and other curatorial systems?		
2	How might you support a shared service approach for an LMS for a consortium?		
3	What new technologies are you most interested in applying to library systems?		
4	Tell us your thoughts on integrating management of electronic items and media not managed by current LMSs.		
5	How will you ensure you provide a stable and reliable platform but still be responsive to changing customer needs?		
6	Can you imagine your company ever selling support for an Open Source library system?		
7	How do you imagine staff workflows could be improved by new library systems?		
8	What changes are needed in the LMS to support improving discovery especially using new discovery interfaces / layers?		
9	Tell us how a linked data approach could fit with your view of the future LMS and discovery.		
10	TAILORED QUESTONS		
	Enter your own question here)		

Sample scoring sheet from the horizon scanning day

Three workshops were held over a period of two weeks: one day was allocated to four vendors; on the other days the staff met a supplier that had put Koha into a number of libraries, representatives of the Library Coop (since disbanded) and a representative from the Kuali Open Library Environment.

The intention was quite straightforward: which supplier or provider or system has a vision of its where its systems are going that is closest to where we want to be?

Proprietary Systems

Taking the commercial vendors first, two distinct service models were presented, with variations (remember, this was mid-2012):

- an incremental upgrade approach, with little change in the basic setup and few enhancements (single-instance systems, supported by the supplier, hosted on- or off-site);
- a major shift to a fully hosted, off-site service based on a large-scale bibliographic database with services wrapped around it.

The supplier who presented the first option was so casual about the approach − which seemed to rely upon the inertia of sites that did not want to go through the process of moving to a different system − that we wrote it off almost immediately (but not without putting it through the same scoring process as all the other options).

The second option can be summed up in the diagram below. In the three vendor cases offering this model, there was only one option, which was to move all library management functions into its externally hosted system. The variations on this approach were that one supplier already had a very large bibliographic database and was proposing to build services around that database whereas the other two suppliers already had library systems but were in the process of building up large databases by ingesting customer data into their new, multi-tenant systems.

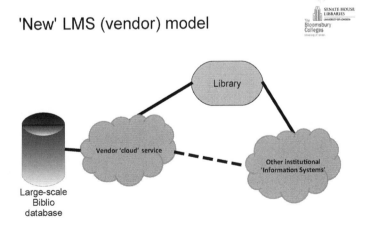

'New' LMS (vendor) model

Noting again that this was mid-2012, and the request was for suppliers to show their roadmaps rather than attempt to sell us something, at least two of the systems we were shown were not yet deliverable and a third was at an early stage, with a number of UK Libraries working as pilot sites to assist the supplier in developing its service.

In addition to the objective scoring, one of the strongest, subjective impressions of all three vendors offering this model was that they wanted our libraries for our data as much as for our money (although the money would be nice).

For the library I was in they will do better with an Open Source system. For a much smaller library or something you might be better with a vended system or being part of a consortium. Some of the large consortia have to have IT staff to run vended systems so they might be better off in the long run to have an Open Source system but a small library itself it might be more the services they can get from either a vendor or a consortium.

I have a background with vended systems. I have a background with implementations, at this point in time I like the Open Source, I like the flexibility, you have to be willing to do the strategic planning for how things will work in the future but I think it puts the library in a better position for the future.   **FM**

Open Source Systems

We had already seen Evergreen and Koha demonstrated, including the session in 2011 led by Staffordshire (the first UK University to implement Koha). The primary European provider of implementation and support services for Koha made a presentation which focused on a general discussion of the benefits of the Open Source approach, using Evergreen and Koha as examples alongside some other systems from its portfolio. The supplier was reasonably open about the strengths and weaknesses of its supported library systems and had also looked at the development of the Kuali Open Library Environment.

The Library Coop was a consultancy group formed by six librarians who came together after having worked with the Software Coop[19] on Open Source library systems in non-academic libraries. Their presentation focused on the benefits of Open Source, using their experience with Koha as an example. They talked about the Open Source ecosystem and alerted us to the problems (at that time) with the Koha code base having 'forked' (divided into two different streams with different support arrangements) and some of the disputes which were in progress. They provided a very useful suggestion that the BLMS ought to aim for Kuali OLE as its preferred system but that it would benefit from an interim migration to Koha as a staging system whilst waiting for OLE to be ready. Their idea was to undertake the work in four stages:

1. migrate to Koha, using the process to clean up all data;
2. implement ERM and Link-Resolver systems;
3. replace the Koha OPAC with a comprehensive discovery system such as Blacklight or VuFind;
4. migrate the back-office systems to Kuali OLE.

Their suggestion was that this might be a five-year process, 2013–18.

We had a presentation on the Kuali Open Library Environment (OLE) from one of its representatives who happened to be in London for meetings with Jisc about another project (a collaboration to build a Global Knowledge Base for e-resources in conjunction with the Jisc KB +, which had been funded by HEFCE under the Universities Modernisation Fund mentioned in the Timeline). He described the origins of Kuali OLE in a 2008/2009 study funded by the Mellon Foundation which resulted in a recommendation to build a new library system from the ground up, operating under the umbrella of the Kuali Foundation, a not-for-profit US organisation founded in 2004 to build Open Source Enterprise Resource Planning (ERP) systems (starting with Finance, moving on to Student and HR).

We are the solution, we are the developer and we are the customer and there is something empowering about how you manage and influence all three of those vectors to gain what your institution needs. It also puts you in the context of doing something greater than your own position, we feel like we are contributing to what libraries should be thinking about. **MW**

Two things were particularly striking about OLE: the way it was being built in a modular fashion on top of a 'middleware'[20] software layer, an essential component of enterprise software architecture; and the strong governance provided by the Kuali Foundation. Unlike most of the presentations, the slides from the OLE session were freely shared (see below). The first slide shows an outline of the software system as it was in 2012. Kuali Rice is the name given to the middleware layer (the software layer providing connections and data exchange between the different modules in the system). As OLE does not include an OPAC, the Discovery API is used to interface to user systems. The DocStore holds the Bibliographic, Patron and Circulation Data for the Describe and Deliver modules, the Finance API provides the basis of the Select and Acquire module. Further APIs provide interfaces to external bibliographic systems, corporate systems and identity management.

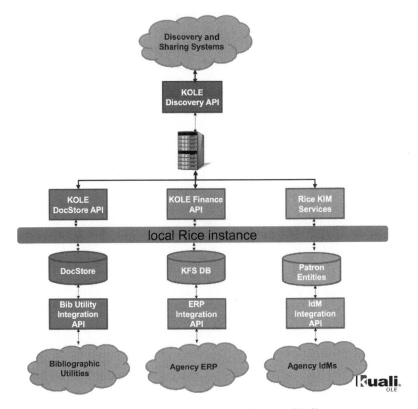

The Kuali OLE software architecture (2012)

This slide led on to a more detailed view of the service architecture. again, the clear description of the open nature of the system was impressive when compared with many other presentations.

Kuali OLE Service Architecture

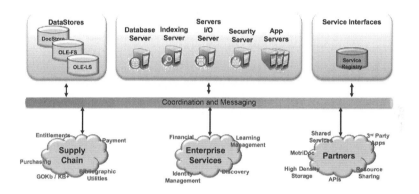

Finally, the Kuali OLE Governance model was set out.

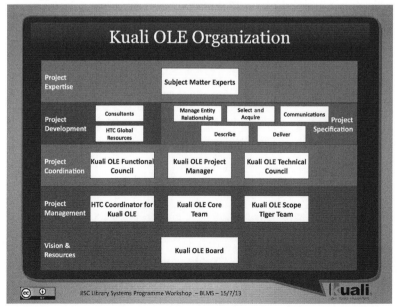

It is fair to say that many of the librarians present at the session, who had engaged over the years with the 'User Group' approach operated by library system vendors, were struck by the degree of involvement of library staff with the OLE project, at several levels, set out in this diagram.

Analysing the Choices

Two exercises were conducted:

1. an analysis of the score-sheets;
2. a SWOT analysis of each of the options which had been presented.

The exercises were conducted by the project executive group supported by the project manager and senior systems librarians. Once the exercise was complete, the decision about direction of travel was made by the Executive, taking into account a number of other considerations.

Score Sheets Outcome
The scores from the two workshops were analysed separately. The first summary sheet is from the supplier workshop.

BLMS Project
Supplier Horizon Day - Commercial - 5th July 2012

1.   **TOTAL SCORES - COMMERCIAL SUPPLIERS**

No.	Vendor 1	Vendor 2	Vendor 3	Vendor 4
1	59	60	54	30
2	49	68	49	40
3	58	55	57	44
4	57	40	49	37
5	54	55	55	36
6	32	49	42	22
7	21	29	25	22
8	30	31	34	26
9	54	48	37	33
10 - LSHTM	60	34	37	13
TOTAL	474	469	439	303
Average	4	4	3	2
WEIGHTED	854	838	778	562

Sample scoring summary sheet from the horizon scanning exercises

This scoring was consistent with comments from the workshop participants, which put the most conventional suppliers offering the next-generation, hosted model ahead of the less conventional supplier, with the 'steady as she goes' supplier last. The impression was that, if we were to go for a consortium approach to procuring a commercial service, there would be a strong response but with reservations about whether any of the suppliers could respond to the more ambitious aspects of the BLMS approach.

The second summary sheet is from the Open Source workshops.

BLMS Project
Supplier Horizon Day - Open Source - 9–10th July 2012

2.   TOTAL SCORES - OPEN SOURCE

No.	Kuali	Library Coop	System integrator
1	39	48	44
2	47	53	44
3	39	44	39
4	37	43	36
5	25	51	50
6	45	48	49
7	28	15	21
8	25	33	37
9	28	30	38
10	26	48	23
11	42	57	44
12	29	45	41
13	30	41	26
TOTAL	440	556	492
Average	3	4	4
WEIGHTED	1078	1326	1194

Sample scoring summary sheet from the horizon scanning exercises

What was interesting here was that the Library Coop, which recommended a phased project using Koha as a stepping stone to Kuali OLE came out first. The 'librarians speaking to librarians' approach found considerable favour amongst the workshop attendees. The comments about the Systems integrator mentioned that the presentation glossed over the forking of the Koha code base and disputes arising from the fork. Kuali OLE was seen by many as ambitious but not ready for a production environment.

SWOT Analysis

A SWOT (Strengths, Weaknesses, Opportunities, Threats) analysis was undertaken for each of the 4 models that were identified through the sessions:

- Proprietary, software-centric;
- Proprietary, data-centric;
- Bespoke, commissioned (Kuali OLE);
- Open Source, build-it-yourself (Koha or Evergreen).

Looking across the analysis, a number of cross-cutting themes were evident.

The Unknown

- Impact of the equity finance model on the future of commercial suppliers and their systems.
- Open Source projects or commercial suppliers backing the wrong horse in terms of technology.
- BLMS is a relatively small player in the global context of LMS, potentially affecting capability to influence development and keep up with HE sector changes in the UK.

LMS Development

- US centric (Open Source and commercial)
- Speed and flexibility of enhancements to suit the Consortium − Open Source being very far ahead

Costs

- High for commercial suppliers − but a known quantity
- Total Cost of Ownership (TCO) unknown for Open Source

Support

- A 'Quiet life' for existing commercial systems by comparison with Open Source
- Unknown requirements for numbers and skillsets for Open Source system support

Governance

- Robustness and reliability of development and release models − clearer with commercial suppliers; solid for Kuali; currently good for Koha; less clear for Evergreen

SWOT Tables

Each model was then analysed in the workshop sessions using the standard SWOT definitions.

Model 1: Proprietary, Software-Centric

Strengths	*Weaknesses*
• Robust, reliable supplier • State of the art for current systems • Comfortable • Proven/established/stable • Established customer base • Support for core operation	• Vendor/technology lock-in • Lack of adaptability • Reliance on supplier's roadmaps • Properties of the user base/market share • Possibly region-specific • You are stuck with it • Have to buy everything from one place • High cost • Long enhancement process • Proprietary customisation languages/scripting • Unresponsive to user needs • BLMS is a small part of the overall market share • Non-UK focus
Opportunities	*Threats*
• Off-the-shelf system for the basics • No need to re-invent the wheel • A quiet life for your systems team • Negotiate price on consortium basis • Core modules work	• Technology dead-end • Quality of support fails • Can't control costs • Funding is locked to product • Left behind sector, not risk-taking enough • Library relies on supplier to adjust to new developments • You're at risk from their future business choices, including: supplier 'betting on the wrong horse': if they choose the wrong technology, support and then product reaches end of life • Few opportunities • Changing market • Suppliers not keeping UK needs in sight • Can't develop system to meet needs • Equity capital model impact on supplier's direction

Model 2: Proprietary, Data-Centric

Strengths	*Weaknesses*
• Innovative end of technology spectrum • Access to massive bibliographic databases • Global reach	• Unclear if systems are production ready • Lock-in to a quarterly update cycle with no opt-out • Few reference sites for any of the examples

(*Continued*)

Model 2: Proprietary, Data-Centric	
• Nimble software development (no Legacy)	• Bib data is only part of the system, can this provide a complete system?
• One variant includes a not-for-profit, membership model	• Who develops the non-bib data stuff?
• Open APIs around one big database allows for development of your own services	• Circulation modules seem tacked-on
	• Content inclusion per site (relevance)
	• Records-matching algorithm weak
• Specifically OCLC, they do know about data on a large scale	• Supplier tie-in
	• Agreements with the right suppliers
• Interesting but flawed	• Unclear on the complete system
• Data structure	• New to market
• Membership model based on NFP	• Production ready?
• Global reach	• Reference sites limited
	• No big research libraries

Opportunities	*Threats*
• Join a future-proof system	• Financial buy-outs in the case of two examples
• Interesting technological trajectory	• All library data is held off-site by the supplier
• Free up systems staff from generic IT allowing them to do cooler library stuff	• You are relying a lot on someone else's systems
• More flexible and responsive than a traditional model	• You're beholden to their future business choices
• Synergies/cost savings with content suppliers	• Challenge of data from different vendors — what if they fall out?
• Tailoring through APIs	• Agreements may only last a short while
• New technology on fascinating trajectory	• Supplier agreements

Model 3: Bespoke, Commissioned (Kuali OLE)	
Strengths	*Weaknesses*
• Rigorous, bottom-up software design	• Software at Alpha stage
• Carefully structured to be fit-for-purpose for academic libraries	• Few early adopters
	• US centric at the moment
• Strong governance model	• There is no finished LMS product
• Interoperability with enterprise systems	• Hard to see how this could be done in our university/organisational constraints
• Integration as a complete system for the institution	• Time commitment
• A solid basis for developing software building on Open Source	• Support
	• No early adopters/reference sites
• Member = shareholder approach; you're your own vendor	

(Continued)

Model 3: Bespoke, Commissioned (Kuali OLE)	
Opportunities	*Threats*

• Bring a European base into the project
• Genuine enterprise system
• Integrate with federated
  ID management
• A great deal of potential for
  this approach
• Influence direction at an early stage of
  the system
	• Small consortium (9 libraries)
	• Seed-funding may run out
	• Unknown costs of future development
	• Uncertainty longer-term, you'd need to maintain
	  the consortium
	• UOL politics
	• US-based
	• Sustainability of resource here
	• Large bill when seed funding ends?

Model 4: Open Source, Build-It-Yourself (Koha or Evergreen)	
Strengths	*Weaknesses*

• Community code base
• Shared/rapid development
• No licensing costs
• Flexibility, nimbleness, you can develop
  your own thing
• 'Of the moment'
• Mutual support from others
  and community
• Flexibility
• Short development cycle
• Tap into community knowledge
• Cost
• 'Ace and interesting'
	• Evergreen does not support Unicode
	• Koha has a forked code base
	• Neither system offers Enterprise architecture
	• Have to work with a community
	• New and different approach, untested
	• Still need to spend money on things from
	  vendors like a big index of journal data
	• Lack of ILL system
	• Support models variety
	• Suppliers still required
	• Evergreen not persuasive
	• Lack of reference sites for both options

Opportunities	*Threats*

• Join a growing bandwagon
• Shared service is an integral part of
  the model
• Could migrate to Kuali OLE at a
  later stage
• A new and exciting approach, much
  more responsive
• We can actually do it ourselves
• Possibility to build on the software
• Ease of programming
• Migration easier
	• Risk of choosing the wrong version of Koha
	• Unknown support costs
	• Skills-base of own staff
	• Need to be realistic about what Open Source is
	  really like
	• Danger of project petering out if you don't have
	  a solid user-base
	• The usual Open Source dangers such as forking,
	  politics in the community
	• Back wrong horse

Further Analysis

The dynamics of the BLMS Executive Group were a significant factor in the process of decision-making. The technology principles outlined above were important, but so was the organisational context. A lot of thought was given to the nature of the collaboration: what was the primary connection between the libraries? What was the common ground and what was the vision for growth of the envisioned shared service?

The diagram below describes the range of connections between the libraries.

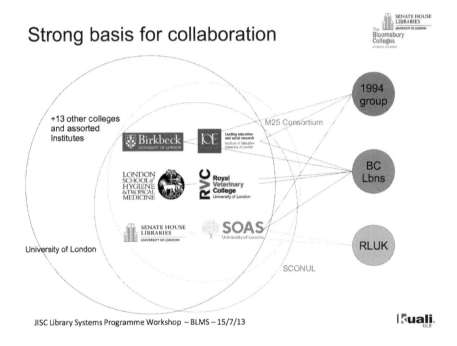

All six libraries were in both SCONUL and the M25 Consortium; all five Bloomsbury College libraries were in the BC Group (the School of Pharmacy by this point was joining UCL); Birbkeck, IoE and SOAS were in the 1994 group (since disbanded); SHL and SOAS were in the RLUK group; all libraries were part of the Federal University of London (along with 13 other colleges and various institutes). Which was the strongest collaboration to feed the aspiration for a pathfinder shared service that would grow?

The role of Senate House Library was important. This library already provided a range of shared services to other parts of the University: access for all staff and students to its collections under the University of London Access Agreement[21]; access to a shared book repository; consortial access to its library management system for the other libraries in the School of Advanced Study.[22] As noted in the introduction, Senate House Library in previous decades had also provided a shared version of LIBERTAS.

SCONUL and M25 seemed too large and diverse to form the basis of a strong collaboration. Given the particular role of SHL, the decision was to envision the BLMS as potentially growing into a University of London Library Systems Association. This decision was to have some far-reaching consequences for the evolution of the project but in the short-term, it provided one very strong driver for the decision: a vision of like-minded, research-intensive academic libraries collaborating on the development of a modern library systems platform which was flexible and extensible – potentially extensible across 18 colleges to enable shared access to resources – firmly branded as a University of London initiative.

It was clear, all other things being equal, that the ethos of the Kuali OLE Partnership had a strong resonance for the BLMS Executive when seen from this point of view.

What's happened here is we recognised that the model needs to evolve in order for us to survive. The original model that we had was based on a Kuali governance model with a Functional Council made up of people who actually used the system, and a Technical Council made up of people who understand the technology and know how to make it work. We still have a project manager who helps the two chairs so the Functional Council and the Technical Council coordinate and try to bring together issues which have some synergy and need to be developed together. In the Functional Council they have a more complex structure, we have subject matter expert groups. So for acquisitions, for cataloging and for circulation each have a subject matter expert. Those subject matter expert groups are made up of representatives from each of the partners, and in these groups they discuss what is important to develop and some various directions which are proposed upwards to the council ultimately. What I'm describing is a group which has had the luxury of being able to have representatives from each partner on each of these groups for full participation. I think that has both helped us and proved to be a little bit of a drag on our decision-making process. We make decisions by consensus and it takes a while to get consensus.   **CR**

Financial Modelling (1)

Some financial modelling was done at this stage of the project, mainly focusing on the potential on-going costs once systems were installed and configured. The most significant early finding was based on a comparison of the financial model in the Open Source options versus the Software Licensing and Support model in the most mature of the 'Model 2' systems.

Open Source does not involve a paid-for license but this does not mean there is no license. Systems are released using a number of different licenses. Theoretically, the software can be downloaded and used without payment but the licenses may involve obligations, for example if the software is modified. The financial implications of this approach were difficult to estimate so it was decided to benchmark against the 'Model 3' system (Kuali OLE) which offered a partnership model with annual fees. Under this model, the BLMS could join as a consortium for an annual fee of around $100,000. This fee provided access to early releases of the code, membership of the various governance bodies and, via that membership, input into the development of the code. Critically for the analysis, the fee remained the same regardless of how many instances of OLE were installed and how large (or small) were the bibliographic databases. Thus, a financial model could be devised in which the cost of the OLE Membership was a constant, shared between BLMS partners and — as the partnership grew — the share per partner would decrease.

By comparison, the leading 'Model 2' supplier asked a lot of questions about the volumes of bibliographic data held by the partner libraries and provided an indicative license price based on the volume. The initial annual price was so high (running to hundreds of thousands of pounds) that some data (volumes of holdings catalogued in the Archives systems) were excluded on the basis that none of the Open Source options under consideration included (at that time) an Archives model. In this model, as new partners joined the BLMS, costs would increase in line with the size of their holdings.

In summary, the Open Source option represented by Kuali OLE offered fixed, predictable software costs (excluding hosting and support) which could be shared across partners, giving rise to economies of scale. By comparison, the most predictable element of the outsourced supplier approach was that licensing costs would increase as new partners joined.

> The basic financial model of the Kuali OLE system is different from other proprietary systems in the sense that you pay a subscription annually and that could potentially be reduced over time so it was seen as very attractive in attracting other libraries to it hence reducing the costs over years to come and therefore the costs would go down. With a proprietary system the costs are likely to rise so the financial model was attractive in that sense.　　　　　　　　**RA**

Further, more detailed financial modelling was undertaken at the Options Appraisal stage of the project.

Follow-up Investigations

At this stage in the project, the BLMS Executive focused on two questions:

1. how to develop BLMS as a consortium;
2. which technology option would have the best fit for the BLMS.

The project manager was tasked with obtaining further information from Kuali and the Library Coop (the Koha option was already well-documented by Staffordshire University) and also tried to get information from libraries which had recently chosen the leading commercial option about their experiences (on the one hand) and costs (on the other). The experiences of the early-adopters of this new system were mixed and the sense that it was a very expensive ('gold plated') option confirmed, although no-one was prepared to reveal full details of their financial arrangements with the supplier.

During the period July−October 2012 the functional specification was completed and an outline Options Appraisal prepared. The executive was strongly drawn towards an Open Source option and saw that Koha or OLE were the only viable choices due to the lack of Unicode in Evergreen. The split in the Koha community gave cause for considerable concern although a lot of time was given to considering the suggestion by the Library Coop.

It became clear that a decision was needed in order to focus on the detailed Options Appraisal which would include financial analysis and business cases for institutional support. With Open Source as the first preference, there was confidence that a commercial option would still exist as a fallback if the Open Source approach proved not viable.

There are a lot of advantages to [Open Source], one of which is financial in terms of costs going forward over years once you have the system in place, that partly depends on a group of libraries working together so it suits that type of arrangement [...] With proprietary systems if you wanted to change something or you need some information from them they will often charge you. [T]hat isn't an issue when you have a group of libraries working together, developing software. One of the key messages that was attractive about Kuali OLE at the start was the fact that they were developing a system and librarians were heavily involved in developing the system as opposed to a company producing a system that they thought librarians would need but it was actually librarians who were heavily involved in creating the system itself so that again is incredibly attractive. **RA**

Decision in Principle

In October 2012 the BLMS Executive published the following statement on its project website:

The Bloomsbury Library Management System consortium has made a decision in principle to develop its 21st Century LMS using Kuali OLE Open Source software as a platform.

Extensive options analysis and specification work over summer 2012 have indicated that an Open Source solution will offer the most flexible and future-proof direction to deliver the visionary shared service.

Strategically, Kuali OLE fully supports the direction and goals of the consortium members whilst also providing best value for money in terms of project and recurrent costs.

Technologically, the roadmap for Kuali OLE and the underlying enterprise technology, is delivering a truly next generation system.

Detailed planning and specification work will continue during the remainder of 2012. The programme of development work will continue during 2013, with a pilot service targeted to go live in late 2013.

The post was followed up by a second post titled 'We scanned the horizon and found something interesting'[23] to provide further detail about the background to the decision. The posting summarised the reasons for the decision in the following terms:

Three things about Kuali OLE persuaded us to make it our preferred option:

1. a group of large university libraries looked at the LMS field and, having decided that nothing on offer addressed their functional requirements, set about building one based on a systematic and detailed analysis of their library workflows, using a combination of their own resources and a large grant from the Mellon Foundation;

2. the Kuali system, developed and maintained by the Kuali Foundation, has interoperability at its core, offering extensive modularity based on the primary principle that data should be managed once in the appropriate place and software modules should be able to address that data directly rather than importing and replicating it;

3. whilst offering its software through the Open Source model, Kuali is a membership organisation with strong governance and high levels of assurance about both the quality and longevity of its systems with members able to have direct and continuing input into the choices about the development of the software and systems.

(Anyone who has struggled to get a vendor interested in its requirements for changes to or developments of its LMS will understand why the third point is so significant.)

In summary, Kuali OLE provides us with the opportunity not only to build a truly next-generation LMS, but to approach levels of cooperation (through the focus on interoperability and data-sharing) which go well beyond the scope of a simple 'shared-service LMS'.

In making its decision in principle, the BLMS executive was aware of the need to assess the impact of its decision on existing systems as it was clear that partnership working with the current vendors would be essential during the development and parallel running stages of the project. It was also clear that a great deal of work was required before the decision in principle was translated into an implementation plan. What was not anticipated was the response of the vendor community.

Fear, Uncertainty and Doubt

It is an unusual experience, to put it mildly, for a library director to find himself or herself more or less pinned against a wall in the middle of a major conference by the representative of a library systems provider who has grabbed him or her by the lapels and is shouting about the 'terrible mistake' which has been made. It is certainly an unusual sales technique but such was the tone of the 'Fear, Uncertainty and Doubt (FUD)' sales technique (invented, some say, by IBM back in the 1960s) which was unleashed by the BLMS decision.

Kuali may not have been a byword in the United Kingdom (indeed, the BLMS statement on its website admitted that it had only come into view quite late in the horizon scanning process) but it was well-known and attracting a lot of attention in the United States, where the competition to be first in the 'next generation ILS' stakes was becoming quite intense. It might be said – in 2012 – that the large suppliers who had coasted for years on the strength of their user-base and the fact that libraries don't change systems very often had been caught on the hop by the speed with which the transition from print to hybrid libraries had changed the landscape for systems support. The money that the Mellon Foundation put, first into the Kuali Finance system, then into the 2008/2009 study which developed the OLE concept, followed by the seed funding for Kuali OLE, had attracted a lot of attention and the 'energy and enthusiasm' for OLE had not gone unnoticed.

> The reason [we] decided to go along with this project was because it is Open Source. We in Library Technology Services have been working with a lot of Open Source technology – we had the Moodle system for our course management software, we had Drupal for our website. On the library side we used VuFind for our discovery layer or catalogue. We were already trying to move away from vendor world and this would be another move to move away from our vendor.
>
> We just saw costs going up and [the vendor] hadn't made many changes to the library system that we were thrilled with – we didn't see much movement towards working with electronic resources but our collections are slowly moving towards electronic resources. We did not see our vendor changing their development at all to take into

> consideration electronic resources – that was a big one – plus we wanted control over our own data and have our system analyst and technology team be able to get their hands into code and look at the code and that you can't do in a proprietary system.   **SW-Y**

For a supplier, winning the business for a consortium which could – potentially – extend across the University of London would be a major coup. More than one supplier lost no time in letting as many librarians as possible – at University of London colleges and across the sector – know what a 'mad' thing the BLMS was doing. A senior manager from the University of London reported that he was approached by a librarian from a different university who told him that the BLMS Librarians were 'barking'.

The decision ended one stage of the project but marked the beginning of the next, in many ways much more difficult phase: to build a robust consortium model which would support the implementation of Kuali OLE in the BLMS partner libraries.

The Moving Horizon

As described above, three years later SOAS Library is on the new system and the other UK libraries are sitting in the wings. The lessons learned about shared service and consortial working are documented below. If we repeated the horizon scanning exercise today, what would we see?

Clearly, the environment has changed dramatically. Not only the local circumstances mentioned above have changed, but also the national environment. The Tory-led coalition, which was in power in 2012, has given way to a Tory government faced with weak opposition and able to pursue its agenda of marketising the UK higher education environment with few constraints. In the autumn 2015 enrolment sessions there were no caps on the recruitment of home and EU undergraduates and – especially for smaller HEIs – the situation is more turbulent than ever in living memory.

The UK Comprehensive Spending Review has the potential to change – again – the funding structures in HE. Central funding for initiatives such as Jisc may vanish. Institutions may be told to find the costs of central, shared services from their (allegedly increased) fee income whilst also attempting to generate strategic reserves to replace their lost capital grants.

The 'cloud' has become a pervasive marketing term which refers to a range of service offerings which might be genuine, collaborative efforts or simple efficiency gains, but might equally be further privatisation of services previously operated as core business by HEIs. To a considerable extent, the public appreciation of this approach to information systems provision has been constructed around the 'free' services delivered by large, mostly American corporations.

It is hard to find a university in the United Kingdom that has not moved its e-mail, calendaring, collaborative document-authoring and much else besides to a 'free' provider. Where not completely free, subscription charges are set so low, and data allowances (measured in tens of gigabytes) so high, that the 'offer' is exceedingly hard to refuse. When asked, 'is it really safe to put our data onto someone else's computer', most of the IT practitioners brokering access to these services mention reassuring pieces of paper but in reality, the answer is, 'nothing bad happened ... yet and besides, it's cheap'.

The Open Data, Open Access agenda has moved dramatically since 2012. Libraries, particularly Research Libraries, are at the forefront of the move back towards the curation, preservation and publication of their institutions' intellectual property. In this context, health warnings about the 'cloud' come in to sharp focus. It is one thing to commit the ephemeral e-mail, calendar and document floods to some vast data centre in the sky (but don't mention this to the social historians); another thing altogether when it comes to the data that is the primary intellectual property of the institution. We spend a fortune securing our physical archives: why would we not give our digital holdings the same attention?

We are completely emancipated from a vendor who owns our data. But from a moral point of view if you work on a system and you invest quite a lot of time and your profession is cataloguer you want to believe that the catalogue record belongs to the institution who is paying your bills, but it never did: vendors owned that data and they would charge you to take it out of their environment. So that is a leap forward in the way the libraries store their data.   **CM**

Looking ahead then, a considerable tension arises between the proprietors of big data, happy to take anything we give them at little or no cost and the requirements of libraries to ensure that their holdings are safe for now and posterity. Once the data leaves the building, the digital Dark Age is really only one light-switch away.

Scholarly Communications and Open Access
The challenge of scholarly communications and the protection of the scholarly record have also come into sharper focus, especially for research libraries. At present, publicly funded research outputs (books, chapters, journal articles) are freely given to large publishing conglomerates who call upon the labour of other academics to 'peer review' the material before publishing it in 'quality', 'high impact' journals or hard-backed volumes which they then sell back to the sector which gave it to them, at eye-watering profit margins. Members of the tax-paying public who in many cases funded the research must stump up their own cash to get the outputs, unless they are lucky enough to be associated with a university or learned society.

In the digital age, it has never been easier to publish. Every academic library that has set up an open access repository is already a publisher, and shared platforms are emerging for the rest. Funders are demanding that research is put on open access as soon as possible after publication and in many cases that should also include the original data so that others can reuse it or at least test the research. There is already evidence of a strong trend for universities to revert to publishing their own material once they have re-established their credentials as authoritative publishers.

In the commercial library systems sector, a number of things have also changed. Through a continuing process of mergers and acquisitions, the number of suppliers is shrinking and it is becoming clear that there is an aspiration amongst some to provide a seamless web of library management, discovery and content services. The Kuali Foundation meanwhile has established a spin-out company to accelerate its goal of providing a comprehensive suite of Open Source Enterprise applications on a managed-service basis and the OLE Partnership is considering where it stands in relation to this initiative.

If we started again today the only thing that is certain is that we would end up in a different place. Such is the nature of decision-making processes: decisions have consequences and often it can take years for the full implications of those consequences to be worked-through.

PHASE TWO: OPTIONS APPRAISAL

It was one thing to make a 'decision in principle' for Kuali OLE but quite another to work out how to put the decision into practice. What models of practice did exist were either to be found in the American libraries considering their implementation plans, or in other enterprises. A number of examples could be found in the United Kingdom of universities taking Open Source software and building effective services: very few of them in libraries.

Three tips for a successful Kuali OLE implementation:

— hire good staff and resource the project properly — it's a project which requires a lot of technical staff, more than we had at SOAS and I would recommend them not to underestimate the skill levels involved rly and often, as I've said it is quite a culture change, it's a community driven project and you need to have the library staff on your side to implement it effectively because pushing against library staff makes the whole thing a lot harder,

— plan well ahead of time; really think about what you are going to need, what the system is going to do. Plan these things out with functional specifications, a project manager for a workflow and business analysis going up with technical specifications — do a lot of planning.

I'd say that OLE needs a couple more years to develop into a mature product, so the state that the software is in now I would say would need a medium size HEI. You need a lot of staff for it, so you need a moderately sized organisation with a good IT department who can hire and assign staff to the project. Conversely you don't want too large a university because of the sheer quantity of data and data analysis and data transformations that need to take place.   **SB**

In order for the BLMS to move from its decision in principle to implementation therefore, a number of detailed options were studied and obstacles negotiated. We also had to prepare business cases for investment by each of the partner institutions, which would be keen to see the financial modelling showing not only the up-front implementation but also the on-going support costs.

First, the obstacles.

Conventional Wisdom

There is a conventional approach to the selection of information systems and services that starts with a specification written up as an Invitation To Tender (ITT, described in the United States as a Request For Proposals or RFP), released to 'the market'. If the value of the system or service is above a certain threshold, the notice of intention to procure must be placed into the Online Journal of the European Union (OJEU) to ensure that anyone in the EU can bid.

Depending upon how it is defined, this approach has the potential to reduce the options for obtaining a service. Universities typically have procurement offices to prepare the paperwork and Vendors are geared up to respond. Procurement can work well when the thing being procured is a commodity such as desktop computer equipment or network equipment but it can create problems if the intention (as in this case study) is to implement an Open Source system. A typical ITT (or RFP) will ask for 'supply and support' of a system or service, possibly (in the case of an information system) including hosting and will ask for reference sites where the bidder has previously installed such a system. This tends to favour the vendors of proprietary systems, leading to vendor lock-in, as few vendors will allow a choice of support providers, meaning that, if one does not like the level of support being provided, one has to migrate to another system with all the costs that involves.

At least one university in the United Kingdom succeeded in obtaining an Open Source Library system via conventional procurement, by specifying Open Source as one of the 'mandatory requirements' in its ITT but many procurement offices will object that such a requirement restricts the 'market', and there are many more examples where the 'pre-Qualification questionnaire' was constructed in such a manner as to exclude almost any bid based on Open Source.

There is some evidence that the ITT/RFP process does not always produce a good outcome. Ken Chad, for example writing in the Jisc 'LMS Change' Wiki, says

> I'm rather against the detailed functional RFP process myself – maybe part of that is the scars I still have from working for a variety of vendors for over 20 years and writing responses to tenders/RFPs ... More recently, as a library consultant I have worked with quite a few libraries to help them determine requirements and I try to avoid detailed feature lists – and yet it seems libraries still seem to cling on to them.[24]

Choices: Purchase, Commission or Build?

In the Bloomsbury case, we avoided this hazard by working through an Options Appraisal approach to answer a basic question: 'are we purchasing, commissioning or building our new system?'

The answer to the first question was quite simple: we had decided on Kuali OLE, which meant that we were not proposing to purchase software. The software was available to us on an Open Source basis, meaning that it was available to download. In point of fact, we had decided to join the Kuali Foundation and the OLE Partnership, giving us a stake in the development of the system and early access to code releases, meaning that we could say, 'we don't need to purchase the software as we already own it'.

This left the other two questions to answer: commission or build? This led to further thinking (again before approaching the Procurement question) about how the service model might operate. The intention at this stage in the project was to scope a shared-service approach to hosting and support. We decided to disaggregate the two questions in order to maximise the flexibility once we moved towards implementation. The diagram below shows how a disaggregated service model might look, based around a 'Cost Sharing Group' (CSG).

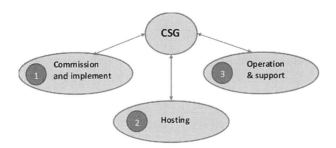

Example of a disaggregated service model based on a Cost Sharing Group (CSG)

Commissioning, Hosting and Support

Hosting was a relatively straightforward question. Most of the partner libraries at that time were based in institutions with IT services set up for local hosting and with one exception, existing Library systems were hosted locally. The situation at Senate House Libraries was slightly more complicated than the others as its internal service (the University of London Computing Centre or ULCC) was also operating as a provider of managed services to other Colleges and external users; hence, it charged back the cost of its services to the library via an internal market. At that time (2012), Infrastructure as a Service (IaaS) was starting to become an option; hence, it was possible to scope various scenarios ranging from local hosting, through managed service from ULCC, to alternative IaaS providers. Finally, the decision on hosting would come down to cost, functionality and security. If local, in-house hosting was the best option, no procurement was required; if outsourced hosting was under consideration, a procurement effort would be required.

Information Technology is idiosyncratic to each institution. At some institutions the Library Dean can have lots of latitude in this area to solve their own problem. At other institutions there's a stronger core to the technical solutions that a university may be pursuing and the library needs to consider the wider organisation. There are strategies they are pursuing that the library needs to be aligned with. A lot of it is being somewhat situational to your specific circumstance. Carlen is in a statewide loose affiliation of libraries that are attached to universities who are trying, as a state university system, to achieve certain types of goals. The libraries have this longstanding relationship with each other of resource sharing and in many cases technology and collection sharing.   **MW**

Putting that question to one side left us with the decision about commissioning or building the new service. We already had some experience in shared staffing, as we had taken on a project manager on a consortial basis and were planning for a shared business analyst. As a benchmark, we calculated the cost to set up a Systems Team of three (senior analyst programmer supported by two analyst programmers), which came out at £190−250K p.a. depending upon how the overheads (office space, computers, etc.) were calculated. We assumed it would take a year for the team to get up to speed and at least another year to commission the systems. An outcome of this approach would be to create a team that could – potentially – form the basis of a shared support service. If all partners bought in to the process from the start, this could be a viable approach.

> We are beginning to look seriously at how does a large organisation work, there are models out there for us, and there are well-established models for Kuali already. There are other organisations that we can look at and say what motivates people to join the partnership and sustain this effort and what are the right mechanisms for participation whereby people feel like they are influencing the outcomes that aren't as participatory as the current. There is a tension between more partners would bring in more income and should drive down costs because you are sharing it among a larger community. On the other hand, a larger community demands more resources, so the support, for example if we got up to 25 partners we may have to hire people to do frontline support, like a helpdesk as a vendor would have. That's a cost we don't need to have right now. **MW**

The alternative was to seek external assistance. The Kuali Foundation was operating a model of 'Kuali Commercial Affiliates' (KCAs): companies that could provide commissioning, hosting and support services for its members (the Foundation at that time did not offer these services directly, focusing instead on administrative support for the various Kuali projects). The OLE Partnership had contracted with HTC (a systems integration company with offices in the United States, India and the United Kingdom) for the development of its system and we contacted the company for an informal estimate in order to compare the cost of build versus commission. The response at that time (early 2013) was 'about £100k per Library plus VAT', provided that all the libraries were commissioning on a similar time frame.

We now had figures on which to base a budgeting exercise. We also had the basis of a model for how to implement the new system: disaggregate the service elements of software, hosting, commissioning/building and support. In order to proceed to the next step, we needed to work out what the service-delivery model would look like.

Financial Modelling (2)

Before that, we needed to provide some notion of what this was going to cost our host institutions. Using the benchmarked staffing model, we came up with some initial costings:

	Option 1: employ a systems team for two years		
	Year 1	Year 2	Year 3 on
Kuali Membership fees	£89,600	£89,600	£89,600
Systems Team	£250,000	£250,000	
Total	*£339,600*	*£339,600*	*£89,600*
Three-way split	£113,200	£113,200	£29,866
	Option 2: outsourced commissioning over 1 year		
Kuali Membership fees	£89,600	£89,600	£89,600
Commission 3 systems	£360,000		
Total	*£449,600*	*£89,600*	*£89,600*
Three-way split	£149,866	£29,866	£29,866

On this model, the net cost per library over three years of Option 1 is £256,266 and for Option 2 £209,598. If Option 1 is chosen and then the Systems Team kept on for support, annual costs are £133,200. The attraction of the second model was the lower annual costs (Kuali fees only) but it left the matter of on-going support unresolved.

Both models demonstrated an economy of scale: if a fourth or fifth library joined, the annual costs would go down by sharing between more partners and the fact that only three were committed at the start was a factor in the decision about whether to go with a local systems team or outsourced commissioning.

On-Going Support Costs

This was the hardest part of the scoping process. What does support for an Open Source library system look like? Our starting point was to look at current arrangements. Each of the partner libraries had a library systems team of some description. As noted above in the analysis of current systems, the involvement of the local IT service (however it was configured)

tended to be relatively basic: keeping the 'lights on' and the terminals connected. Beyond that, technical support for the system itself came from the
suppliers and the library systems teams were operationally focused, treating
the system by and large as an appliance and supporting library processes.

One of the tensions which had grown over the 2000s, leading to the
impulse to look for something better, was the expansion of the Library
System into a cluster of systems alongside the need to support the management of electronic resource access, for which the legacy systems had no
meaningful support.

Individual members of the library systems teams in the partner libraries
had branched out into innovative areas. Birkbeck, for example had implemented a VuFind system to replace its legacy OPAC because the local
Systems Librarian became interested, persuaded IT to give him a server to
play with, and configured the system. A Systems Librarian at IoE had also
been looking at Data Analysis tools, using VuFind and this shared interest
led to a very productive collaboration which resulted in two of the BLMS
libraries putting up VuFind systems that were very well received by library
users. SOAS had been an early-adopter of the UK Access Management
Federation[25] which used the Shibboleth implementation of SAML[26] to
manage off-site access to electronic resources, a project which led to a very
productive collaboration with the section in the local IT service which operated the SOAS Identity Management system.

Other systems librarians had had to become familiar with turnstile control systems and self-issue and return systems. When the systems librarians
had their regular meetings it became clear that, taken as a group, they had
developed a considerable range of technical capabilities.

I have used other systems and I have always found the most help and
the most collaboration is not with the vendor as much as with other
customers, so in our last system, if we had a question and we knew
the institutions that were a little ahead of us or had done some functionality that we hadn't done yet, we would call them directly, we
wouldn't go through our vendor so I think this is a good point to
make about the Open Source we were very collaborative with each
other and we could solve some problems with each other too which
was really nice with our data and our tables and getting into our
tables which under a closed system we couldn't get into like the
underpinnings of the data.   **SW-Y**

The ingredient missing in each instance (with notable exceptions) was productive engagement with IT staff. It was still quite common at that time for conversations to go along the lines of, 'there are corporate systems, and there are library systems'. For some reason, many IT staff simply didn't see library systems as 'serious'. For their part, many library staff were intensely frustrated that their requests for assistance seemed always to be parked in the 'pending' tray at the local IT service.

It became clear that a number of libraries in the United Kingdom had resorted to setting up their own IT support teams for the simple reason that it was the only way to get things done. The BLMS model therefore considered what a dedicated library support service might look like.

Putting to one side the process by which the team could be formed, the obvious solution was to create a Library Systems Technical Support team with the skills required to support the configuration and operation of the chosen Open Source systems. The work had already been done to scope an in-house implementation team and this formed the basis for a simple financial model, building on the scoping work for the implementation phase.

Item	Annual cost
OLE Partnership dues	£89,600
Senior analyst programmer/developer (team leader)	£55,000
2 x Programmer/developers (team members)	£88,000
Office provision (assumes located in a partner college)	£31,500
Allowance for administration costs	£20,000
Travel	£10,000
Total	*£294,100*
Rate per partner if split three ways	£98,033
Rate per partner if split four ways	£73,525
Rate per partner if split five ways	£58,820
Rate per partner if split six ways	£49,016
Rate per partner if split seven ways	£43,104

The model excluded infrastructure costs as these were absorbed locally under a range of different arrangements. It was benchmarked against the net spend of the partner libraries on their current arrange-

ments (software licenses and support by the suppliers). It became clear
that three libraries was not a large enough group to make the model
viable but from five libraries onwards, the cost of the support model
came close to what the libraries were already spending and hence affordable on a like-for-like basis. It was pointed to some kind of banding
model would that need to be developed to account for the different sizes
of the partner libraries.

Choosing an Implementation Method

At this point, with three libraries definitely planning to implement, it was
decided to share the costs of the OLE Partnership fees but to put the other
shared support elements on one side pending new partners joining
the consortium.

The follow-on decision from this was that employing a Systems Team
for the implementation was risky for two reasons: the time taken to recruit
and bring them up to speed; the burden upon the institution which took
the lead as employer if either or both of the other partners pulled out, leav-
ing it to pick up the employment costs.

The commissioning option was therefore selected on the basis that

(a) it was a fixed cost; and
(b) the supplier had indicated the work could be done in a year.

Following from this, a procurement effort was required to secure
the services of a commissioning company. Two of the three partners
had procurement offices and the respective managers were consulted. It
was agreed in both cases that a single-supplier procurement was justified as (at that time) there was only one company available with the
expertise and experience to implement a Kuali OLE system. The third
partner was willing to take the advice of the procurement officers. The
commissioning company was then engaged in detailed contractual
negotiations.

This decision left the matter of on-going support in abeyance. Work was
required to determine how a support team could be employed in such a
manner as to engage effectively with all partners, open options for new
partners to join, and avoid unnecessary VAT charges.

The decision also triggered invitations to any number of seminars about the future of library systems, launched several staff from BLMS partners across the Atlantic to Kuali OLE planning meetings and set in train planning for a 'Kuali Days UK' conference at the Senate House of the University of London in 2013.

I didn't actually go to Chicago and Lehigh but I went to two Kuali conferences and a couple of other events in the States, where the Kuali OLE community got together, talked about the project, did programming. We got together and discussed OLE, the direction of the project overall. Those face-to-face interactions were incredibly valuable on getting that long-term perspective on what the software would achieve, where it would go, how it would develop, not only in terms of technical stuff, what code basis but in terms of how it would reach and communicate with other libraries, get more people to adopt it [with] a long-term view to adjusting the library systems market place. Also as part of my role I attended online meetings every week so I was on the technical council and the functional council of OLE. We would meet on WebEx every week and talk through an agenda, highlighting any outstanding issues and particularly when SOAS went live talk about our experience and warn other people about potential problems. **SB**

PHASE THREE: PLANNING THE SHARED SERVICE MODEL

Three things make for a successful shared service:

1. partners already having a strong basis for collaborating with one another, including a clear understanding of their shared values;
2. partners sharing a clear need for a system or service that they are going to have to obtain in any case, with a business case for investment which will stand up in their institution, and senior management support for proceeding collaboratively;

3. the option of buying, building or commissioning the system or service through a collaborative model giving better value or delivers a better outcome than the partners could obtain working on their own.

These factors certainly obtained in the early stages of the BLMS project. They also apply to the members of the Kuali OLE Partnership and the success of the partnership to date is testament to these factors being present.

[To be successful at Open Source] you need to

— setup a good project,
— make sure you have a really good test system,
— get data into the system as soon as possible and be looking at your own data as soon as possible,
— build into the schedule a good testing thing, that's not just an Open Source thing that's true of any implementation.

Don't schedule a bunch of other things if you are going to try to implement this. Reward people for making the change and moving into the new way of doing.

You would want to make sure that you have a couple of good technical people and that they can work with the other technical people from the other libraries, because that's what Open Source really is like. It works well with programmers and technical people because they like to do that.   **FM**

The Innovation and Shared-Service Spectra

In a series of workshops, the Bloomsbury Libraries considered where they wanted to be on the shared-service spectrum, the innovation spectrum and their appetites for risk. The workshops were attended by representatives from all 6 of the original partners. A discussion-based approach was taken to positioning their appetite for taking on the various categories of risk associated with the project (e.g. financial, reputational, technical, service delivery, political):

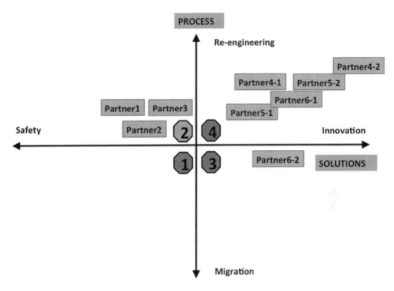

Partner positioning on the risk appetite grid

On this grid, three of the partners appear twice (Partners 4, 5 and 6) as there were different risk appetites between their directors and systems librarians.

The next grid places partners on the shared services spectrum:

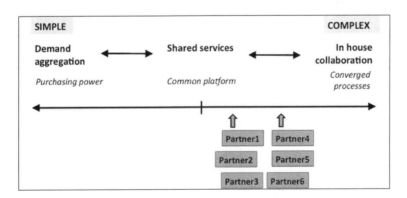

Parter positioning on the shared services spectrum

Based on this work, there was a clear appetite to move beyond collaborating on a Procurement exercise that would most likely result in a shared purchase of a proprietary system, to the creation of a common platform with options to converge some library operations.

Models of Provision

In order to proceed to build a shared service, a service model is required. There are two aspects to this question:

- how are the services put together?
- what is the governance model for the service partners?

As noted above, the decision had already been taken to disaggregate the primary service elements in order to offer maximum flexibility for the partners. (A risk-mitigation feature was that the detailed functional requirement and technical specification documents had been drafted in such a way that, if a partner decided not to proceed into the shared service, it still had something to take away: a set of documents which could be adapted into a conventional systems Procurement exercise.)

Service models were produced, setting out the context in which the new systems would operate, how the service elements would be commissioned and detailed work on the possible systems architecture.

Models of Governance

Key to success was finding a governance model that gave all partners a high level of assurance that they were working as equals. This was important because one of the partners (the University of London) was considerably larger than the others (the Bloomsbury Colleges) and the University was already a provider of managed services to the colleges, through its library, its International Academy, its accommodation and counselling services, and the University of London Computing Centre (ULCC). The clear direction from senior management at the colleges was to avoid going in a direction that would result in a library system delivered by the University as a managed service. (Whilst this might seem to be a constraint placed upon the project for political reasons, where questions of governance and autonomy are at stake, negotiating local politics becomes essential.)

Governance models were also an important part of the decision to join the Kuali Foundation and OLE Partnership. The view was that the well-developed Kuali model provided a high level of assurance that the software would be sustainable, and partners' requirements would be met.

Several models for the BLMS were considered:

- a lead institution (not the University) commissioning or procuring the shared service elements and employing the staff, billing back to the partners;
- a 'Joint Activity Not An Enterprise' (JANE) in which service elements are distributed around the partners, billing back to each other as appropriate;
- a Joint Venture delivered through a company.

The Bloomsbury context already had a number of examples of the first two models. In these cases, the billing-back process involved VAT with the potential to increase costs (e.g. a salary paid at one partner institution when billed-back to the others became a service subject to VAT).

Around this time, the UK Treasury announced some changes in taxation regulations, which gave rise to the development of 'cost sharing groups'. Once this became a possibility, there was further work on which service model would provide such a benefit. Detailed advice was obtained from

- HEFCE,
- BUFDG (British Universities Finance Directors' Group), and
- Commercial Accountants.

The BLMS was strongly advised to form a Company Limited by Guarantee Having No Share Capital, based on a number of examples of other such arrangements (UCISA, RLUK, SCONUL, LMN, M25, Jisc, etc.).

The need for each partner to have an equal voice was also important. The Joint Venture in a new Company was the best means to protect the partner interests and it was clear that the maximum VAT benefit derived from using the Joint Venture as an employer of shared staff. The basis of the VAT exemption, as explained by the accountants at that time, was that a membership organisation might be able to avoid some or all VAT on services provided to its members (depending on the category of service) hence there would not be the 20% uplift on salary costs which would be seen in the model where one partner employed staff and billed back the costs to the other partners.

The model developed to the point where draft Articles of Association were prepared and a Shadow Board drawn from Senior Management at each potential partner formed.

At the time the concept was so new that the BLMS the would have been first implementer of a CSG (Cost Sharing Group) in the United Kingdom and would have been a test case for HMRC.[27]

Planning for Company Formation

A 'swim lanes' style roadmap towards the preferred Shared-Service model was used extensively in discussions during 2013/2014, summarising the Work Packages 1 through 8 that fed into the preferred outcome:

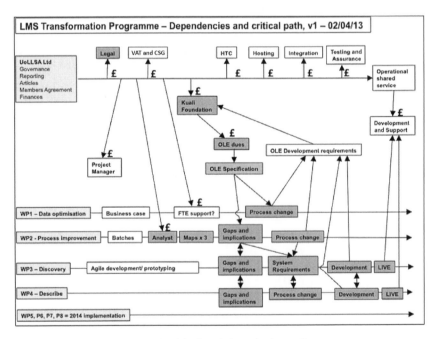

Programme critical path in swim lanes format

Throughout 2013, the partners worked on the assumption that this roadmap would be followed. As the plans progressed, the Articles of Association were prepared by a firm of solicitors and the contracts prepared for the commissioning of a system for each library. But when the moment came to sign the various documents, the partners hesitated. By December 2013 it was clear that SOAS was ready to proceed but the other partners were moving towards a 'wait and see' position.

By April 2014 there was still some hope that one of the other libraries would start its implementation but by July it became clear this was not going to happen during 2014. The Shadow Board for the proposed joint venture company met for the last time, the Articles of Association were consigned to the bottom drawer, and SOAS continued to work towards its implementation of the Kuali OLE system, making it the third library in the world to move to this system, following the libraries of Lehigh University in Bethlehem Pennsylvania and the University of Chicago.

Stepping Back from the Brink

What made the partners hesitate at the point of moving into the Joint Venture? The Shadow Board had a loss of confidence. Why?

Moving from a conventional approach to systems replacement to a novel approach where several variables are changed at the same time (Open Source, shared support, joint venture, consortial membership of a US Foundation and Partnership) requires strong and continuous input from the champion at each partner.

The change in the BLMS approach was the outcome of circumstances beyond SOAS' control. To summarise:

- first the School of Pharmacy and later the Institute of Education merged with University College London, reducing the Bloomsbury Colleges' alliance from six to four;
- the Librarian at Birkbeck, a strong advocate for Open Source systems, retired;
- the Librarian at Senate House Libraries, a strong advocate for the BLMS, moved on;
- the Librarian at LSHTM moved on;
- the Registrar at SOAS, a supporter of the BLMS, moved on;
- the Director of SOAS, a supporter of the Senate House Library, libraries in general and the BLMS project in particular, retired;
- the atmosphere around the notion of 'shared service' had cooled, when not actually obscured by the 'clouds' which have become the lingua franca of the managed service brigades in all their variations (CoLocation,[28] Joint Tenants,[29] SaaS,[30] IaaS[31]).

At this point, the robust insistence on each partner having something to take away at each stage of the project came into play. It was agreed that partners could commission their systems at different speeds, with local hosting (as this was cost-neutral compared with existing arrangements); the joint venture would go into abeyance, with its focus moving onto the need for shared support — once three or more partners were up and running on the new system.

The concept is still a great one, this sense of libraries working together on an Open Source system has a lot of potential to it and if indeed SOAS are able to create some momentum behind the system and other libraries join in, the financial model does work very well — if you get a group of libraries then the costs go down and it's really good. The costs vary depending on the number of libraries involved. The costs were a bit vague at the beginning and alarm bells were raised at that point especially among senior management at Birkbeck when it wasn't clear at that first board meeting what the cap on the budget was. All senior managers are fairly fearful if you have a project where it doesn't seem to have a cap. But it was a new concept and that added to the risk element, so I think people were a little bit wary about that but as I say the concept is still an interesting one and could potentially work.   **RA**

The shared project management and business analyst arrangements were confirmed. SOAS became the lead partner, charging back the shared costs to the other partners.

Lessons Learned?

The lesson for any potential collaboration is that, when things change, it can be difficult to carry on if the original premise is not strong enough to carry the activity through the bumps along the way. It is essential to have good risk mitigation in place so that changes can be accommodated. SOAS therefore was able to lead the way on implementing Kuali OLE for its library management system during 2014–2015, successfully going live in April 2015.

> The only other thing that happened was that Senate House began to get cold feet as well [...] and the fact that Senate House's involvement as far as we were concerned was quite important as they're a flagship library and once they started dragging their heels on the project it was looking like just us and SOAS, it began to be a slightly less attractive prospect. The vision originally was built on the idea of lots of libraries joining in on the shared service and it just seemed to that another library was pulling out, a key library in our view, and that had financial implications [...] Without that potentially ourselves and SOAS would have to pay more. So all of this was gathering momentum which made us want to draw back from the project rather than go towards it. **RA**

The shared service ethos continued as, by the point that SOAS went live in 2015, it was a member of an international shared service in the form of the Kuali OLE Partnership. This is a highly collaborative community, whereby development, technical support and governance are shared across its members.

The Kuali OLE community's full partners pay an annual fee, abide by a Memorandum of Understanding – and all have an equal voice in the development and support of the OLE software.

Most of this collaborative group are major US research universities, with SOAS the only full international partner. SOAS has therefore had a critical role in channelling UK and European requirements and priorities through into a shared software development community.

At the time of writing (January 2016), the Mellon Foundation has made another grant to the OLE Partnership, its membership has grown to include two German Library Service Consortia and two new US Universities and it is considering its options for developing from a Library Management System to a true Library Services Platform using a new technical architecture delivered via a re-vamped 'Agile' development process.

REFLECTIONS (1): OPEN SOURCE TECHNOLOGY AND CULTURAL CHANGE

At the beginning of this journey, there was a clear aspiration to work colla-boratively and use – if possible – Open Source software for library systems. The impulse arose from a number of factors, some top-down (the enthu-siasm of the library directors for a new approach) and some bottom-up (the frustration expressed by many library staff with their current systems).

Whilst collaboration between libraries was seen as potentially transform-ing, leading to a shared service approach, what was less understood at the start was the potential for the new initiatives to disrupt and, potentially, change working practices within libraries. The problems that this disrup-tion needed to address manifested in a number of ways which can be described through scenarios.

Scenario 1: Capability Gaps

This scenario varies depending upon the size of a library and the ways in which it has developed its staff. For a relatively small library, it is not unu-sual to find a 'library systems team' of one or two people. This was cer-tainly the case across most of the BLMS partners. In the case of the SOAS Library, a single post was allocated to this function, with a further half FTE within one of the corporate systems teams allocated to the 'systems administration' function.

The Systems Librarian was able to interact with the proprietary system via its client software or its 'dumb terminal' interface for those functions which could not be operated via the client (its web interface was limited to provision of an OPAC). Some key functions in the system, or troubleshooting of pro-blems, or application of patches, could only be done by the vendor. For most of the time during which the system was in operation at SOAS (a period of almost 20 years), the vendor's help desk was located on the west coast of the United States, which added an 8-hour time-zone difference to the mix. One of the tasks of the Systems Librarian therefore was to try to explain problems to the help desk towards the end of the UK working day and then, the next morning, see whether the problems had been solved overnight.

In a pinch, the Systems Librarian knew how to re-start the application but not how to reboot the system. The Systems Administrator, on the other hand, knew how to reboot the system (a server running the Sun Solaris ver-sion of UNIX) but not how to restart the application. The maintenance agreements on the Sun hardware and software lapsed when Sun was purchased by Oracle and the system was two releases out of date on its operating system, with no patches having been applied for a number of years.

At the point where the limits on the capability of the Systems Librarian to diagnose a problem was reached, problems tended to go unresolved as the vendor help desk did not see its role to include diagnosing problems and was quick − in the case of problems interfacing to other systems − to pass the buck. Hence, in one particularly frustrating example, an online payments module purchased for the Library System (at considerable expense) took more than four years to configure whilst the various systems vendors blamed each other for the problems and the local staff lacked the capability to identify the source of the problem and hold the correct vendor to account. This pointed up the difficulties which manifest in another scenario.

Scenario 2: Internal Stand-Offs

As already noted, it was not unusual during conversations with staff in corporate systems to hear them describe 'library systems' as, somehow, *other* ('we look after corporate systems not library systems'). This extended in the early days of the project to a range of stand-offs between Library and IT staff, who sometimes seemed to live in different universes. For example

- an interim Librarian left his job early because he 'liked the Library, but would prefer never to have to deal with IT again'
- a request to upgrade one of the servers handling an important piece of Library software (a link-resolver) was repeatedly delayed until the machine in question failed, leading to an emergency replacement using kit which had to be sourced (by the library director) via eBay
- a new discovery service from a library systems vendor took several years to configure because of a dispute about network security and the firewall rules
- an EzProxy system took three years to get working whilst arguments raged about who would pay the license fees
- the need to update computers in the library running the OPAC software was repeatedly deferred due to disputes about whose responsibility it was to maintain the computers
- a librarian demanded the removal of most of the non-OPAC computers in the library because the 'noise of the keyboards' was annoying users in

the silent spaces and no-one in the IT section was prepared to consider the possibility that better keyboards might solve the problem

In general terms, the attitudes on each side could be characterised as a mixture of frustration and anger: Library staff had the distinct impression that IT staff would say 'yes' to their requests (possibly to get them to go away) but then do nothing; IT staff saw the demands of the library as a nuisance to be avoided. One IT Manager, when challenged about his lack of interest in the users in the library declared 'I don't support users, I support IT'.

Scenario 3: Abjection

In the face of intransigence from the local IT service and an almost completely moribund approach by the main external library systems vendor (happy to take 10s of 1,000s of pounds each year from the library in return for a remote help desk and very occasional software patches), Library staff had become resigned to the point of abjection about the possibility of any improvement in their systems environment and online services to users. Any real progress that had been made, generally arose from external engagement, for example

- the Jisc-funded 'LEAP' project for Research Repositories led to the Library using ePrints on a local server, but installed and supported by staff at the University of Southampton,
- another Jisc-funded project ('SHIBBO-LEAP') led to the Library becoming an early adopter of the UK Access Management Federation replacement for the centrally funded ATHENS service, with most of the initial effort provided by staff at other LEAP Libraries.

It became commonplace to hear Library staff declare there to be 'no point' in asking for systems improvements because none of their requirements ever seemed to become priorities at IT Support. This situation was ripe for disruption.

REFLECTIONS (2): DISRUPTIVE INNOVATION

Two innovations happened at SOAS that have – over a 7-year time-span – led to significant changes in the working culture of the Library:

- the Library was moved, in 2009, into a new 'converged services' directorate alongside IT, MIS and AV services under a single director;
- the Library joined the BLMS project.

Disruption by Reorganisation

The first innovation created the circumstances for the second to produce a successful outcome.

[As an aside: when comparing notes with the other two libraries which were early-adopters of the Kuali OLE system, it became clear that there was a common thread between all three of the early adopters. In each case, the Library was either part of a converged service (Lehigh and SOAS) or had a very strong, long-standing relationship with its local IT service (Chicago). This was an important success-factor for early adoption of an Open Source library system.]

Over time, the notion – at SOAS – of an 'IT department' has been eroded, alongside an initiative to re-engineer Library and IT user-facing services as 'customer services'. The SOAS Library & Information Services directorate is organised into three divisions: Customer Services & Operations (CSOPS); Information Systems (IS); Research Library Services (RLS). The Customer Services & Operations division is the most converged of the three, combining what was Library Reader Services with the former IT help desk and the audio visual service under an assistant director. A service model has been put in place under which front-line enquiries which cannot be dealt with at the first point of contact by CSOPS staff are escalated to specialists in the IS or RLS divisions. Where responsibilities cross management boundaries between divisions, working groups meet regularly, combining relevant staff from the divisions and teams to ensure a coherent service provision.

Some of our managers are on the subject matter expert teams, so we all had a part in writing specs for the functionality and suggesting how the functionality in OLE should work. We never as functional people in libraries had that opportunity before to work with developers to set the functionality we needed and work with developers to see how they were going to build the code, we never had that communication line to a developer before. I think that brought us closer to

the technology side. We are very close to our systems analyst and our
own library so we've learned a whole new world of technology that
functional people never had to know before and I think that's a real
benefit because our systems analyst and our developers now know —
we go back and forth saying this is the spec that we need this is the
functionality but it is so powerful. There are many libraries in the
1970s that developed their own library system and then we went to
vendors doing it and now it is time for us to get our data back and
do our development together as well as letting our systems analysts
locally have a chance to contribute code.   **SW-Y**

With these arrangements in place, the environment was created in which
the BLMS initiative, once it moved into its implementation phase, could, in
principle, be supported by appropriate cross-divisional teams (provided
relevant managers and team leaders engaged pro-actively with the project).
In addition to this, the business case for implementation of a new system
(as part of a new suite of library systems which also included repositories
and research data management) included a new analyst programmer post
that was added to one of the corporate systems teams with a brief specifically to support library systems.

Disruption by Technology

I have described above how the decision to adopt an Open Source library
system meant working against the grain of conventional approaches to
system procurement. This approach also disrupted the normal ways in
which library staff were used to interact with the technology provider.

As noted above, the attitude of many library staff towards their systems
was one of powerlessness, bordering on abjection. To a considerable extent
they saw themselves as the passive users of the system. Indeed, for some staff
who had started their library careers in the 1960s and 70s, and had been
through the entire life-cycle of 'library automation' (from cataloguing on
3"×5" cards and book issuing via rubber stamps, through 'retro-conversion'
to online systems addressed via 'dumb terminals' and the introduction of
bar-codes, to the system they had been using since the mid-1990s), their conceptual model of 'Library data' was what they saw on the screen when
logged in to the Library system.

I think it's fair to say that people did get a little discouraged when they ran into bugs and we couldn't move some of our records through like our order process. For a little bit things were getting held up, but once we resolved those I think the staff felt like they had some skin in the game because they identified the problem and they got to work with our system analysts who worked with the developers so I think people felt like they could have a direct effect on it. Our serials cataloguers and serials acquisitions suffered the most but I think other than that most people just carried on with what we could do and left open certain projects we couldn't move ahead on until a bug patch got put in. Because we had direct line into the developers to tell them what we were running into and what we needed straightened up and our system analysts could tell them what part of the code wasn't working, they could even see the code well enough to find out that piece of code needs to be changed. We could have never done that in a proprietary system.   **SW-Y**

The selection by the BMLS project of the Kuali OLE system was heavily influenced by the aspiration to empower Library staff to become much more actively involved in the selection, configuration and operation of their systems, not merely wait for the replacement system to be dropped onto their desks, delivering a 'like for like' service in a brighter, shinier web interface. Indeed, the Kuali 'community source' software approach (as encapsulated in the quote from the 2009 report at the start of this document) set out to involve library technology users in the entire life-cycle of the software from scoping, through specification, design, coding (with certain caveats), to testing and implementation.

The community-source, peer-support processes in the Kuali approach are examined in detail below. On the technology front, for the BLMS libraries, there were several stages of disruption based on specific choices.

Discoverability

Jisc did a great deal of work during the first decade of the 21st century on 'discovery to delivery'.[32] This led, by the second decade, to a widespread appreciation, in research libraries and beyond, of the need for 'discoverability'. With the exception of a small cohort of researchers willing to come into the library and dig through card catalogues, indexes and other paper records, for the vast majority of library users, if material cannot be discovered online, it might as well not exist.

The first deliverable from the BLMS project was a set of new Library Discovery systems. Several Open Source systems were evaluated and VuFind[33] from the Falvey Memorial Library at Villanova University[34] was chosen. Development of this system was a truly collaborative effort by the systems librarians from all the Bloomsbury College Libraries (at that time) and Senate House Libraries, resulting in new systems being put into production at Senate House and SOAS, with upgrades to the existing system at Birkbeck and a system managed by the IoE Systems Librarian used for the analysis and cleansing of bibliographic data.

For Electronic Services Librarians in particular, the creation of this system was an eye-opener. It was the first resource discovery system that they had seen, which was not delivered by an external supplier. Having struggled for several years with the difficulties of configuring the proprietary link-resolver and federated search systems, they were given a new system which provided, through a single interface, discovery of print materials, serials and repository holdings, with direct click-through to electronic sources where available. Configured and installed locally, by local staff, with no licensing costs. Meetings about discovery systems, which had previously become bogged down in complaints about the faults in the proprietary systems turned quite rapidly to discussions about how best to present material to users, what kinds of faceted searches should be available, how to lay out the interface: all elements which could be defined and configured locally.

PHASE FOUR: IMPLEMENTING THE SYSTEM

Library Systems Specification

A business analyst was employed, shared between the three BLMS Libraries planning early adoption of the new system. The analyst spent time with many of the functional teams in the libraries, talking through their work processes and documenting them with special software that generated diagrams. She layered up processes and use cases to produce 'the wall', which was an invaluable communication and change tool when looking at implementation and efficiency gains. The wall was built up from a series of process maps. See below.

The process analysis "wall"

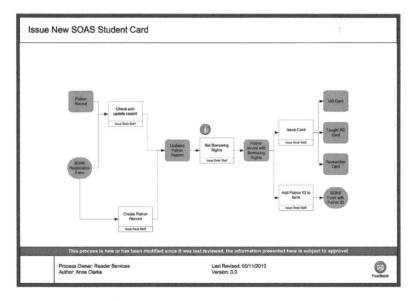

Example of a detailed process analysis

Which was then worked into a Use Case:

SOAS Enquiry Desk

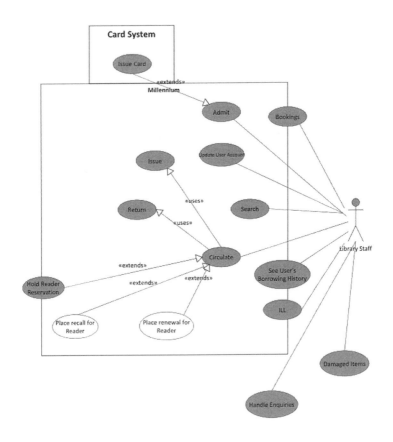

This iterative process, repeated across teams and libraries, laid the groundwork for two kinds of expectation:

1. that library work processes were worthy of study and possible improvement (not something everyone took for granted); and
2. that the process of implementing a new system provided opportunities to obtain a greater alignment between library work process and the underlying systems.

This latter expectation was, for a number of library staff, also a novel thought in a context where their work had been tied to the capabilities of a particular system for such a long time.

This work led into the processes which were kicked off at the point when a contract was signed and systems implementation could begin.

Systems Implementation

Implementing an Open Source system using differs in a number of significant ways from working with a vendor, particularly when it comes to the 'acceptance testing' criteria for the new system. On the one hand, with a vended system, it is likely that the contract will make payments dependent upon results so that, if there are bugs or faults in the system, it is the responsibility of the vendor to fix them with a financial incentive to do so. On the other hand, if there are features missing and they were not specified as 'mandatory requirements' in the procurement process, the vendor is likely to say 'tough' or, if feeling generous, 'we'll put them in the roadmap'.

With Kuali OLE, there was no vendor in the conventional sense: the OLE Partnership is responsible for the development of the system. As a member of the partnership, the library (in this case, the SOAS Library) is directly involved in the process of specifying the system requirements and testing the software as it is delivered. This was explained to library staff through the simple statement: 'we are the vendor'. If there are bugs or faults in the system, the library can report them through the partnership via the governance structure and, depending upon priority and criticality, they will be fixed. If there are features missing, the library can propose them for development via the relevant SME or, if it has the resources, develop the features locally using whatever programming talent is available.

As an early adopter of the system therefore the SOAS Library (in common with the other two early adopters) was simultaneously loading its data onto the system, testing the functionality against its own requirements and testing the software itself against the specifications recorded by the partnership. Many issues in the software did not become apparent until it was loaded into a development and test environment using the full data sets exported from the old system in an iterative process. The SOAS Library, through its contract with HTC (the company also contracted to the OLE Partnership for software development) was able to have some issues resolved directly and contribute the fixes back to the code base, whilst others were flagged for attention by the partnership.

Library staff had already been exposed to a systems development environment during the implementation of the Open Source VuFind discovery system, becoming familiar with the idea that software is loaded onto multiple systems called Development, Test and Production and terms such as code releases, patches, upgrades, jiras and test scripts. The production system is the one which the library users connect to. New features or bug fixes (the 'patches') are loaded onto the test server and library staff are asked to follow the test scripts, checking that the system is safe to move into production. Major new software releases are first loaded onto the development system for more extensive testing before being considered as candidates for moving into test and production.

For library staff used to complaining about a moribund system that never seemed to change, and a supplier that never delivered much in the way of improvements, this approach was a dramatic change in their work practices. It is fair to say that some staff took to it much more enthusiastically than others. For some, there was a lot of mumbling and grumbling about job descriptions and how 'we are librarians not software people'. For others, it was a breath of fresh air and they were soon pointing out deficiencies in the screens, faults in the data and − most usefully − reflecting on the work practices that the system was designed to support.

Phasing in the New System

One of the most controversial aspects of the implementation was the decision to phase the system in over an extended time period with basic functions configured first, to the point where it was adequate to move full service across from the old system, and other functions enabled progressively. This decision was taken for a number of reasons:

- the old system was operating at risk as the hardware on which it was running was out of date;
- a number of the features in the OLE system were either untested, or still in development;
- staff had been working on preparations for the new system for most of 2014 and were starting to question whether it would ever be ready.

One of the things that we did at SOAS which no one else did, is to deploy the system in a phased approach rather than in a full functioning system. Chicago and Lehigh went live in September/ August before we did, and they turned on everything and found many things to be missing. So we turned on the sections that we knew were working, having learnt from our predecessors, and we learnt that one part. My intention was to turn on other parts of the system later. If the staff were engaged they would have known that more was coming, but they weren't they just complained about it. We turned on the basic circulation functionality, then focused our efforts on testing the rest of the functionality and turned it on when ready.

So that's an approach that we took that was different, the other two institutions that are coming after us have not learnt from that approach and are still going for a big bang. What they're doing is they know some of the functionality is not there so they are delaying their start. I feel in this type of environment that is ill advised because it is only when you try to go live and start using the system that you truly test and prove it. They have yet to realise that, because there is no vendor responsible for getting the software better, then waiting longer is not going to make it unless they're engaged with it. **CM**

The implementation had originally been planned for a switch-over in July 2014. This was initially delayed until December 2014 when it became clear that key elements of the circulation system (the OLE 'Deliver' module) were not ready. The delay gave time for the technical issues to be resolved (mostly associated with the operation of the self-issue and return machines) and also for library Customer Services staff to spend more time in training and familiarisation sessions. By December, the Cataloguing ('Describe') and Acquisitions ('Select & Acquire') modules were configured and ready for use but there were still problems with the Deliver module, which turned out to be the most complex part of the system. A further delay was agreed, with the new go-live date set for Easter 2015.

In the event, the implementation schedule was as follows.

Process	Go live Date	Rationale and Challenges
Phase 1: cataloguing and acquisitions	December 2014	Bibliographic records migrated into production-ready server acquisitions and Subject Librarians as targeted group to enrich existing records

(Continued)

Process	Go live Date	Rationale and Challenges
Phase 2: Basic circulation and full cataloguing and acquisitions	April 2015	Circulation: borrow, return, renew
Phase 3: Reservations	June 2015	Circulation: holds and recalls via OLE Client and VuFind
Phase 4: Notices and fines	September 2015	Courtesy and overdue notices – fines triggered and paid via OLE Client only
Phase 5: Online fines payment	January 2016	Technical difficulties with interfaces requiring further programming effort

One benefit of this approach (for library users) was an effective fines amnesty from Easter 2015 onwards, with fines only re-started in the 2015/2016 session.

At the time of writing (January 2016), the implementation work is on-going. SOAS is using version 1.6.2 of the OLE system. Versions 2 and 3 are scheduled for release during the first half of 2016, offering new features (an Electronic Resources Module) and improved user interfaces. During the first part of the implementation, considerable improvements have been made to systems integration functions, particularly in relation to authentication, the issuing of ID cards, and interfaces to access control systems. The next phase of the work will focus on further improvements, particularly in the interface between the Select & Acquire module and the central Finance system, with the aim of eliminating a lot of redundant manual processes.

PEER-SUPPORT NETWORKS AND 'AGILE'

Starting with their collaborative ethos and aspirations – expressed at the start of the project – to be part of a shared service, the BLMS partners saw the Kuali OLE Partnership as an exemplar of both. The OLE shared service has succeeded and is growing (whilst the BLMS has gone on hold). There are a number of reasons for this to do with the way in which the partners have signed formal agreements and committed funding and labour, which is mobilised via a formal structure. Partners who have implemented – or are about to implement – the new system look to the partnership for support. What is less apparent, seen from the outside, is the way in which the OLE

Governance Model (referenced in the 'Options Appraisal' section) delivers a comprehensive peer-support network for staff in the partner libraries.

Research into Open Source or Community Source development and governance models reveals a wide field and – as expected – strident criticisms of the various approaches by proponents of alternative approaches. It is clear there is no general model of what 'works', just as there are a variety of Open Source licences, some more open than others. It is not the intention here to interrogate the various models other than to comment that the Kuali OLE Partnership model derives from the models put in place by the Kuali Foundation since its formation in 2003 and these models are now under review in the face of aspirations to accelerate the software development processes. What is of interest here is the ways in which the development and governance models provide library and technical staff with support for their own professional skills and development, alongside the production of the software. The metaphor of a jigsaw could be used to describe the ways in which the various groups interact.

By way of reminder, here is the diagram of the OLE Partnership governance model presented at the Horizon Scanning stage of the project.

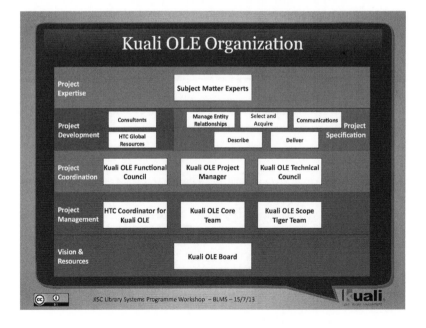

Jigsaw Pieces (1): Subject Matter Experts (SMEs)

SMEs are a fundamental piece of the Kuali governance jigsaw, providing the basis for staff to focus on the functionality required in a system which supports their daily working practice. In the OLE Partnership, there is an SME for each of the modules: Describe, Select & Acquire, Deliver, Systems Integration. The concept is reasonably simple: the SMEs define the functional requirements for the modules, log these into 'Jiras' (an online bug-tracking and feature request system) which are passed along the chain for review and potential inclusion in the 'work packages' which make up the systems development 'roadmap'. SMEs then play a key role in testing software releases and 'patches' to ensure that their functional requirements are met.

For staff in the Partner libraries, this manifests as a regular (weekly or fortnightly) schedule of virtual (online) meetings, supplemented by 'face to face' meetings once or twice a year. Depending upon the particular SME, staff joining the meetings might be cataloguers, acquisitions librarians, systems librarians, counter staff, subject librarians, e-resource librarians, programmers, ICT staff or corporate systems managers. What is fascinating, for those staff who have joined these groups and call in to the regular meetings, is the opportunity for regular, detailed conversations with their peers in other libraries who are all, they discover, grappling with the same sets of problems and challenges. Engagement with the SMEs is a two-way street: staff find they take away from the engagement as much as they put in.

One Partner library provides an 'SME lead' (essentially, the chair of the group), a role which rotates around the Partners from time to time. These leads are an important in the next pieces of the jigsaw.

Jigsaw Pieces (2): Functional Council (FC)

The job of filtering the input from the SMEs into a coherent, deliverable system roadmap falls to the OLE Functional Council. The Council is formed from the SME leads plus additional members to ensure that all Partners are represented. Members are defined as 'Voting Members', 'Alternates' and 'in attendance'. When decisions (e.g. on the prioritisation of work packages) cannot be reached by consensus, a vote is taken.

The FC also considers the medium-term view of the system development, referring back to the original vision (referenced at the start of this chapter), testing to see whether the current line of development is consistent with the vision. From time to time, major decisions are required which need Board sign-off. For example, on one occasion, the needs of the early-adopter partners (important test-beds for the viability of the system) were prioritised over some of the 'nice to have' features in the requirements coming up from the SMEs; on another occasion, FC provided detailed commentary on proposals by a 'Commercial Affiliate' to invest in a significant overhaul of the underlying systems architecture.

Jigsaw Pieces (3): Technical Council (TC)

Each partner nominates at least one Voting Member and perhaps an Alternate to the TC. This council is tasked with considering the technical architecture of the system. It also suggested that it has a role in Quality Assurance (QA) of code contributions, acting as a gatekeeper to the code repository, into which partners who have signed a Code Contribution License (CCL) may deposit source code that they have written or modified as part of their implementation processes (whilst there is a member of OLE staff working on the QA process, in practice the gatekeeping role had defaulted to the Lead Developer from HTC to which OLE has contracted-out the programming effort).

The councils were artificially separated and there were flaws in the Technical Council who never saw their brief being the nitty-gritty, let's figure out how the system works and ensure we have a system of quality they never saw that as a brief. The Functional Council stayed with lofty ideas of what the aims were not the nitty gritty. This particular governance model did not work: it could be a symptom of the disparate services where it's not a single site. If it worked as a single site with one development house and everyone working in a core location that could have worked. **CM**

Jigsaw Pieces (4): The OLE Partnership Board

Each full partner nominates a voting member (possibly an alternate) to this Board, which has the authority to determine the use of partnership funds, the overall strategy, applications for membership, hiring of staff and other matters which are typically dealt with at Board level. Members of this Board are, generally, chief librarians or library directors from partner libraries (in the United States they are often known as Library Deans or Vice-Provosts in addition to the formal title of Librarian). The FC and TC chairs and a representative of the Kuali Foundation are 'in attendance' (without voting rights).

> The issues [with consortia] and the thinking can appear to be different so there is politics involved as well as what is happening with development. As more consortia come on and we gain more experience we will be able to manage those situations. For anyone working with a consortium, even the proprietary systems, it is different. You are not just talking with the hands on people about what's needed, you are talking with a whole other layer and there's a whole other layer of politics. It is a mini community with all kinds of conflicting desires and interests. If you have a very good executive director of your consortium; everyone will be closer to the same page. If you don't have someone, or your philosophy is loose it is a lot more difficult to organise and get into any system.   **CR**

Putting It Together: A Group for Every Peer

The outcome of these arrangements, taken together, is a comprehensive set of groups that many members of library staff, from cataloguer to director, can join. Whilst it is undoubtedly a time commitment with a certain workload attached (an issue for some staff), the process of engagement can also be rewarding and encouraging at both a systems and personal level. It is of no small import that the libraries contributing to these groups include large and prestigious US universities such as Cornell, Chicago, Duke, Penn,

Indiana, Maryland, Lehigh, Villanova, NC State and Texas A&M, two large German Library consortia and representatives from HTC and EBSCO.

The degree of engagement of SOAS staff with these peer-support networks has been slow to take off, as the process of cultural change works its way through the various teams. There is still some resistance to the notion that library staff become confident with IT-related questions and likewise IT staff (particularly corporate systems) still tend to see the 'business systems' as taking priority. On the positive side, some staff have had opportunities to attend conferences and workshops in the United States, with further events planned (including events in the United Kingdom and other parts of the EU). As the work progresses on the next phase of the implementation and the OLE approach changes, the benefits of the peer-support networks will become more evident.

Working collaboratively with other libraries and high-level professions and the passion they have for the system is refreshing and encouraging. I'm not from a library background but I want to believe that if more of my colleagues that currently work in the library had had the time to engage with the other libraries it would have been a much better experience for them. The US colleagues chat amongst each other quite freely and exchange ideas with each other freely. If SOAS had managed to change the cultures to engage the staff into this experience they would be better for it.   **CM**

The Move to 'Agile'

The OLE Partnership has recently reviewed its organisational structure to ensure a more 'Agile' approach to software development. This term has a precise technical meaning in systems development terms as well as the implied colloquial meaning of developing in a more rapid, responsive manner. A new organisational structure has been proposed to support this approach.

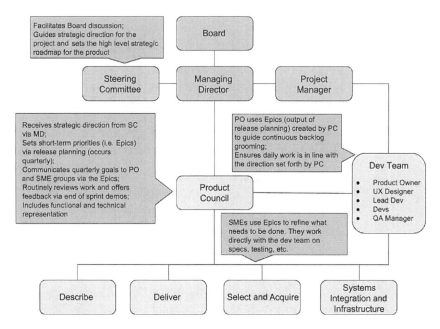

The OLE Partnership model re-organised around "Agile"

The SMEs continue to have a critical role in this structure, along with the Board, whilst some of the functions previously allocated to the FC and TC are redistributed to the Steering Committee and the Product Council. The introduction of a managing director post recognises that the Board members are generally too busy to attend to detailed operational planning and needed to have someone to whom to delegate this work. The structure has also been adapted to work with a distributed development model in which a number of partners will either host or fund development teams.

I've learnt a lot and I would have a strong voice backed by evidence arguing against similar collaboration in the future. Collaboration is not needed, what you need is a single driver. Parts of the system that work better have been principally driven by Chicago who had very specific needs who developed a relationship with the lead developer and got what they wanted. That's how systems work.   **CM**

For members of SMEs, the outcome will be that agreed functional requirements are wrapped up into 'sprints' (rapid development of software components) and they will be asked to test the components. This will require more input, but the result should be a more rapid delivery of the software improvements.

> We are the solution we are the developer and we are the customer and there is something empowering about how you manage and influence all three of those vectors to gain what your institution needs. It also puts you in the context of doing something greater than your own position, we feel like we are contributing to what libraries should be thinking about. **MW**

Outcomes for Library Staff

The net effect of this approach on library staff and their working practices has been quite dramatic. It is now well-understood that they are no longer *consumers* of library systems software, but *collaborators* in a process of continuous testing, feedback, upgrades and improvements. The sense of abjection in the face of impenetrable systems is markedly reduced. Library staff meet regularly with their peers in other libraries as well as local project, ICT and corporate systems staff to review progress on the development of a suite of library-related systems – most of them Open Source – that are now recognised to be as important to the institution as the 'hard admin' systems (Finance, HR, Student Records). As a process, the question of whether this represents a true 'convergence' of the IT and Library functions at SOAS, remains to be seen.

REFLECTIONS (3): VOICES OF THE PARTNERS

> I have been in a leadership role from the very beginning and one of the things about working in a community project is that you may be supervising staff in other institutions so I have had responsibilities for supervising staff in various places, we don't work in the same office so

its remote, right down to writing annual staff evaluations. That's something that even though you work collaboratively in many other environments I have never before had the experience of actually supervising someone who doesn't work for my organisation. What we have described is this is a new paradigm of working together, it's not the first collaborative project but the way we have approached it has made it somewhat unique. Particularly in managing staff that work in other organisations is one of those key issues, there will be more and more projects like that in the future but we are one of the earlier ones.   **CR**

There is a cultural element here about change. I worked in the public sector for many years before moving into education and I worked with three other universities namely Kent, Greenwich and Canterbury Christchurch. It came to a moment where there is a lot of resistance against any kind of change. Even the best intention change has to be conveyed in the most meticulous way. It is not just the library management it is a whole cultural issues. Even if Kuali had the perfect from the beginning I say we would have had the same level of resistance. What I never stopped doing, my team is the largest and the main users of the product, I never stopped educating. Right from the beginning I do weekly communications every Friday when I write to people about new features, what's changed and what you need to tweak. I have also seconded members of the team to the project team to help with refining the project and because of the frontline experience of how it works they have been able to translate their distress into the design. So whenever the designers are doing something wrong they will quickly say this will not work on the frontlines. Because of these measurements and because it is on-going, I find that the complaints are just dying. Now people practically report stuff to me and we don't get many things going wrong, before I would write 10 or 20 things on weekly comms I now struggle to find things to write.

At the beginning before we went live we made champions from the user group, people in archives or special collections had to nominate a champion. We had the most champions but it was a distraction because they still had their day to day work to do and also had to engage in technical design. They were not doing the technical work, but had to explain things to the project team to make sure they didn't get it wrong. The project team did not have library experience, they were just designing a tool. I still have two people seconded to that team, they have been there for months now and it is likely to carry on until January next year. But they are not complaining, this is a secondment I advertised and it took off. **AA**

Even though the partnership is small we have included a larger number of people and everyone has adopted the same values and proceeded down the road from the same path as much as possible. Beyond that I have met some longtime colleagues and friends who will know each forever. The dedication of every individual I have worked with, the skill sets have been phenomenal. That mutual regard has helped us move forward. **CR**

SOAS and to a certain extent Senate House were in a more urgent position in terms of changing their library system than we were. We were quite keen on the idea, we [...] still have a system which is relatively old and we would like to change it at some point. [...] I don't think we've quite got that sense of urgency so what we've done at the moment is leave it as it is and we are taking a more leisurely approach. That's not to say that we are not interested in the Kuali OLE concept [...] but it would probably be something where we would look for SOAS to be running it successfully for a period of time. They went live with it in Easter this year so it is definitely early days and we are certainly interested in talking to SOAS about how that develops and we will be interested in some point in looking at the system again [...] **RA**

I left the project when the system had been in place for 3–4 months. It was well bedded in, it was established. I think it was a success. It could have gone a lot worse. The system was running fine, it still needed some support and some development around it but I left it in a good position for people to build on the work that had been done, with clear objectives as to what needed to be done and what needed to be implemented technically. I think it would be about the same if not longer[for a vendor system], because the thing with the OLE project and Open Source software in general is that it requires more upfront planning so we had planned to the nth degree up front for the implementation and we well aware of everything that needed to be in place whereas with vendor-led software it tends to come along very suddenly, the vendor does a lot of work up front but the library staff don't necessarily see that or feel the benefits of that and so suddenly a new system appears and it takes a while for them to get used to it, whereas with OLE with all the user-acceptance testing and bug reports everyone was well aware of what the software looked like before it was implemented.   **SB**

I would advise any potential adopter of this system to come in as soon as possible, to become part of the collaboration to make the next stage of the product better, this initial stage feels like a pilot. Future adopters will have more robust code. The challenge is that the benefit they get is directly related the amount of effort we put into documenting, which is not something we have found the capacity to invest into. If you haven't written it, it is not there.

Definitely when it comes to the governance the amount of resources that need to be in-house that will duplicate the cost of the vendor relationship during that initial stage in order to transition to a non-vendor system. We won't go for a vendor but the resources will go into the implementation. But we need those resources then, permanent staff to come in beyond the staff you have.   **CM**

CONCLUSION

As flagged at the beginning, SOAS has a next-generation library system, Open Source, as part of a shared service. It is not the system or service it imagined at the start, but the impulse remains. What are the key lessons that can be taken away by others who might wish to follow the same path?

A sceptic might ask (indeed, more than one sceptic has asked), 'if the BLMS failed, why did SOAS carry on?'

The first point to make is that the BLMS did not actually fail; it was merely put on hold as a result of the various changes in circumstance detailed above. The concept remains intact and it would only require one or more of the UK libraries currently 'reviewing their options' to decide to move ahead with OLE to get it moving again. As set out in this document, the notion of a shared approach to the support for − if not the operation of − library systems is sound and is validated each time a Librarian comes to SOAS and asks, 'when can you offer this to me as a managed service?'

This highlights a second point: the relationship between libraries and their IT services is uncomfortable at best and distinctly difficult at worst. It is no accident that many libraries are attracted to the idea of managed services, as they want to minimise their dependency upon IT beyond the basics (PCs and Macs which are up and running, connected to the network, able to access external services). Clearly, it also suits vendors to push the line that 'we are the experts in the delivery of service X, don't worry about the details, we'll deliver the service to you for a price, with an SLA'.

It's not a failed system, it's failed only for the people who didn't understand there was going to be a phased installation, so we put in parts that we knew worked when we thought they were good enough. If staff were more engaged they would have understood that and then been more proactive in making do with functionality rather what we got was just complaints that the system was not the vendor system.

It was a learning experience, slowly people are coming round and you see glimmers of hope. It was a challenge and I think small institutions would need to consider the practicality of this Open Source there are companies that give you a managed service, so you get the Open Source but they manage it for you, its halfway between. The part-serviced solution might be what I recommend for people considering any Open Source initiatives: don't do it on your own, it's too much! **CM**

SOAS did not get to the point of operating Kuali OLE as an internally hosted and supported service as part of a consortial approach to software design and delivery by setting out to separate itself from its IT service. On the contrary: the SOAS Library is part of a service 'directorate' which includes Learning services, Classroom services, IT support, ICT services and Corporate Information Systems. The SOAS Library is faced with the challenge not only to modernise its back-office systems and improve its working processes, but also to deal with the need – as a major UK Research Library – to support Resource Discovery across a complex field, Research Repositories, Open Access Publications and Research Data Management, all of which must be integrated with its existing Teaching and Research Support operations. As a large Library in a relatively small college of the University of London, the SOAS Library simply cannot afford to take each of these functions as a managed service from an external provider. The only viable strategy is for it to build up its library digital services suite and support expertise around a cluster of Open Source systems. In this context, the choice of OLE is as much about the need to build capability within the library, and to move the library culture on from being consumers of software to collaborators in the development and support of software as it is about the specific need for a back-office library management system.

Two other key factors apply. Firstly, as a Research Library, the SOAS Library is acutely aware of its need to develop, preserve and present its unique and distinctive collections. Traditionally these were the books, serials, rare books, manuscripts, archives and other materials, which it collected in line with its institutional and national remit. In the modern era, a large portion of this material comes in digital form. Digital curation and preservation operates to the same standard as traditional curation and preservation, which requires that the 'vital' data be held as close to home, and as safely, as possible. Such an approach is not – in the present environment – compatible with most of the so-called 'cloud' offerings from major vendors. Collaborative work with other libraries is feasible, but not yet mature. Hence, the SOAS Library must build capability and expertise. Working with OLE alongside the other Open Source providers is consistent with this approach.

Secondly, the SOAS Library does not operate in isolation from its institution. One of the original functional requirements for a new library system was enterprise integration. In order for the library to go about its daily business, its systems need to inter-operate with student systems, HR systems, finance systems, authentication services, access control systems, printing systems, discovery systems and a range of other infrastructure and corporate services. This presents a challenge: how can we move library staff, on the one hand, to recognise that they are also information technologists, and corporate systems staff, on the other, to treat library systems as having equal importance with the other 'hard admin' systems?

We got here, then, because this is where we need to be. It is not an easy place to be, nor is it necessarily a comfortable place to be. The Kuali OLE system is currently at version 1.6.2 and the SOAS Library is still only the third library in the world to be using to operate its services. There are many rough edges in the system: some things don't work as well as they should; some things work differently from what we are used to. Whilst SOAS is planning for its upgrades to version 2 and then version 3, the software architects are already talking about the 'next generation' of 'middleware' which will change the underlying structure of the system to make it even better at the enterprise integration and outward-facing inter-operability which was — for SOAS — one of its unique selling points.

The other points remain: it is an open system, with open architecture, based on Open Source principles. SOAS has already achieved things with this system which it could not have managed with its previous library system but there is a long way to go and the biggest challenge remains a cultural one: moving from 'the supplier should fix this' to 'we can fix this'.

Signs of the Times

What does this mean for SOAS and its (currently dormant) BLMS partners in the larger Kuali context? It comes back to my primary thesis about ethos, collaboration and technology. For libraries to survive the technological onslaught they must look to their values, the ethos they share with other libraries and their host academic institutions. Without collaboration, they face a serious risk that the technological imperative embodied in the vast data-gathering conglomerates will overwhelm them. Computing technology as it currently operates has a fundamental drive towards large-scale, centralised data models in which content is reduced to data-flow and consumers become the consumed. Some might call this a tendency towards technological totalitarianism.

Libraries are the inheritors of the Age of Enlightenment, custodians of the knowledge that makes reason possible. Do we stand back and allow this knowledge to be taken from us and put somewhere that appears to be accessible, but in fact is only given back at the whim of the 'provider'? Or do we work together to preserve the knowledge and wisdom of the previous and current generations, for the generations to come? The choices may not be obvious today, and the offer to 'put it in the cloud' — where we don't have to worry about all the messy technologies — can be quite seductive, but is this the right thing to do?

Meanwhile, not that far from London, in places which are of particular interest to SOAS, malign forces are at work, seeking to return entire regions to the Dark Ages sooner rather than later. 'Terrorist' incidents have become almost a daily event but remember: not all barbarians come brandishing swords and Kalashnikov rifles.

Enlightenment: the casting of light upon the darkness. Libraries have an important role to play, even if it is just to ensure that the stocks of candle never run out.

NOTES

1. http://www.london.ac.uk/2895.html (accessed May 2016).

2. For an excellent survey of the field in the late 1990s, see Tedd, L. A. 'Library management systems' at http://hdl.handle.net/2160/719 (accessed May 2016).

3. http://blogs.staffs.ac.uk/informationlandscape/2010/12/10/staffordshire-university-chooses-koha-for-its-new-library-system/ (accessed December 2015).

4. https://en.wikipedia.org/wiki/Koha_%28software%29 (accessed December 2015).

5. https://en.wikipedia.org/wiki/Evergreen_%28software%29 (accessed December 2015).

6. Society of College, National and University Libraries http://www.sconul.ac.uk

7. Research Libraries UK http://www.rluk.ac.uk

8. The M25 Consortium of Academic Libraries http://www.m25

9. Ligue Bibliothèque Européennes Recherche http://www.liber-europe.org

10. Chartered Institute of Library and Information Professionals http://www.cilip.org.uk

11. American Research Libraries http://www.arl.org/

12. American Libraries Association http://www.ala.org/

13. http://www.webarchive.org.uk/wayback/archive/20140614104505/http://www.jisc.ac.uk/whatwedo/programmes/di_informationandlibraries/emergingopportunities/lmschange.aspx (accessed December 2015).

14. http://lmsguidance.jiscinvolve.org/wp/sitemap/ (accessed December 2015).

15. http://www.sconul.ac.uk/page/library-and-general-shared-services-resource-links (accessed December 2015).

16. A list of these can be found on the SCONUL pages at http://www.sconul.ac.uk/page/library-and-general-shared-services-resource-links (accessed December 2015).

17. See also the reference to this aspect of LMS in the SCONUL Business Case for a shared-service approach to LMS delivery at http://helibtech.com/file/-view/091204 + SCONUL + Shared + Service + - + for + distribution.pdf (accessed December 2015).

18. Sadly, deleted from his site at https://libtechrfp.wikispaces.com/ but still available at https://web.archive.org/web/20120427174127/http://libtechrfp.wikispaces.com/LMS + ILS + Specification

19. http://www.software.coop/products/koha/

20. https://en.wikipedia.org/wiki/Middleware − in summary, a software layer which enables data-exchange between applications.

21. http://www.london.ac.uk/libraries_agreement.html

22. http://www.london.ac.uk/2399.html

23. http://www.blms.ac.uk/scanning-the-horizon/ (accessed December 2015).

24. http://lmsguidance.jiscinvolve.org/wp/about-lms-change/ (accessed December 2015).

25. http://www.ukfederation.org/ (accessed January 2016).

26. Security Assertion Markup Language: a system which exchanges user credentials between 'identity providers' and 'service providers' using encrypted data channels exchanging anonymised credentials.

27. Since that time, Jisc has done a major analysis of this approach, resulting in a situation in which its membership subscription invoices do not attract VAT.

28. A shared facility (power, cooling, data, security) in which a client can put its own equipment, managed by itself.

29. A single, out-hosted, managed service which is used by multiple, separate clients.

30. 'Software as a Service' in which a client can subscribe to an out-hosted, managed service in which it gets access to a software platform dedicated to its requirements, where it manages the content but not the application layer.

31. 'Infrastructure as a Service' in which a client can rent access to a complete platform upon which it loads its application and data, managed by itself.

32. http://www.webarchive.org.uk/wayback/archive/20140614100238/http://www.jisc.ac.uk/whatwedo/programmes/resourcediscovery/d2dateandm.aspx

33. http://www.vufind.org (accessed January 2016).

34. https://library.villanova.edu/ (accessed January 2016).

INNOVATION AND INFORMATION

Jo Smedley

ABSTRACT

Purpose — *The effective and efficient analysis and application of information lies at the heart of success in today's world. Greater emphasis is now on the quality of information and the confirmation of its value through effective analysis and review. This includes engaging in dialogue to enhance understanding, the empowering role of technology and the versatility that information provides.*

Methodology/approach — *The chapter considers the innovative use of information from different perspectives to encourage readers to reflect on their own experiences and think about their individual and organisational uses of information with a view to being creative and exploring new avenues of use. Two case studies are included to demonstrate possible approaches — not as a definitive way ahead but more as examples of possibilities.*

Findings — *There will continue to be new ways of innovating information — some of which we know, others which we don't yet know. The creative thinking approach that is key to being unafraid to explore and use information to best effect is the overall finding of this chapter.*

Originality/value — *With the continually changing landscape of technology, the creative and original use of its application is the key to*

Innovation in Libraries and Information Services
Advances in Library Administration and Organization, Volume 35, 227–241
Copyright © 2017 by Emerald Group Publishing Limited
All rights of reproduction in any form reserved
ISSN: 0732-0671/doi:10.1108/S0732-067120160000035016

continued entrepreneurial outcomes. Some suggestions for the innovative use of information are included – certainly not a definitive list – to encourage reflection, inspire creativity and stimulate thinking with the overall aim of gaining value from information.

Keywords: Information; innovation; people; technology; change; learning

Today's world is one of change. Whether we like it or not, nothing stays the same forever – however hard we may try to keep it so. Keeping things as they are can be seen as providing a constant, giving reassurance and maintaining standards. However, on closer scrutiny and reflection, it is important to consider whether this view is one of consistency to maintain standards or a fear of what change could bring, preferring to associate it with emergent problems.

DEFINING INNOVATION

To innovate is defined as making changes to something established, by introducing new methods, ideas or products (*Oxford Dictionary*, 2015). Innovation is defined as being a new idea, a more effective device or process. It can be viewed as the application of better solutions that meet new requirements, articulated needs or existing market needs (Maranville, 1992). This is accomplished through more effective products, processes, services, technologies or ideas that are readily available. It can also be defined as something original and more effective that 'breaks into' the market or society (Frankelius, 2009). While a novel device is often described as an innovation, in economics, management science, and other fields of practice and analysis, innovation is generally considered to be a process that brings together various novel ideas in a way that they have an impact on society.

This then sets the scene for positive change with the powerbase lying in the appropriate and timely sharing of information in appropriate languages, whether linguistically or subjectively cultural, to maximise engagement and enable collaboration to achieve the maximum possible outcomes.

INNOVATION AND INFORMATION

In the 21st century, technology has enabled change to develop apace at a rate far exceeding expectations of decades ago. The development of the Worldwide Web in the 1980s unlocked the doorway to information accessibility and enabled generations to engage and realise the power of information in ways that had never been imagined. Nowadays, it is a growing expectation that the majority of the population readily have access to technology to access information for business and general everyday purposes (Czaja & Lee, 2006). This represents a considerable change from some 50 years ago where paper and land-based mail approaches dominated with technological focused approaches reflecting more limited information transmission, that is wire messages, telegrams and the telephone. This technological engagement has raised implications for skills development among the population as a whole. It is now common-place for younger age groups to readily engage and progress at a pace which challenges their tutors who, historically, would expect their younger charges to passively accept information which they didactically passed onto them (Bennett, Maton, & Kervin, 2008). Now, while there may be initial engagement with tutors, increasingly it is apparent that the students themselves become more centre stage in the learning with the tutors engaging in a more mentoring and facilitative role (Hamilton-Jones, 2000). While this makes for a more collaborative learning experience, it introduces new challenges – particularly if the tutors themselves do not relish the change.

It is with this background that today's information filled learning environment presents opportunities and challenges to inform and enable continuing collaborative developments. The information world now will continue to change and update. With so many information channels readily available through Internet-based sources, that is text, music and video, it is increasingly important to be able to recognise the importance of managing information to extract relevant components – rather than become overwhelmed by quality and peripheral aspects. In today's 24/7 working world with so much information available, it is the ability to assess information quality, whether from an individual or organisational perspective, which enhances opportunities for innovation, creativity and enterprise. Hence, using information to achieve its best effect and greatest impact.

If we reflect on how we deal with information on a day-to-day basis, the best approaches come from establishing and building on a familiar system, enabling new opportunities to grow and be nurtured (Nonaka & Konno, 1998). This allows weaker sections to be subsumed or assisted with a collective whole of achievement. Change which happens too quickly or which occurs at an inappropriate time risks disturbing the embryonic foundations with resultant uncertainty and subsequent wider implications (Kotter & Schlesinger, 2008). Too little change risks lack of overall progress and a reduction in engagement, given that other external factors are enabling and expecting developments. So change is in the equation whether we like it or not and it is a case of moving forward at an acceptable pace within a local environment but which also is comfortable from a global perspective – very much a challenge!

INNOVATION AND CHANGE

So who is responsible for implementing change in the management of information? Is it the role of managers? If so, how do they know what needs to be done? Or maybe it is the role of those involved in 'doing' – after all, they perhaps have first-hand insight of the operational aspects and could suggest ways to improve and enhance systems and outcomes. Or maybe it is a collective responsibility – in other words, it is the role of everyone to 'own' change and the need for it in their local world while also being aware of the global priorities. This then suggests that the most important aspect of change are the people involved in it. For change to succeed, everyone needs to see the purpose of the change, be clear about its intended impact and benefits and also own their parts of the solution in implementation. People are the key to successful change in terms of strategy, its implementation, its operation and its outcomes.

With this background, there is a need for a vision to encourage the 'green shoots' of innovation enabling individuals and groups to gain a sense of ownership of change within a strategic purpose. A sense of engagement is often thwarted at a first hurdle through a lack of understanding of terms used implying a lack of value, a perception of change for the sake of it and challenge at local levels. So often the 'language' of innovation gets in the way of progress and opportunities for quick wins in implementation are lost due to misunderstandings and confused intentions with resultant lack of sharing, engagement and collaboration, thereby losing the collective 'whole'.

ORGANISATIONAL INFORMATION INNOVATION

With rapid communication changes, today's entrepreneurs continuously look for better ways to satisfy their customers through improved quality, durability, service, and price through innovation from advanced technologies and organisational strategies (Heyne, Boettke, & Prychitko, 2010). In an organisational context, innovation is often linked to positive changes in efficiency, productivity, quality, competitiveness and market share with an increasing expectation of the consequent achievement of tangible performance improvements (Salge & Vera, 2012).

The world of work has changed through the increase in the use of technology and businesses are becoming increasingly competitive. Maintaining competitive advantage requires the creation and nurturing of an environment of innovation. This involves breaking away from traditional ways of thinking and using change to individual and organisational advantage. While it can be seen as a time of risk, it also provides even greater opportunities.

Organisational innovation has three main components; recognised need, competence with relevant technology and financial support (Engelberger, 1982). However, innovation processes usually involve identifying customer needs, macro and meso trends, developing competences, and finding financial support. Organisational innovation is achieved in many ways, with much attention now given to research and development (R&D) for 'breakthrough innovations'. Innovations can be developed by less formal on-the-job modifications of practice, through exchange and combination of professional experience and by many other routes. The more radical and revolutionary innovations tend to emerge from R&D, while more incremental innovations emerge from practice.

As a result, organisations may incorporate users in focus groups (user-centred approach), work closely with so called lead users (lead user approach) or users might adapt their products themselves. The lead user method focuses on leading users to develop breakthrough innovations through generating ideas. User innovation expects that a great deal of innovation is done by those actually implementing and using technologies and products as part of their normal activities. User innovators often have some personal record motivating them. In selling their product, they may choose to freely reveal their innovations, using methods such as open source.

Programmes of organisational innovation are typically tightly linked to organisational goals and objectives, to the business plan and to market competitive positioning enabling the setting of growth objectives. Goals can involve improvements to products, processes and services and dispel a popular myth that innovation deals mainly with new product development. Most of the goals could apply to any organisation be it a manufacturing facility, marketing firm, hospital or local government.

Common causes of failure within the innovation process in most organisations relate to goal definition, alignment of actions to goals, participation in teams, monitoring of results and communication and access to information (O'Sullivan, 2002). Success then depends on appropriate planning, engagement of people and the setting and timely achievement of realistic targets. Thus, collective organisational outcomes require effective communications throughout. Without it, opportunities for celebrating interim successes are missed, morale becomes low and mission drift occurs through lack of engagement and increased urgency.

INFORMATION INNOVATION – FROM THE INSIDE OUT

As well as design and development, for innovation to be truly effective, it involves having a full understanding of activities dealing with issues of cost, production, quality, performance, reliability, serviceability and user features. Consideration of all these factors are an important part of making the resulting product attractive to its intended market as well as being a successful contributor to the business of the organisation that intends to offer the product to that market. This 'reverse product engineering' approach of extracting knowledge or disassembling information from manmade systems or products and re-producing products based on the extracted information (Eilam, 2011) is a crucial part of sustained resultant success. This analysis of systems and processes is an important aspect of gaining a deeper understanding of how innovation can work from an organisational perspective.

INNOVATION AND LEARNING

Societies and economies have transitioned from an industrial to a knowledge base with global drivers increasingly to the fore in developing '21st century competences'. There is a growing realisation that traditional educational approaches are insufficient and require supplementary more informal approaches to full equip learners for the world of work. Moving beyond achievement levels and shortcomings to desirable change requires a deeper understanding of how people learn effectively. Enabling learners to display transferable proficiency encourages and enables upward mobility in employment. Every tutor aims to create a learning environment to foster students' love of learning. However, it is often difficult to define or pinpoint exactly what the criteria are for an innovative student experience. The aim is to develop self-directed learners who possess 'adaptive expertise' which they 'own', use confidently and apply creatively to a variety of situations (Groff, 2013).

Innovation – in systems, in technologies, in institutions – can be thought of as examples of flexibility (Barnett, 2014). However, flexibility and innovation are sharply different ideas. A new digital platform or delivery system or mode of communication may become so dominating that it becomes a fixed part of the landscape not to be tampered with. Particularly when driven forward as a matter of fact, innovations can quickly become ideologies that act as a brake on creative thinking and subsequent action. Tensions may result and a concern to bring about learner flexibility may call for autonomy and professional responsiveness and so a heightened degree of teacher flexibility. Such pedagogical flexibility at the heart of the teaching process may conflict with a drive to establish new systems aimed at a greater flexibility at the national or institutional levels.

The changing Higher Education market has pushed flexible delivery into new approaches through the deliberate creation of new markets in higher education. Private providers, new interactive and global technologies, more sophisticated expectations from employers and the labour market generally, and heightened expectations from students that their higher education experience should match their particular wishes and situations, are calling for new levels and forms of responsiveness on the part of universities. Hence, a flexible and responsive academic approach with a more commercial outlook is a necessity rather than a choice. Responsiveness is a major challenge to enable measures of flexibility to be injected into educational systems and processes to provide the necessary levels of continuing responsiveness. Paths beckon towards educational provision less limited by time, less located in particular places and with more open relationships between tutor and learner. Ethos and collective understandings are not easily modified. New style organisations are emerging (especially in the private sector) that are ready to establish new educational systems infused with an ethos of responsiveness.

Flexibility brings complexity not just in systems and technologies but in ways of understanding just what an institution of higher education might be and what a valid student experience might look like. The very concepts of 'higher education', 'teaching', 'learning' and 'student' are all challenged fundamentally and continuously (Barnett & Davies, 2015). There needs to be consistent flexibility in our ways of thinking about Higher Education to maximise opportunities.

INNOVATION AND THE LEARNING ORGANISATION

Any environment where learning takes place needs to be vibrant, challenging, positive and supportive to enable students to be stretched to maximise their potential. It is a tough balance to prevent both coasting and overloading and enable students to experience both academic success and the challenge of discovery. Group work can help to achieve this as students at different levels work together and help one another. Understanding the connections between subjects and ideas is essential for the ability to transfer skills and adapt. Learning has limited meaning if students do not understand why the knowledge will be useful to them and how it can be applied in life. Assessments are important to gauge how to structure the next learning input for maximum effectiveness. It needs to be meaningful, substantial, and shape the learning environment itself.

Many of these ideas are second nature to good teachers, but they can feel hard to achieve within education systems that are slow-moving, bureaucratic and resistant to change (Schneckenberg, 2009). It is important to be open to innovation while realising that there are expectations of the experience with student success and workload as frequent factors (Kyriacou & Kunc, 2007). If the learning culture does not encourage experimentation, negative reactions can be mitigated against by framing the ideas in a way that will be accepted, or by bringing in outside resources to be appropriately persuasive. It is always useful to test out ideas with students before implementing them. Students often feel uncomfortable if they become aware that they are part of experimentation. It is important to maintain enthusiasm so that resultant collaborative learning experiences are achieved.

INNOVATION AND LEARNING CONTENT

The concept of reuse is not new. Many industries have turned to reuse to reduce costs, increase productivity and standardise their processes. In particular, the manufacturing and computer industries have been using reuse strategies for years with the technical communication industry developing content reuse strategies in the early 1990s. For example, Creative Commons (CC) licences enable content to be more useable as the licences grant permission rights to reuse the content (Creative Commons, n.d.). The metadata and rights expression language (REL) within each one makes them more searchable. The metadata adds information about the licensed work to the file which is machine-readable, that is the title, creator and licensing information. This has many useful advantages, that is search engines can distinguish between Creative Common and 'All Rights Reserved' material.

Content reuse is fundamental to a successful unified content strategy by enabling effective and efficient use of existing content components to develop new documents without having to rewrite it for distinct purposes. Although the majority of reusable content is text-based, graphics, charts and media are wider varieties of content types which can all be reused. Content can often be reused through copying and pasting. This works well while the content is current. However, when it is updated, it becomes time onerous to source each occurrence to update, resulting in inconsistencies and inaccuracies. Over time, these inconsistencies result in two completely different content sources. A better approach to reuse is one of linking to an element of reusable content where it is displayed in the document being worked on but does not actually reside there. When the reusable element is updated, it changes wherever it occurs − hence saving time and effort in keeping information up-to-date (Rockley, Kostur, & Manning, 2012).

INNOVATION AND LEARNING TECHNOLOGIES

Enhancing learning through technology involves a complex system of technologies and practices and, consequently, takes time to implement change. There is clear evidence that innovative educational technologies such as e-learning, simulation and m-learning provide opportunities for learners to acquire, develop and maintain the essential knowledge, skills, values and behaviours needed for safe and effective learning. Successfully embedding significant learning through technology innovation involves looking beyond product development and paying close attention to the implementation approaches. Significant innovations are developed and embedded over periods of years rather than months. Sustainable change is not a simple matter of product development testing and roll-out. Successful learning through technology innovation includes informed and directed exploration of the technologies and practices required to achieve an education goal. It involves experimentation to generate fresh insights and a creative use of available resources. It also requires engagement with a range of communities and practices through different approaches to maximise engagement and impact. Evaluations provide the means for evidencing resultant impact which is a powerful motivator and influence for subsequent developments. This measures the impact of the past but it also determines how future aims will be achieved.

INNOVATION AND PEOPLE

Communities of practice have been identified as playing a critical role in the promotion of learning and innovation in organisations (Swan, Scarborough, & Robertson, 2002). While innovation may be facilitated within communities of practice, radical developments frequently occur at the intersections between communities. Managers play a key role in constructing, aligning or supporting such communities during their development phases through informal interactions and consequent lack of formal noting. Hence, a facilitative management style using social networking often produces a more positive outcome than a more direct approach (Bjork & Magnusson, 2009) resulting in enhanced quality of innovation ideas.

Despite innovative ideas being available, learner engagement is widely recognised as an important influence on achievement and learning and as such has been and continued to be widely theorised and researched (Bryson & Hand, 2007). An important factor in maximising retention is to consider the styles of learning and how these impact on the learner experience (Crosling, Heagney, & Thomas, 2009). Learners are more likely to engage if they are supported by tutors who are engaged with and supportive of the learners, are knowledgeable in their subject and are skilled in the teaching process. Engaged learners are more motivated to stay for the duration of their course, whatever the duration, and thereby maximise achievements and potential. Hence, innovation can be present in the learner environment and ideas can be plentiful but it is crucial to encourage and enable creativity in gaining engagement to enable the fulfilment of innovative learning in achieved outcomes throughout a learning community.

INNOVATION THROUGH LEARNING ENTERPRISE

Entrepreneurial teaching and learning has various meanings and connotations in different parts of the world and in a diverse range of contexts.

It could be suggested that it is a process through which learners acquire a broad set of competencies or for an individual's ability to turn ideas into action (European Commission, 2011). The development of the entrepreneurial mindset is a common thread throughout developing European policy and reports published by the European Commission suggesting that education is critical in helping to develop such thinking. The Quality Assurance Agency (QAA, 2012) suggested that 'Universities and colleges should take the lead in fostering a culture of enterprise and entrepreneurship for students across disciplines'.

To encourage ideas to become actions and to propagate the skills, behaviours and attitudes that underpin the entrepreneurial spirit and to engage students in doing so − requires a significant paradigm shift. This means stepping away from traditional teaching and learning practices and developing greater focus on experiential learning opportunities, through people-led enquiry and opportunities of discovery and collaborative practice.

Learners require learner-centred pedagogies and real-world experiences to develop their understanding and skills. 'Clearly, the implication of these changes for teachers is substantial. They mean nothing less than a new role for every teacher: that of learning facilitator' (European Commission, p. 3).

Traditional models of educational management portray a serial model linking teaching styles implemented by lecturers with students as more passive participants of their learning experience (Fig. 1). Hence, the arrows on the diagram reflect a one-way flow of information.

A revised, and more innovative and collaborative, model of student-centred learning offers a more dialogical approach of implementation. It also offers enriched opportunities to support and influence staff to update their teaching styles through student feedback with the overall outcome of enhancing student learning experiences (Fig. 2).

The strategic direction remains the same with a direct link to the middle managers which then link to the operational staff. However, this time there are additional opportunities for the strategic leaders to link directly with operational staff through market research to inform continued practices. Represented diagrammatically, this demonstrates that there is now an additional flow of information to support the change. This time, the operational

Fig. 1.   Traditional Top Down Management. *Source*: Smedley (2013).

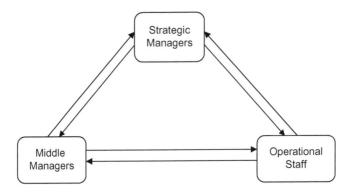

Fig. 2. Top Down and Bottom Up Management Styles. *Source*: Smedley (2013).

staff can now influence change at the middle management staff level who in turn may feed comments back to the strategic managers.

Two case studies are considered here highlighting the innovative use of information gathering informing continuing professional development and enhancing academic practice. The first case study reflects a reward and recognition focus from information gathered by students in the Student-Union-facilitated student-led teaching awards. The second highlights the involvement of students and staff in sharing information and working together to enhance learning experiences of all.

Case Study 1: Reward and Recognition

The Centre for Excellence in Learning and Teaching (CELT) at the University of Wales, Newport (now the University of South Wales) success-fully gained funding to design, develop and implement a student-led teaching awards initiative in 2011. Led by the Student Union and developed by four students working on work-placement, these awards enabled the 'student voice' to nominate those across the University (staff, students, employers and others) who had positively impacted on their accredited or co-curriculum learning experience. Consequently, it encouraged students to think holistically about their learning experience and its components as an important part of their lifelong learning journey. This links to aspects of an entrepreneurial approach to learning and preparing students for lifelong engagement, as a result of the risks that staff take as learning facilitators, by using more learner-centred pedagogies that provide a joined up learning experience for the students. It also enabled staff to reflect on comments made by students regarding their learning experiences and thereby inform their continuing professional development.

This cross-University learning and teaching initiative provided work-experience for four students (1 undergraduate and 3 post graduate). As well as providing invaluable market positioning from the student perspective, this also enabled them to work in an inter-disciplinary manner and gain further informal and formal inter-personal skills.

Alongside gathering and sharing information, outcomes from this innovative learning exercise (now firmly embedded within the University's annual celebration of practice) provided additional insight of impact factors to guide strategic decision-making and benefit current and future student focused developments.

Case Study 2: Supporting Innovative Dialogues in Learning and Teaching

At the University of South Wales, Innovation Grants from the Centre for Excellence in Learning and Teaching (CELT) promote and enable enhanced academic practice and scholarship in learning and teaching by supporting innovative developments. They are designed to create a sense of learning communities where students and staff are engaged in academic discussion about the nature, content and delivery of their courses.

CELT Teaching Innovation Grants promote creativity and innovation by providing funding to support the freeing up of staff time to work on specific projects. Each project includes at least one student work-experience opportunity. The scheme is open to academic and non-academic staff. Faculties and departments are expected to encourage potential applications and support staff, as appropriate.

CELT Learning Innovation Grants are student-led projects which team staff and students in partnership to instigate projects to enhance learning and teaching experiences and benefit the whole University community. Building on CELT Learning and Teaching Grants, CELT Learning Innovation Grants encourage learning communities across the University where students and staff work together in academic discussion about the nature and delivery of their courses. An important aspect of the CELT Learning Innovation Grants is that the students lead the projects — rather than being passive recipients of the learning experience. Faculties and Departments are expected to encourage potential applications and support staff and students, as appropriate.

REFERENCES

Barnett, R. (2014). *Conditions of flexibility: Securing a more responsive higher education system.* New York: Higher Education Academy. Retrieved from https://www.heacademy.ac.uk/sites/default/files/resources/FP_conditions_of_flexibility.pdf. Accessed on July 24, 2015.

Barnett, R., & Davies, M. (2015). *The Palgrave handbook of critical thinking in higher education.* New York, NY: Palgrave Macmillan.

Bennett, S., Maton, K., & Kervin, L. (2008). The 'digital natives' debate: A critical review of the evidence. *British Journal of Educational Technology, 39,* 775−786. doi:10.1111/j.1467-8535.2007.00793.x.

Bjork, J., & Magnusson, M. (2009). Where do good innovation ideas come from? Exploring the influence of network connectivity on innovation idea quality. *Journal of Product Innovation Management, 26*(6), 662−670.

Bryson, C., & Hand, L. (2007). The role of engagement in inspiring teaching and learning. *Innovations in Education and Teaching International, 44*(4), 349−362.

Creative Commons. (n.d.). *Creative commons.* Retrieved from http://www.creativecommons.org. Accessed on May 16, 2016.

Crosling, G., Heagney, M., & Thomas, E. (2009). Improving student retention in higher education: Improving teaching and learning. *The Australian Universities' Review, 51*(2), 9−18. Retrieved from http://search.informit.com.au/documentSummary;dn=1592254072 05474;res=IELAPA. Accessed on July 25, 2015.

Czaja, S., & Lee, C. (2006). The impact of aging on access to technology. *Universal Access in the Information Society, 5,* 341−349.

Eilam, E. (2011). *Reversing: Secrets of reverse engineering.* Hoboken, NJ: Wiley.

Engelberger, J. F. (1982). Robotics in practice: Future capabilities. *Electronic Servicing & Technology.*

European Commission. (2011). *Entrepreneurship education: Enabling teachers as a critical success factor.* Brussels: Entrepreneurship Unit of the EC.

Frankelius, P. (2009). Questioning two myths in innovation literature. *Journal of High Technology Management Research, 20*(1), 40−51.

Groff, J. (2013). *Principles for innovative learning.* Retrieved from http://labs.pearson.com/principles-for-innovative-learning/. Accessed on July 24, 2015.

Hamilton-Jones, J. (2000). Supporting tomorrow's managers: The Coca-Cola and Schweppes in-house degree programme. *Education and Training, 42*(8), 461−469.

Heyne, P., Boettke, P. J., & Prychitko, D. L. (2010). *The economic way of thinking* (12th ed.). Upper Saddle River, NJ: Prentice Hall.

Kotter, J., & Schlesinger, L. (2008). *Choosing strategies for change.* Retrieved from http://www.slsglobal.com/wp-content/uploads/2012/06/Choosing-Strategies-for-Change-Kotter.pdf. Accessed on May 16, 2016.

Kyriacou, C., & Kunc, R. (2007). Beginning teachers' expectations of teaching. *Teaching and Teacher Education, 23*(8), 1246−1257.

Maranville, S. (1992). Entrepreneurship in the business curriculum. *Journal of Education for Business, 68*(1), 27−31.

Nonaka, I., & Konno, N. (1998). The concept of "ba": Building a foundation for knowledge creation. *California Management Review, 40*(3), 40−54. doi:10.2307/41165942

O'Sullivan, D. (2002). Framework for managing development in the networked organisations. *Journal of Computers in Industry, 47*(1), 77−88.

Oxford Dictionary. (2015). Oxford University Press.

Quality Assurance Agency. (2012). *Enterprise and entrepreneurship: A new approach to learning.* Retrieved from http://www.qaa.ac.uk/Newsroom/PressReleases/Pages/Enterprise-and-entrepreneurship-a-new-approach-to-learning.aspx. Accessed on November 20, 2012.

Rockley, A., Kostur, P., & Manning, S. (2012). Fundamental concept of content reuse. In *Managing enterprise content: A unified content strategy.* Indiana: New Riders.

Salge, T. O., & Vera, A. (2012). Benefiting from public sector innovation: The moderating role of customer and learning orientation. *Public Administration Review, 72*(4), 550–560.

Schneckenberg, D. (2009). Understanding the real barriers to technology-enhanced innovation in higher education. *Educational Research, 51*(4), 411–424. doi:10.1080/00131880903354741

Smedley, J. K. (2013). *Supporting change through collaborative dialogue.* Internal paper. Wales: University of South Wales.

Swan, J. A., Scarborough, H., & Robertson, M. (2002). The construction of communities of practice in the management of innovation. *Management Learning, 33*(4), 477–496.

PUBLIC LIBRARIES AND INNOVATION IN GREECE: AN OPTION OR A NECESSITY?

Evgenia Vassilakaki and
Valentini Moniarou-Papaconstantinou

ABSTRACT

Purpose − *Innovation is proven to be an essential element of every organisation that wants to achieve survival and sustain its presence. Libraries as information organisations are transformed into innovation incubators because of the fluid information environment, the social and economic influences and their desire to advance the public good. The Greek public libraries of Nafpaktos, Levadia and Veria are known examples of libraries that have successfully embraced change and innovation. This research aims to identify, through a content analysis of these specific public libraries' websites, the innovative services they offer to the community.*

Findings − *It was found that the chosen public libraries offer a wide range of innovative services (e.g. Media Lab, Information Centres). No matter the challenges the Greek public libraries are facing, they have*

Innovation in Libraries and Information Services
Advances in Library Administration and Organization, Volume 35, 243−255
ISSN: 0732-0671/doi:10.1108/S0732-067120160000035017

developed the necessary internal mechanisms to change the difficulties into opportunities and chance for excellence.

Keywords: Public libraries; information professionals; innovation; Greece; information services; innovative services

INTRODUCTION

The economic, political, social and technological developments have forced information organisations to adopt change in order to respond to the information needs of the modern society (Jantz, 2001). Furthermore, changes in consumer expectations and behaviours as well as changes in community involvement affected innovation (Rowley, 2011). Evidence suggests that organisations innovate mainly for reasons of survival and success in a fluid environment (Jantz, 2012a; Rowley, 2011).

With respect to public libraries, there are increased demands for redefining their roles (e.g. being a social meeting place, supporting lifelong learning, serving as a provider of employment) (Julien and Hoffman, 2008; Sigler et al., 2011). In this changing environment, it appears that innovation is not a consideration but a necessity (Brundy, 2015; McBride, 1999). One of the often-cited definitions of innovation is given by Damanpour (1996) who defined it as 'the introduction into organization of a new product, a new service, a new technology, a significant improvement to an existing product, service or administrative practice' (Damanpour, 1996, p. 694).

In Greece, the public libraries are public sector organisations and part of a wider scheme. The recent reform of the Greek local government structure resulted in a reduction of municipalities with serious implications for public libraries (Vassilakaki, 2015). Public libraries, like most information organisations, are suffering from reduced budgets, professional staff cutbacks and staff redeployment because they rely primarily upon public funding (Moniarou-Papaconstantinou & Triantafyllou, 2015; Semertzaki, 2014). In these challenging times, public libraries, regardless of their size and mission, are expected to prove their value and to embed innovation in their culture and approach developing services (Kostagiolas, Margiola, & Avramidou, 2011).

This chapter aims to examine the nature of innovation in specific public libraries in Greece and the factors for successful implementation of the innovative information services. Specifically, it focuses on the information services that these Greek public libraries provide that constitute innovation. This study contributes in informing information professionals' understanding of innovative information services developed and offered with restricted human and economic resources in order to anticipate and meet users' changing needs.

This chapter is structured as follows. First, a critical analysis of the literature on libraries offering innovative information services is performed. Second, details regarding the methodological approach adopted are illustrated. Third, the specific innovative services of the selected Greek public libraries are described in detail. Finally, a discussion of these services with the ones presented in the relevant literature is performed whereas limitations and implications are identified and future research is proposed.

LITERATURE REVIEW

Libraries constantly record and identify their users' needs and develop information services that would address these needs in the most appropriate, effective and efficient way possible. In an attempt to create more value, libraries and specifically public libraries, need to adapt to change, formulate strategic plans and promote innovation (Brown and Osborne, 2012; Deiss, 2004). Change results to the development or offering of a new service. Strategy would enable information organisations to make important decisions on identifying, implementing and promoting innovation in all levels (Brown and Osborne, 2012; Deiss, 2004; Rowley, 2003, 2011); whereas innovation would enable them to create and offer added-value information services to their users (Deiss, 2004; Kostagiolas et al., 2011). Innovation in libraries is directly associated with the creativity of staff, vendors and users (Deiss, 2004). In particular, staff need to acquire a set of specific skills in order to develop and support innovative information services namely outreach and marketing skills, data mining and analysis, entrepreneurship, technology, logistics, operational control, legal knowledge, training and recruitment (Brundy, 2015), critical thinking, problem solving, communication, collaboration, cross-disciplinary thinking and creativity (Anthony, 2014).

The desire to advance the public good is the main motivation behind the adoption and promotion of innovation (Jantz, 2012a, 2012b). Information organisations innovate mainly in order to survive short-term, and then to thrive over the long-term. Innovation can occur at different levels. There is namely strategic innovation, organisational structure innovation, performance innovation, product innovation, service innovation (Brundy, 2015; Deiss, 2004; Jantz, 2012a; Rowley, 2011). Public libraries are more focused on service innovation in order to keep existing users and attract new (Deiss, 2004). Specifically, innovative services are thought to promote 'what users can do' in terms of allowing users to do what they want and need in the most beneficial way (Deiss, 2004). Therefore, exploring users' information seeking behaviour could assist information professionals in their quest for future innovative services. Identifying the potential factors (e.g. political, societal, economic) that would influence the adoption of innovation services, could assist in the formulation of the strategy for developing and marketing these services (Brown and Osborne, 2012; Deiss, 2004; Sheng & Sun, 2007; Rowley, 2011). Libraries need to address a series of internal barriers namely organisational stability, standards, expertise, performance-oriented cultures, adherence to certainty (Deiss, 2004; Koch and Hauknes, 2005; Moss Kanter, 2002; Ulrich, 2002). External factors also challenge the innovation process mainly because (a) libraries are part of the state which is resilient to change and (b) of lack of collaboration among libraries and other information, public, voluntary and non-profit organisations (Rowley, 2011).

Innovation, as already stated, is 'the introduction of something new'; however, not all new developments are innovative and cannot be considered innovative in every community (Anthony, 2014). Innovation is directly related to novelty, usefulness and most importantly to value (Anthony, 2014; Deiss, 2004; Rowley, 2011). Innovation needs to solve problems even before users express the desire to address a specific need. Therefore, understanding users' needs and their specific characteristics as well as the needs of the community they live in would allow information organisations to provide innovative information services of added value (Anthony, 2014). Innovation is all about sustaining continuous improvement and progress in formulating policy and strategy, in addition to the development and offering of information services.

There are a series of innovative information services public libraries around the world provide. Specifically, 'Knowledge Centers' were developed to solve daily problems of the community (e.g. accessing public and health information). These were situated in different buildings in the community with easy access, equipped with all the relevant information resources and hardware (e.g. computers, printers, cameras), Internet connection and with skilled librarians in order to promote community empowerment and engagement (Higgins, 2013). In the same line, 'Community

Technology Centers' (CTCs) provided access to computers, information resources and thus, education. Furthermore, 'Information Literacy (IL) programs' were offered to specific groups (e.g. women) in order to make education accessible to everyone (Higgins, 2013). IL classes are also offered in 'Information Commons' places that are equipped with computers and recording hardware whereas 'Maker space' aimed to allow users to 'make actual things' (Alcorn, 2013; Peachey, 2014; Zickuhr, 2013). The idea of 'Pop-up-stores' is based on the concept that libraries are storefronts that need people engagement to thrive and disseminate their services to new audiences. These stores were seen as a way to address the problem of population ageing and address libraries' fear of losing the audience that was used to going to the library. Finally, the 'People's Library' offered people in central public places with books to pass their time. It was thought of as a 'hyper-local, low-infrastructure model' which further proved that bookshelf libraries are still in need of (Alcorn, 2013; Peachey, 2014; Zickuhr, 2013).

One could claim that the type of innovative services offered by the public libraries focuses on two axis: technology and education. Emerging new technologies namely mobile phones, tablets, GPRS and 3d printers, are adopted and placed either in designated buildings or specific rooms in the library. On the other hand, information literacy programs regarding the use and exploitation of such technologies are developed and offered to the public, fully customised to the specific needs and characteristics of the user groups (e.g. children, elderly, workers, farmers, unemployed). Overall, it appears that public libraries driven by technological and social changes offer innovative services in order to remain key players in the changing information landscape, to enhance education opportunities for all members of society, to increase citizens' involvement and to provide solutions for daily problems.

METHODOLOGY

The method of content analysis (Forman and Damschroder, 2007) was used to identify the innovative information services offered by the Greek public libraries. Specifically, Forman and Damschroder (2007) argued that qualitative content analysis is based on categorising data by using generated categories which emerge inductively and 'in most cases ... through close reading'. They defined qualitative content analysis as the method that 'also includes techniques in which the data are analysed solely qualitatively, without the use of counting or statistical techniques' (Forman and

Table 1. Use of Qualitative Content Analysis in the Study.

A/A	Forman and Damschroder (2007)	Implementation in This Study
1	Data management	Identification of the websites of the Greek public libraries and selection of the specific three
2	Develop a code scheme	Codes based on innovative services
3	Code the data	Coding the services found on the websites
4	Analysis with the use of coding categories	Common features of the innovative services identified
5	Interpretation	Presentation of innovative services

Damschroder, 2007, p. 40). Specific steps were proposed for performing content analysis in a qualitative way (see Table 1).

Specifically, searches were performed to identify the websites of the 46 Greek public libraries, from these, the websites of three public libraries: Veria,[1] Nafpaktos[2] and Levadia[3] were considered for the purposes of this study. These specific public libraries were chosen because they are considered as the libraries that mostly promote innovation in Greece (Higgins, 2013).

The considered libraries' websites were visited during the last week of July 2015. A thorough investigation of the public libraries' websites revealed the specific information services offered. For each information service, the specific features were identified as well as the factors for the implementation of the innovative information services whereas an emphasis was placed on the features that signified an innovative service. These features further revealed the innovative services and enabled their comparison in order to identify similarities and differences.

FINDINGS

The public libraries of Nafpaktos, Levadia and Veria share some common characteristics. They all sustain presence on a significant number of social networking sites namely Facebook, Twitter, Instagram and Scoop.it. All three libraries promote collaboration with other public libraries as well as information literacy to the wide public. They participate in national campaigns that enhance the library's presence and children's engagement (see Table 2). Notably, the public library of Veria has received the Bill & Melinda Gates award of excellence which has boosted its creativity and innovation.

Table 2. Characteristics of the Three Selected Greek Public Libraries.

Characteristics	Public Libraries		
	Nafpaktos	Levadia	Veria
Presence on social networking sites	×	×	×
Collaboration with other libraries	×	×	×
Collaboration with other public authorities		×	×
Participation in national campaigns	×	×	×
Participation in international campaigns		×	×
Participation in European funded projects			×
Award winning		×	×

In terms of the innovative services that these three Greek public libraries offer to their clientele, a wide range of these services is offered to address users' needs. All three libraries provide some common services namely a Public information centre, free wireless access, digitised collection, organisation of events (e.g. book presentations), information literacy programs, book readings clubs (e.g. children, young adult, subject specific book clubs) and online tutorials (see Table 3).

The public library of Veria offers the highest number of innovative services (19) while the public library of Nafpaktos the lowest (8). Levadia public library keeps a balance between the two with 13 innovative services in total (see Table 2). Both public libraries of Levadia and Veria offer Media labs, e-book readers (i.e. tablets, kindles), job seeking assistance, press display and mobile library services. Nafpaktos public library promotes volunteering by offering an online form for everyone interested to support the different activities and events that the library organises and offers to its community. In addition, Veria public library offers an *American corner* that was created in 2003 in collaboration with the office of Public Affairs of the American Embassy in Athens and aims to promote American culture and language in the population; a *Maker space* for hosting information literacy courses, courses to promote creativity and innovation and finally, courses to support high-school students' preparation for the exams; a *Brain pulse* place designated to accommodate group meetings, staff meetings of different companies to perform tele-conference video-calls (i.e. skype calls); a *Robotic lab* fully equipped to promote innovation and creativity; *3D printing* facilities and finally, *e-Gov services* to assist the public in performing some basic but important transactions with the government (see Table 3).

Table 3. Innovative Services Offered by the Three Greek Public Libraries.

Innovative Services Offered	Public Libraries		
	Nafpaktos	Levadia	Veria
Public Information Centre	×	×	×
Free wireless access	×	×	×
Digitisation of collections	×	×	×
Events organised	×	×	×
Educations programs to high school students	×		×
Information literacy programs	×	×	×
Book reading clubs	×	×	×
Online tutorials offered	×	×	×
Media Lab		×	×
E-book readers loan		×	×
Job seeking		×	×
Online volunteering form		×	
Press display		×	×
American corner			×
Mobile library		×	×
Maker space			×
Brain pulse			×
Robotic labs			×
3D printing			×
e-Gov services			×

DISCUSSION

Libraries have started offering a range of innovative services in order to survive, succeed and sustain development. In fact, the number of innovative services is constantly increasing, proving that libraries are incubators of innovation (Anthony, 2014; Ulrich, 2002). The three selected Greek public libraries have succeeded innovation at the level of developing information services. Specifically, they offer the same type of innovative services namely Media Lab, Information Centres, Mobile Libraries, free wireless access as identified in the relevant literature (Anthony, 2014; Higgins, 2013; Peachey, 2014; Ulrich, 2002). It appears that Greek public libraries stay up-to-date with recent technological developments and most importantly, they experiment with customising the innovative services they offer to the community.

The type of innovative services that these three public libraries offer are both technology-based and education-related further confirming Alcorn (2013), Peachey (2014) and Zickuhr (2013). Innovation is developed by examining what is available, analysing different contexts and synthesising them again in new and innovative ways (Jantz, 2012b). Therefore, Greek public libraries need both to further stay in line with international developments in the field of Information Science and to continually examine users' needs to provide high standard services to their users.

Furthermore, the specific innovative services of the Greek public libraries are designed in such a way in order to enhance creativity among the public. Specifically, libraries need to provide all the necessary means to promote innovation not only on behalf of the library but from their users as well. It should be noted that currently the selected libraries focus on young people and children in order to promote creativity and innovation.

In addition, the offered innovative services address the needs of a range of age, gender, ethnic and occupational groups, which is in accordance with the scope of the public library further confirming Deiss (2004) and Rowley (2011) who pointed out the need to explore and identify the public's needs. Overall, the selected public libraries proved to have a very good understanding of the users' needs and thus, have successfully developed customised, innovative services.

In terms of the internal factors affecting the selected public libraries' innovation, libraries' participation in various projects both nationally and internationally, formulation of coalitions and collaborations with other libraries and organisations as well as acceptance of awards signify that these libraries have embraced change. Overall, the selected public libraries manage to provide these innovative services by having staff committed to innovation, establishing a trust between users and library, achieving involvement of the community and promoting the new services through national and international campaigns. Furthermore, they were able to embrace innovation by adopting flexible management approaches in order to overcome administrative obstacles and looking for funding opportunities outside the traditional financial system (e.g. sponsorship, donations, competitive European funded projects, crowdfunding). As a result the usage of libraries is grown every year. With respect to the library of Veria it should be mentioned that 62% of the Veria population are registered users whereas the library is considered the third more popular place in terms of frequency of visits after home and the work place (Kathimerini, 2016).

Nafpaktos library has currently 7.466 members, which is one quarter of the city's population (Municipality of Nafpaktia, 2016).

It seems that understanding the need to change, led them to adapt their strategy for developing innovative information services. As a consequence, these libraries have been transformed from passive institutions to active engagers that support lifelong learning and provide collaborative spaces (Anthony, 2014). The libraries are accepting the new roles of the incubator of creativity, innovation, knowledge provider and educator (Vassilakaki & Moniarou-Papaconstantinou, 2015) whereas a clear emphasis is placed on developing the public's skills and expertise in order to address the needs of the current social, economic and political environment.

Currently, Greek public libraries face challenging external factors. The current economic climate, the constant and unpredictable social changes, the anxiety and stress among the public are only a few of the factors that public libraries need to take into consideration in order to formulate strategies and innovate (Vassilakaki, 2015). Although the barriers are serious, it seems that these selected public libraries are using them as an opportunity to adapt and evolve.

This research identified some implications. Library and Information Science (LIS) schools need to adjust their offered curriculum in order to provide the future information professionals with all the necessary skills and competencies to promote innovation. In addition, LIS education needs to provide the space and tools to encourage students' creativity and innovation in an attempt to formulate innovative professionals.

Limitations were also identified. This research focused only on three Greek public libraries, which were considered to promote innovation. However, there are still a lot of public libraries in Greece that provide innovative services that might have not reached the degree of maturity that the selected libraries have. This research also considered the information that was only available on the specific public libraries' websites in a specific time period (end of July) due to time constraints.

CONCLUSIONS AND FUTURE WORK

Innovation is crucial for any organisation because it assists in succeeding its survival and in sustaining its long-term development. Libraries were thought to embrace innovation and nowadays, have really turned to be innovation incubators (Alcorn, 2013; Anthony, 2014; Higgins, 2013; Peachey, 2014). The public libraries of Nafpaktos, Levadia and Veria are three very good examples of public libraries in Greece that encourage creativity and promote innovation at the level of information services. They offer a range of innovative services to different user groups in order to efficiently and successfully address their information needs. However, all Greek public libraries face several challenges: is the public ready to accept an innovative service? Is the social, political environment ready to accept and assist the development of innovation in Greece? Are the information organisations in Greece ready to diffuse innovation? Which are the factors for successful implementation of the innovative information services?

Public libraries in order to establish innovation need to consider the local circumstances and community needs, adapt innovation to the existing context (e.g. political, societal) and create value in people's lives. Innovation is grounded on the community needs and public libraries need to turn more outward in order to succeed sustainable and continuous innovation. Overall, they need to become centres of creativity, research and collaboration, all for free.

Future research should focus on exploring other Greek public libraries innovative services offered, as well as other types of libraries (e.g. academic, research). Interviews could be conducted with the directors' of these libraries' in an attempt to investigate their opinions on preparing, planning, developing, and offering innovative services to their community as well as of their future plans. In addition, to understand which they think are the driving forces or the barriers to innovation. Innovation can take place at different levels and thus, future research could focus on other types of innovation in Greek public libraries namely strategic innovation and organisational innovation.

NOTES

1. http://www.libver.gr/ (accessed on July 29, 2015).
2. http://vivl-nafpakt.ait.sch.gr/ (accessed on July 29, 2015).
3. http://libLevadia.wikidot.com/ (accessed on July 29, 2015).

REFERENCES

Alcorn, S. (2013). *5 innovations that show libraries don't have to die*. Co.exist | ideas + impact. *Fast Company*. Retrieved from http://www.fastcoexist.com/1681678/5-innovations-that-show-libraries-dont-have-to-die. Accessed on July 12, 2015.

Anthony, C. A. (2014). *Innovation in public libraries*. Public Libraries Online. Retrieved from http://publiclibrariesonline.org/2014/02/innovation-in-public-libraries/. Accessed on July 12, 2015.

Brown, K., & Osborne, S. (2012). In S. P. Osborne, O. Hughers, & W. Kickert (Eds.), *Managing change and innovation in public service organizations*. London: Routledge, Retrieved from https://www.google.com/books?hl = el&lr = &id = GloRgOwZrEwC& oi = fnd&pg = PR3&dq = innovation + public + library&ots = jQJ4TOjSJ2&sig = DXUW9 VHSA9SVwNFzBJojtonrgSY. Accessed on May 22, 2015.

Brundy, C. (2015). Academic libraries and innovation: A literature review. *Journal of Library Innovation*, 6(1), 22–39.

Damanpour, F. (1996). Organizational complexity and innovation: Developing and testing multiple contingency models. *Management Science*, 42(5), 693–716.

Deiss, K. (2004). *Innovation and strategy: Risk and choice in shaping user-centered libraries*. Retrieved from http://www.ideals.illinois.edu/handle/2142/1717. Accessed on May 22, 2015.

Forman, J., & Damschroder, L. (2007). Qualitative content analysis. *Advances in Bioethics*, 11(1), 39–62.

Higgins, C. (2013). *4 innovative libraries transforming lives around the world*. Mental-floss. Retrieved from http://mentalfloss.com/article/52525/4-innovative-libraries-transform-ing-lives-around-world. Accessed on July 12, 2015.

Jantz, R. (2001). Knowledge management in academic libraries: Special tools and processes to support information professionals. *Reference Services Review*, 29(1), 33–39.

Jantz, R. C. (2012a). A framework for studying organizational innovation in research libraries. *College & Research Libraries*, 73(6), 525–541.

Jantz, R. C. R. (2012b). Innovation in academic libraries: An analysis of university librarians' perspectives. *Library & Information Science Research*, 34(1), 3–12.

Julien, H., & Hoffman, C. (2008). Information literacy training in Canada's public libraries. *The Library Quarterly*, 78(1), 19–41.

Kathimerini. (2016). *Public library of Veria did it again* [in Greek]. Retrieved from http://www. kathimerini.gr/858674/gallery/politismos/vivlio/h-veroia-ekane-pali-to-8ayma-ths. Accessed on May 15, 2016.

Koch, P., & Hauknes, J. (2005). *On innovation in the public sector*. Retrieved from http://citeseerx. ist.psu.edu/viewdoc/download?doi = 10.1.1.104.3988&rep = rep1&type = pdf. Accessed on May 22, 2015.

Kostagiolas, P., Margiola, A., & Avramidou, A. (2011). A library management response model against the economic crisis: The case of public libraries in Greece. *Library Review*, 60(6), 486–500.

McBride, R. C. (1999). Implementation of organizational innovation. Studies of academic and research libraries. *Library Quarterly*, 69, 253–254.

Moniarou-Papaconstantinou, V., & Triantafyllou, K. (2015). Job satisfaction and work values: Investigating sources of job satisfaction with respect to information professionals. *Library & Information Science Research*, 37(2), 164–170.

Moss Kanter, R. (2002). Creating the culture for innovation. In F. Hesselbein, M. Goldsmith, & I. Somerville (Eds.), *Leading for innovation and organizing for results* (pp. 73–86). San Francisco, CA: Jossey-Bass.

Municipality of Nafpaktia. (2016). *Municipality of Nafpaktia*. Retrieved from http://www.naf-paktos.gr/wellcome-to-nafpaktos. Accessed on May 13, 2016.

Peachey, J. (2014). *Four of the UK's most innovative libraries*. Public leaders network. *The Guardian*. Retrieved from http://www.theguardian.com/public-leaders-network/2014/ sep/01/four-of-the-uks-most-innovative-libraries. Accessed on July 12, 2015.

Rowley, J. (2003). Knowledge management: The new librarianship? From custodians of history to gatekeepers to the future. *Library Management, 24*, 433–440.

Rowley, J. (2011). Should your library have an innovation strategy? *Library Management, 32*(4/5), 251–265.

Semertzaki, E. (2014). *Socio-economic aspects of changes in Greek libraries?* EBLIDA 2014. Athens, Greece.

Sheng, X., & Sun, L. (2007). Developing knowledge innovation culture of libraries. *Library Management, 28*(1/2), 36–52. Retrieved from http://www.emeraldinsight.com/doi/abs/10.1108/01435120710723536. Accessed on May 22, 2015.

Sigler, K., Jaeger, P. T., Bertot, J. C., McDermott, A. J., DeCoster, E. J., & Langa, L. A. (2011). The role of public libraries, the internet, and economic uncertainty: Librarianship in times of crisis. In *Librarianship in times of crisis* (pp. 19–35). Bingley, UK: Emerald Group Publishing Limited.

Ulrich, D. (2002). An innovation protocol. In F. Hesselbein, M. Goldsmith, & I. Somerville (Eds.), *Leading for innovation and organizing for results* (pp. 215–224). San Francisco, CA: Jossey-Bass.

Vassilakaki, E. (2015). Greek public libraries in economic crisis: The past, the present and the future. *The Bottom Line: Managing Library Finance.* Retrieved from http://www.emeraldinsight.com/doi/abs/10.1108/BL-12-2014-0033. Accessed on June 22, 2015.

Vassilakaki, E., & Moniarou-Papaconstantinou, V. (2015). A systematic literature review informing library and information professionals' emerging roles. *New Library World, 116*(1–2), 32–66.

Zickuhr, K. (2013). *Innovative library services "in the wild".* Retrieved from http://libraries.pewinternet.org/2013/01/29/innovative-library-services-in-the-wild/. Accessed on July 12, 2015.

LEADING THE INNOVATIVE AND CREATIVE LIBRARY WORKFORCE: APPROACHES AND CHALLENGES

Graham Walton and Paul Webb

ABSTRACT

Purpose — *This chapter explores the roles that library leaders have in ensuring libraries demonstrate innovation and creativity in their services, systems and facilities. This is grounded in the pressures for innovation resulting from the 'disruptive technologies' identified by Christensen (1997). 'Obliquity' (Kay, 2011) is inter-related around how innovation can be used to meet the challenges. The areas proposed where library leadership can contribute to innovation are leading by example, shaping organisational culture/values, ensuring appropriate training/development takes place, helping develop appropriate organisational structures and establishing appropriate reward and recognition.*

Methodology/approach — *Both theoretical insight and practical experience are used to inform the chapter. Management and leadership theories/research provide the context within which library leadership and innovation is explored. This is complemented by the authors between*

Innovation in Libraries and Information Services
Advances in Library Administration and Organization, Volume 35, 257–275
Copyright © 2017 by Emerald Group Publishing Limited
All rights of reproduction in any form reserved
ISSN: 0732-0671/doi:10.1108/S0732-067120160000035018

them have experience in developing innovation in libraries and also in delivering leadership training on innovation.

Practical implications − *For any library looking to demonstrate innovation and creativity, the chapter identifies some clear responsibilities for leaders. The five specific roles for the leader are crucial in libraries being innovative. A further element of the work is that it explores some of the challenges a library leader will face in moving in this direction.*

Originality/value − *Having joint authorship by people from different backgrounds ensures that the chapter is based on a blended insight of theoretical understanding and practical experience.*

Keywords: Innovation; creativity; leadership roles; libraries

INTRODUCTION

In 2011, a *Harvard Business Review* blog was posted by two creativity and innovation specialists. Mark Sebell and Jan Terwilliger (Govindarajan, 2011). The blog lists nine critical success factors needed to achieve innovation:

- A compelling case for innovation
- An inspiring, shared vision of the future
- A fully aligned strategic innovation agenda
- Visible senior management involvement decision making
- Model that fosters teamwork
- Multi-functional dedicated team
- Exploration of the drivers for innovation
- Willingness to take risk
- Well defined execution process

In the context of this themed issue of *Advances in Library Administration and Organization*, central to all of the above is the role of the leader. This is applicable to leaders across all sectors who aspire to deliver creative services/products. The leader's involvement can range from being an integral part of a creativity team to driving forward and implementing a creativity and innovation strategy. Creativity was acknowledged back in 2008 as being important to the continuing success of libraries and this role has not diminished (Walton, 2008). The purpose of this chapter is to focus on the library leader/manager and explore five specific aspects of their work and function that are part of the innovation and creativity spectrum:

- leading by example,
- shaping organisational culture and values,
- ensuring appropriate training and development takes place,
- developing appropriate organisational structures and
- ensuring appropriate reward and recognition

In many ways, the need for innovation and creativity in libraries can be directly linked to new technologies including Bring Your Own Devices (BYOD), social media and the Internet. The impact of these technologies has been explored by Christensen (1997). Disruptive technologies are those that bring a different set of values to work. Initially they underperform established products but they also improve at a faster rate. When they first appear, they are not seen as being much more than a toy but very quickly they become cheaper, faster and better. As far back as 2004, Lewis (2004) realised the relevance of Christensen's ideas for the future of academic libraries. In 2004, he listed three areas where disruptive technologies were having an effect on libraries:

- Collections: institutional repositories will provide a cheaper and more effective way to disseminate research papers than the traditional route via academic journals published by commercial publishers
- Bibliographic control: Amazon was used in 2004 by many as a substitute for the library catalogue. Even then, the purpose and function of the catalogue was being challenged
- Reference: 12 years ago, Google was making an impact as a search engine that people were increasingly becoming reliant upon.

The influence of disruptive technologies is much more significant now than it was in 2004. Lewis (2004) acknowledged that library leaders needed to ensure their libraries displayed innovation and creativity to adapt to disruptive technologies. This included changing the culture and organisational structure to allow easier collaboration, provide staff with motivation to explore, innovate and change and also to allow ideas and information to flow into the library and out again. Lewis' insight is more relevant in 2016 than it was in 2004.

To develop leadership approaches to best incorporate disruptive technologies, John Kay's (2011) ideas around 'obliquity' are very relevant. His work was inspired by observing Sir James Black, the successful pharmaceutical researcher. The basic principle is that success is businesses and service delivery is best run by enthusiasts who pursue excellence in their specialty. If financial goals etc. are the primary objective, the services/business will then lose its vigour and may fail. The external environment where libraries function abounds with uncertainty and complexity. There is a lack of clarity about the problems encountered. The purpose of the library is being challenged and circumstances in which they operate are changing continually. In this situation, Kay proposes that the 'obliquity' approach is the one most likely to succeed whereby complex goals are often best pursued indirectly.

There is recognition that complex objectives tend to be imprecisely defined. These objectives contain many elements that are not necessarily or obviously compatible with each other. If library leaders base their work around obliquity theories, they will seek to set develop the library staff to experiment and discover. When there are complex objectives, a product of the discovery and experimentation will lead to the objectives being achieved. The library leader's concerns if seeking to apply obliquity is to ensure staff are not driven by Key Performance Indicators (KPIs) or objectives. Instead they should be allowed to allow their passion and interest in delivering the services. If the passion and interest is there, the objectives will be achieved (but the path will be circuitous and not straight). Having passion and interest are integral to innovation and creativity.

An assumption is made in this chapter that the case for innovation and creativity in libraries has been made elsewhere. It is taken as read that libraries need to be creative and innovative to thrive in the turbulent world. It has been highlighted that there are very few empirical studies on innovation and creativity (Brundy, 2015; Jantz, 2012a). For example, Rowley (2011, p. 251) states that 'there has been little discussion of innovation and its processes in the information management professional or academic literature'. All is not lost, as Brundy (2015) highlighted that in the 29 published studies on innovation in libraries, 10 have been published since 2010. The lack of library based innovation studies means that this chapter is grounded in both general management and librarianship literature. This blended approach is supported and reflected by the chapter's authorship which is shared between a practicing librarian and a management academic. This approach has been used elsewhere when considering innovation and libraries (Goulding & Walton, 2014). Most of the librarianship studies on innovation focus on the academic library sector. This should not be seen as indicating that innovation does not occur in other library sectors as this is obviously not the case (Ipsos MORI & Shared Intelligence, n.d.).

The importance of the library leader in innovation and creativity has been argued well by Jantz (2012b). There is a correlation between Jantz's views and the success factors for innovation (Govindarajan, 2011). Prime responsibility for generating and articulating the vision/strategy lies with the leader. There is a real tension facing the library leader needing to support at one level the traditional library functions based upon bureaucratic hierarchical structure whilst at the same time making sure the library is flexible and delivers creativity projects and ideas. Another tension is the library strategist identifying direction and outcomes which involves them giving up power and control to employees as part of the innovation and creativity processes (MacDonald & vanDuinkerken, 2015). This chapter very much focuses on how the leader can contribute and influence the innovation friendly library.

LEADING BY EXAMPLE

Unless the library leader can demonstrate to colleagues that they have innovation/creativity skills themselves, there is limited chance in the attributes occurring in the wider workforce. In order to explore the role of the library leader and innovation there needs to be detailed examination of the concept of 'leadership'. A simple definition of leadership is not immediately obvious, many academic texts explore the subject area in depth and many students explore the topic on undergraduate and Master's programmes. In the portfolio of leadership skills, it is sometimes not clear whether creativity is less significant than either the bottom line of cost control or the need to attain 'quality standards' expected and demanded by most sectors.

Based on practical experience, it is not necessarily the 'leader' that is in the highest position in the organisation, rather it is the individual that on paper best matches the remit for that role. Consequently, organisations facing difficult and challenging times find themselves with Senior Management at the helm who possibly have limited (or indeed no) leadership skills but are there because of circumstance, career trajectory or it just happened they were in the wrong place at the wrong time. In certain organisations, the leader may well not be at the pinnacle of the organisation but may still offer a stimulus and inspiration to others without necessarily the power base to enforce this commitment. It is counterproductive when those at the top of the organisational structure demonstrate limited leadership innovation and creativity skills as these impact on the motivation of the rest of the organisation.

To understand this, there is a need to consider the different forms of leadership in the library (and other) professional contexts which are strongly influenced by historical best practice, governance and public accountability. It is also important to understand how the leaders can keep abreast of or ahead of that other major issue in modern day management: continuous change needed in response to those external factors that organisations have no control or awareness.

In most professional organisations such as libraries there is a division of staff into strategic and operational roles with clear lines of responsibility drawn for these two roles. The assumption is that management will take responsibility for the strategic direction and the operational staff will concern themselves with the day-to-day operational requirements. These two roles are then clearly defined in job descriptions, limits of responsibilities and reporting structures. The key issue is that whilst this model may have been perfectly acceptable in historic static or stable sector conditions, it is unlikely to be relevant to libraries (and others) with the current trends of significant change.

Across the world, the various library sectors have leadership programs and leadership academies in place. Their purposes are to define the various facets of leadership and potential characteristics of individuals which may identify them as 'leaders of the future'. At the international level, IFLA (International Federation of Library Associations and Institutions) (2016) have set up the International Leaders Programme which will take two years to complete and is designed to increase the cohort of leaders who can effectively represent the wider library sector in the international arena, and to develop leaders within IFLA. In the United States, the Association of Academic Libraries in the USA has developed the ARL Leadership Program (Association of Research Libraries [ARL], 2016) which is an executive leadership programme designed and sponsored by ARL member libraries. It is intended to facilitate the development of future senior-level leaders in large research libraries and archives. In the United Kingdom, CILIP (CILIP, 2016) piloted a new programme in leadership which was intended to create additional leadership capacity both within the profession and within the CILIP membership. The programme is intended for CILIP members with some leadership experience (e.g. leading a project/working group, leading a team) looking to further develop their leadership skills. Aurora Foundation (2016) is the Australian programme that 'builds leadership capacity in the library and information management professions by developing and providing innovative and challenging programs'.

The potential for a library to have an innovation strategy has been explored by Rowley (2011). This strategy has seven facets, one of which is innovation leadership. In this strategy, promoting and encouraging innovation is seen as a major role of the library manager and leader. Work by one of the authors, Paul Webb from 2000 is used to outline that if the library leader is to support creativity they need to be candid, highly communicative and open to participation by others in the decision making process. The leader has to be able to co-operate extensively and on an equal basis with other colleagues. The other six facets of the model include innovation capabilities and cultures: innovation processes; the innovation portfolio; innovative and creative teams; open innovation and collaboration and user engagement in innovation. This approach is advocated because there is a need to look beyond the operational management of having projects which are about creativity.

Within libraries there is conflict between professional purpose and the broader technology driven sector that faces 'explosive' levels of technological change (Germano, 2011). Critical in this regard is the need for a shift in librarian leader's world view and by extension the library leadership identity, which is where leadership drives innovation and creativity. Visionary leadership is essential in allowing libraries to transform themselves as strong competitors within the overall information industry. This is a 'leadership that also invites followers to engage in creative responses to a strategic vision that promotes increased organisational success, despite existing institutional values and cultures as well as financial limitations' (Germano, 2011, p. 12). There are various trait based leadership styles (autocratic, democratic, bureaucratic and laissez-faire) which can be interpreted as personality types. Risks do exist around a strategy based upon the cult of personality − where innovation and leadership are tied to one person and one person alone. In these circumstances, reliance on charismatic leadership can be a barrier for continuity and succession.

The power-based exchanges between leaders and followers (often termed transactional and transformational leadership models) are important. A key theme is that under transformational leadership, with the encouragement of risk taking and seeking new solutions, the outcome is often enthusiastic staff seeking new ways to solve problems. Transformational leadership is considered as 'providing the strongest support for change, creativity and sustainable innovation' (Germano, 2011, p. 14).

Transformational library leaders (like those in other sectors) drive and sustain environments that produce change by evaluating innovation, identifying creative people, developing an innovative climate, assessing tolerance for change, understanding customer wants/needs. If library leaders wish to transform people and processes to improve customer experience they must fully support both innovation and creativity.

SHAPING ORGANISATIONAL CULTURE AND VALUES

Library cultures and values were explored by Jantz (2012b) where he investigated innovation in academic libraries and the perspectives of university librarians. Four questions were posed to librarians from four USA institutions:

- What are the characteristics of innovation as understood by university librarians?
- How are university librarians involved with innovation at their institutions?
- In the view of university librarians, what are the processes and forces that stimulate innovation or, alternatively, act as barriers to innovation?
- How is innovation, as perceived by university librarians, effecting scholarly communication, especially with respect to professional roles and specific user groups?

A number of innovations were identified in the sector both technical and administrative and by both product and process (see Table 1). Clearly since

Table 1. Innovation by Type and Attributes.

Product	Process
Technical	• Cooperative preservation
○ Archiving research data	• Copyright advisory office
○ Compact shelving	• Creation of new standards for
○ Faceted browsing in OPACs	e-journal publishing
○ Information commons	• Creating new library services
○ Institutional repository	• Joint publishing with the university press
○ Publishing e-journals	• Leasing library space
○ Shared digital repository	• Library outposts (reference services)
○ Shared annexes for storage (so library	• Mass digitisation
space can be used in a different way)	• Selling library services
○ Shelf-ready books	• Service − provide faculty assistance
○ Streaming video to classrooms	with technology
Administrative (Innovations would	• A revenue producing unit
include products that support the	• A standing R&D budget
administrative structure. There were	• Associate university librarian for
none cited.)	digitisation projects
	• Budget reallocation to digital projects
	• Business plans for new projects
	• Digital programme office

Source: Reprinted by permission of Jantz (2012b).

then other innovations have been further identified (e.g. in the widespread use of social media in an educational/academic setting).

In rapidly changing and turbulent times, leadership is crucial and this is hampered by bureaucracy and hierarchy which are perhaps the main ones in holding back greater innovation in the sector. Jantz (2012a) returned to this theme in a later study, proposing a detailed (and richly complex) theoretical framework and model for studying innovation in research libraries based on a number of propositions. He proposed that research libraries can be considered members of a class of organisations referred to here as institutional non-profits. Not only do research libraries inherit many of the innovative properties that these service organisations possess, they also have other unique characteristics. Jantz uses institutional theory to explain the forces that are acting on the research library and draws on research from organisational learning and structural contingency theory. Typologies of service organisations are applied in establishing a more encompassing innovation framework. The literature review, the theoretical framework, and empirical studies are linked to present a process model and this develops propositions that characterise how the research library might innovate. The conclusions are interesting in that they discuss the fact that most innovation in the sector is incremental. This is a result of organisational constraints invariably bring about a mainly homogenised sector approach — with each institute resembling each other in most respects. The challenge again seems for effective leadership that promotes flexibility over bureaucracy to ensure real innovation. At the same time, there is a need to sustain and support traditional library functions that are essential to provide high level service quality that is in-line with the university community expectations.

Another interesting study that informs innovation and leadership in libraries was conducted by Leonard and Clementson (2012). They considered the innovative characteristics of business librarians within the context of the culture in which they operate. A key outcome was the restrictions that result when there is not a consistent definition across the library. If an individual manager extensively supports innovation in their team, there will be tension if this is out of step with other teams. If there is a culture that fosters entrepreneurship across the organisation and then it is allowed to flourish, then success is more likely. Organisational support is needed and noticed when absent. Continuous user-centred process, product and service improvement are highly desirable but have to be made with constraints that are real. A realistic balance is needed in generating new services but also streamlining other existing services or making them more cost effective.

For the library leader, it again comes down to that balance between encouraging innovation and risk taking It is also crucial to determine those elements that discourage innovation and eliminate them and thus to encourage library employees to 'contribute to their greatest potential'. A major influence on the ability of an organisation to be creative and innovative is its culture (and values). Library leaders have to invest time and effort into maintaining and developing a culture which is appropriate. At the same time, the leader has to work on the library itself having values that help maintain the innovation and creativity. This is in the context of other departments and support functions arguing the same case, competing for scarce budgetary resource. The key approach the library leader can put forward is that investment in the library and its ability to embrace new technology and approaches should benefit the entire organisation not just a single unit.

If the library leader is to develop a supportive culture, there is an imperative to understand reasons why innovation may not flourish in a not for profit organisation. The following reasons were identified by five management academics with over 60 years' experience (Webb & Page, 2015).

- There is an obsession with fixed planning cycles and committee structures
- Possible top down centrist thinking directed from the most senior staff
- Possible dominance of standards and procedures which prevail over customers' needs
- Risk aversion of new ventures yet continuation of often seemingly pointless projects (highlighted previously as highly likely to be prone to failure, but serving some 'strategic' political and PR purpose)
- Other skills and attributes are seen as being more important than creativity and innovation
- Leaders possibly pursuing their own career agendas at the expense of strategy and organisational enhancement
- Peer pressure to adopt the same strategies as others in the sector
- Silo mentality between different parts of the organisation
- Lack of clear communication between different parts of the organisation
- Inability to recognise those with expertise in areas such as innovation and creativity
- Creativity takes time and there is reluctance to give people that time and space

Culture and values are often (usually) those of management − not the workforce. Non-creative (conservative) management quashes innovation rising from below. This is frustrating and potentially dangerous as the world is changing so rapidly that there is a need for creativity, innovation and a changing mind-set of employees to remain competitive as societal demands change. The leader (not necessarily manager) needs to be a visionary and has to enthuse staff to evolve and develop. In this regard, Germano (2011) states that leadership is needed that drives innovation and creativity in order to mitigate some of the anger and frustration, both for librarians and users. This is caused by the traditional library goal of ensuring ordered and reliable access to a body of knowledge despite an increasingly disordered and technologically unpredictable information universe.

Castiglione (2008) provides an in-depth review of the conceptual and practical tools required to engage the creative potential of staff members. The chapter is concerned with facilitating organisational creativity whilst being aware of those barriers that are always in place and (as others have suggested) points out that creative staff respond well to supervisors that encourage creativity and innovation. The conclusions state that the greatest success will come from an organisational structure that encourages employees to think independently, anticipate and adapt to change, express their opinions about problems facing the library openly, grow professionally and share ideas and experiences with colleagues and other departments.

ENSURING APPROPRIATE TRAINING AND DEVELOPMENT

During lean times, it may be that expenditure on training and staff development is the first thing to be cut back or even go altogether. However, this does not make business sense. Innovative and culturally aware organisations should realise that actually it is during these lean times that spend on training and development should increase not decrease. Giving employees the skills needed for an ever more dynamic and rapidly changing future is what will make organisations flexible enough to adapt to the flux of tomorrow's business environment, and thus remain competitive for tomorrow's world.

In the context of the library culture and the constraints of budget, library leaders need to put forward coherent strategies that embody the need for constant and on-going staff development. They also need to instil to authorities their belief that this change will be consistent and unpredictable and thus their staff require on-going training and development to be able to adapt to whatever the future might bring.

It is unrealistic to expect library employees to acquire innovation and creativity skills without support and direction. Careful consideration and planning is needed by the library leader to set up innovation and creativity training that is delivered through different channels that staff can choose from. Ongoing support strategies are also needed to help staff progress in the right direction. Viewing an organisation holistically often highlights issues, problems, and barriers to innovation and change that just cannot be uncovered by more traditional problem solving techniques. This is why, in many instances, change management programmes tackling organisational issues are at best only partially successful, and at worst a complete failure.

This is because solutions to these complex organisational issues and problems cannot be easily resolved, and managers need to 'think outside of the box' to achieve innovative results that are organisationally desirable as well as effective and efficient. There is a need to realise this holistic perspective, and to develop the skills to provide innovative solutions to complex organisational and innovation problems. Manager development workshops and exercises are useful to provide knowledge skills in creativity and soft approaches to organisational thinking and problem solving. Various studies demonstrate how some libraries have developed training and development in creativity for their staff. An experimental staff training programme was developed in which library staff engaged in 'play' to encourage creativity. The programme entitled Innovation Boot Camp was based on the 10 approaches to Innovation termed 'faces of Innovation' (Bergart, 2010). Leong and Anderson (2012) outline a cultural change and innovation programme at an Australian University Library. This provides a blueprint for how to galvanise an organisation into action to encourage leadership development and cross unit working group amongst other approaches, Gifford (2014) discusses change issues in a small non-profit Australian University where there is an ageing workforce. A future vision of what the existing services could be was translated into a single 'consolidated integrated service' consisting of five key strategies: discovery and access, data into information, partnerships, staff development and profile raising.

A training programme model for creativity has been developed by Page and Webb (2015). This programme of developmental workshops is intended to last six days in total − one day per week for three weeks followed by a short reflection period, then a further one day per week for another three weeks. The first three training days are given over to understanding about 'soft' and 'creative' problem solving and learning how to use a range of soft and creative tools and techniques. The following three days are facilitated workshops to use techniques learned with 'live' problems the breakdown of topics covered in each session are covered below:

- Session one: Understanding why traditional problem solving techniques often fail. Understanding the difference between hard and soft problems. Recognising the need for 'soft' and creative thinking. Learning to recognise problems that require soft and/or creative thinking. Introduction to 'wicked' problems. Learning how to use such a technique followed by application of this in one or more exercises
- Session two: Importance of individual perceptions and 'world views'. Innovation and thinking differently. The role of metaphors and 'holons' in creative thinking and problem solving. Learning how to use a technique followed by application of this in one or more exercises
- Session three: The role of organisational culture and 'tribes'. Developing a framework for characterising 'wicked problems' and problem solving technique selection. Learning how to use a technique followed by application of this in one or more exercises
- Session four, five and six: Facilitated, structured workshop utilising one or more techniques learned to date to tackle a live 'wicked' problem in the organisation (as identified by course delegates)

Finally, in Session Six, a closing exercise based on sector scenarios is undertaken, followed by delegate reflection and feedback to the facilitators on the perceived value of the programme of learning to themselves and the organisation.

DEVELOPING APPROPRIATE ORGANISATIONAL STRUCTURES

Invariably the work of the management theorist Henry Mitzenberg is introduced when organisational structures are considered. He proposed that a new structure will emerge from the interaction between the organisation's strategy, the external environment and the existing structure. Mindtools. com (n.d.) has used Mintzberg's theories to give an overview of organisational understanding. There are five different organisational types identified by Mintzberg with three being specifically types of organisation relevant to discussions around libraries and innovation: entrepreneurial, machine and innovation.

- Entrepreneurial organisation: has a simple, flat structure with few senior leaders. Informality and a lack of standardised systems allow the organisation to be flexible.
- Machine: work has many routines and procedures with much standardisation. There is a tight vertical structure allowing central control from the top. There is much specialisation which can result in different sections being isolated from each other. Machine organisations work well when precise tasks and services are needed.
- Innovative: this structure works well when there is a need to innovate and be creative in a fast and responsive manner. Even light touch aspects of centralisations, bureaucracy and complex structure can be counterproductive.

This pressure to have library structures that support creativity were voiced over 20 years ago with the post hierarchical library as a 'flattened organization, unlimited by the traditional hierarchy, anti-bureaucratic, with empowered cross-functional teams, fewer people, constant learning, and redefined and re-engineered work process focussed on customer service' (Sweeney, 1994 p. 62). The rationale for this is that the stable external environment leads to highly controlled mechanistic structure but this machine structure does not cope well with the turbulent world we currently live in now. The above discussions point to the library leader trying to have the machine structure is still needed to support services such as the substantial library transactions whilst at the same time having the entrepreneurial and innovative structures more relevant in 2015. A good example of an entrepreneurial/innovative structure is shown in the Times 100 Business Case Study of Capco (Times 100 Business Case studies, 2015) where teamwork is central.

One of the conclusions from a recent literature review on enhancing organisational creativity (Morris, n.d., p. 12) is that employees will be 'most creative when the organisational structure and systems support people to feel motivated primarily by the interest, satisfaction and challenge of the work itself'. There is an obvious challenge when libraries have previously recruited some staff who find a machine organisational structure comfortable, re-assuring and stable. These staff are unlikely to have the attributes and approach that the entrepreneurial and innovative libraries need. As a result of the hierarchical structure, there is also the challenge of library middle managers who see that flexible structures challenge their role and purpose. Within this context of complexity and concern, the library leader has to identify a path moving away from the rigid hierarchies to the structures where creativity can flourish. The following actions can make significant progress in making the library organisational structure more likely to generate innovative ideas and services:

- Establish working groups: people from different part of an organisation are brought together for a specific fixed term purpose. The aim of the library working party is to enable staff to be stimulated by each other's ideas. People should be chosen for working groups who are from different teams, from different backgrounds and who have different skills. Working groups have to be facilitated by knowledgeable people who care about the chosen focus for the working group and who know how innovation is nurtured.
- Develop more project work: collaborative project work can be used as a process for generating innovation. The processes behind successful project working can be managed and focussed specifically to encourage creative ideas and plans. Indeed, coming with creative ideas can be seen as a major driver for a project's existence. The projects have to be challenging enough to stretch library staff but also not too challenging that they cannot make any contributions. Their intrinsic motivation is likely to grow if they feel the library project has allowed them to develop and further refine their skills and ideas.

The overall aim of these actions is to move towards collaborative practice where library staff are continually working together, developing ideas together and providing each other with help. The process itself is useful as some of the competitive attitudes and silo mentalities still present in libraries will be questioned. The purposes of these strategies are to create a library atmosphere in which creativity and innovation can thrive. The Times 100 Business Case studies (2015) has shown that these groups (both short term and long term) need to share a common purpose. There has to be mutual respect and support with everybody having a commitment to achieving the targets. Each group/team member has to understand both their roles and the roles of colleagues. Each group has to communicate openly and be good at both generating and sharing ideas.

Similar views have been provided by Rowley (2011) who has used work by West to show what factors determine the level of group innovation. Innovative teams will deliver if the tasks are complete, have varied demands, provide opportunities for social interaction and learning and be significant group knowledge diversity and skills. Much is to be gained if tasks explore new areas to discover new approaches and link ideas from many sources. Tasks should bring together people from different backgrounds, experiences and personalities to see issues from lots of different angles. Tidd and Bessant (2013) see *fit* as being one of the key challenges in leading innovation and they highlight the challenges posed by structures created for stability. They reinforce what is outlined above by emphasising that innovativeness is more likely when team working, participation in problem solving, flexible cells and flattening hierarchies is achieved.

REWARDING CREATIVITY IN LIBRARIES

The library leader needs to have a thorough insight into the theories around motivation and creativity if they are to successfully reward library staff for being innovative. Indeed, it is possible for a leader to set up a reward strategy with the best intentions which actually has the adverse effect. Burroughs, Dahl, Moreau, Chattopadhyay, and Gorn (2011) outlines how rewards such as bonuses, one-off payments erode creativity levels in an organisation. These kinds of rewards reduce a person's intrinsic motivation (i.e. where a task or activity is completed for its own sake). If reward is monetary it causes a change in how people engage with the creativity process. They stop being driven by pure interest and instead see creativity as being an end in itself rather than as an opportunity to explore and play.

The American Productivity and Quality Centre (Leavitt, n.d.) found that to drive innovation in an organisation, there needs to be innovative approaches to rewards and recognition. Library leaders have to therefore not seek to reward innovation by paying staff more (even if they have this opportunity in these financially constrained times). Instead they need to be much more aware about how the library employees' intrinsic creativity motivations to create are supported and enhanced. The intention must be to have a deeply engaged library workforce who wants to make real progress. There is very little in the library literature about reward and recognition but these are some ideas from other sectors that can be applied on supporting and developing people's intrinsic motivation (Breen, 2014; Burroughs et al., 2011; Leavitt, n.d.; von Stamm, 2008):

- have creativity awards
- mention creativity achievements in newsletter
- allow staff to choose next role/project
- consistently acknowledge those who contribute ideas, etc.
- ensure success stories are disseminated

- encourage peers to identify where colleagues show strong creativity skills
- make sure that staff have the time and space needed to be creative

When library leaders set up a project, they need to include people not solely on their experience levels but also in terms of their interests. Judgements are needed to strike the right creativity balance in project membership. People are most creative when they care about their work and they are being stretched in terms of skills levels. If the creativity task is below their skills levels, they will become bored whereas if they are being expected to show skills beyond their abilities, they will experience frustration.

The library leader has to set up a work environment where creativity is supported valued and recognised. It is hoped that this will be reward enough for creativity to thrive in a library. It is also not appropriate to expect the library leader to isolate the various angles they take to support a creative workforce. The approaches described in this chapter are all inter-related and inform each other. This is demonstrated in research completed by Burroughs et al. (2011) into creativity in 20 private firms. It was found that that intrinsic motivation of employees was enhanced if there was a dedicated creative training programme.

CONCLUSION

Hopefully this chapter will demonstrate that one of the most important roles that the library leader can take is to create an environment where creativity and innovation flourish. Tidd and Bessant (2013) highlight work that shows 15% of difference in performance of organisations is directly influenced by the leader. An additional 35% is contributed through the choice of strategy. The library leader cannot only supply a passive, supportive role to encourage innovation in their library. There is a complex relationship between the library leader and the levels of innovation in the library. These have been effectively captured in a review of 27 empirical studies on this relationship (Denti & Hemlin, 2012). For the teams showing high levels of innovation, the role is to show support and non-controlling actions to include them in decision making. A different approach is needed where innovation is not present where the leader needs to actively promote innovative and creative behaviour. The leader can make innovation flourish by encouraging team reflection processes such as debates, open communication and divergent thinking. Libraries across the world are investing time and effort into impact assessment and effectiveness when services are evaluated for the difference they make. The library leader has to extend this commitment to evaluation to show levels of innovation in the library workforce. The intention of this chapter has been to demonstrate the centrality of the library leader in their library's innovation capabilities. There is no expectation that it will be easy or straightforward but it cannot be argued that it is not crucial.

REFERENCES

Association of Research Libraries. (2016). *ARL leadership fellows program, ARL*. Retrieved from http://www.arl.org/leadership-recruitment/leadership-development/arl-leadership-fellows-program#.VzRARsv2aM8

Aurora Foundation. (2016). *What is the Aurora Foundation?* Retrieved from http://aurorafoundation.org.au/

Bergart, M. J. (2010). Innovation: The language of learning libraries. *Reference Services Review, 38*(4), 606−620. doi:10.1108/009073210110907

Breen, J. (2014). *The 6 myths of creativity*. Retrieved from http://www.fastcompany.com/51559/6-myths-creativity

Brundy, C. (2015). Academic libraries and innovation: A literature review. *Library Innovation, 6*(1), 22−39. doi:10.1108/01435121211279858

Burroughs, J. E., Dahl, D. W., Moreau, C. P., Chattopadhyay, A., & Gorn, G. J. (2011). Facilitating and rewarding creativity during new product development. *Journal of Marketing, 70*(1), 53−67.

Castiglione, J. (2008). Facilitating employee creativity in the library environment. *Library Management, 29*(3), 159−172. doi:10.1108/01435120810855296

Christensen, C. M. (1997). *The Innovator's dilemma: When new technologies cause great firms to fail*. Boston, MA: Harvard Business School Press.

CILIP. (2016). *CILIP leadership programme, CILIP*. Retrieved from http://www.cilip.org.uk/cilip/about/projects-reviews/cilip-leadership-programme

Denti, L., & Hemlin, S. (2012). Leadership and innovation in organizations: A systematic review of factors that mediate or moderate the relationship. *International Journal of Innovation Management, 16*(3). doi:10.1142/S1363919612400075

Germano, M. A. (2011). Library leadership that creates and sustains innovation. *Library Leadership and Management, 25*(3), 1−14. Retrieved from https://journals.tdl.org/llm/index.php/llm/article/viewFile/2085/2958

Gifford, A. (2014). Deconstructing for change: Innovation for smaller libraries. *The Australian Library Journal, 63*(4), 313−319. doi:10.1080/00049670.2014.956390

Goulding, A., & Walton, G. (2014). Management and leadership innovations. In A. Woodsworth & W. D. Penniman (Eds.), *Advances in librarianship* (pp. 37−82). Bingley, UK: Emerald Group Publishing Limited.

Govindarajan, V. (2011). Innovation's nine critical success factors. *Harvard Business Review*. Retrieved from https://hbr.org/2011/07/innovations-9-critical-success/

IFLA. (2016). *IFLA international leaders programme: 2016 Call for applications*. Retrieved from http://www.ifla.org/leaders

Ipsos MORI and Shared Intelligence. (n.d.). *Envisioning the library of the future: Phase 1: a review of innovations in library services.* Arts Council England. Retrieved from https://www.ipsos-mori.com/researchpublications/publications/1563/Envisioning-the-library-of-the-future.aspx

Jantz, R. C. (2012a). A framework for studying organizational innovation in research libraries. *College and Research Libraries, 73*(6), 525–541.

Jantz, R. C. (2012b). Innovation in academic libraries: An analysis of university librarians' perspectives. *Library and Information Science Research, 34,* 3–12. doi:10.1016/j.lisr.2011.07.008

Kay, J. (2011). *Obliquity: Why our goals are best achieved indirectly.* London: Profile Books.

Leavitt, P. (n.d.). *Rewarding innovation.* American Productivity and Quality Center. Retrieved from http://www.providersedge.com/docs/km_articles/rewarding_innovation.pdf

Leonard, E., & Clementson, B. (2012). Business librarians and entrepreneurship: Innovation trends and characteristics. *New Review of Information Networking, 17*(1), 1–211. doi:10.1080/13614576.2012.671715

Leong, J., & Anderson, J. L. C. (2012). Fostering innovation through cultural change. *Library Management, 33*(8–9), 490–497. doi:10.1108/01435121211279858

Lewis, D. W. (2004). The Innovator's dilemma: Disruptive change and academic libraries. *Library Administration & Management, 18*(2), 68–74.

MacDonald, K. I., & vanDuinkerken, W. (2015). Libraries surviving as entrepreneurial organizations: A creative destruction perspective. *New Library World, 116*(7–8), 406–419. doi:10.1108/NLW-01-2015-0005

Mindtools.com (n.d.). Mintzberg's organisational configurations. *Mind Tools.* Retrieved from https://www.mindtools.com/pages/article/newSTR_54.htm

Morris, W. (n.d.). *Enhancing organisational culture: A literature review.* Futuredge Ltd. Retrieved from http://www.future-edge.co.nz/Files/Organisational.pdf

Page, S., & Webb, P. (2015). *Creative thinking for managers – Developmental workshops, training materials, Page & Webb creative management consultants.*

Rowley, J. (2011). Should your library have an innovation strategy? *Library Management, 32*(4/5), 251–265. doi:10.1108/01435121111132266

Sweeney, R. T. (1994). Leadership in the post-hierarchical library. *Library Trends, 43*(1), 62–94. Retrieved from https://www.ideals.illinois.edu/bitstream/handle/2142/7941/librarytrendsv43i1f_opt.pdf?sequence=1

Tidd, J., & Bessant, J. (2013). *Managing innovation: Integrating technological, market and organizational change* (5th ed.). Chichester: Wiley.

Times 100 Business Case studies. (2015). *Organisational structure and teamwork – Capco.* Retrieved from http://www.google.co.uk/url?sa=t&rct=j&q=&esrc=s&source=web&cd=1&ved=0CCMQFjAAahUKEwipufP2qo3JAhXGbxQKHSqrAU8&url=http%3A%2F%2Fdownload.businesscasestudies.co.uk%2Fretrieve_capco_18_Y2FwY28vdGVhY2hlcnMvMTgvbGVzc29uLXJlc291cmNlLW9yZ2FuaXNhdGlvbmFsLXN0cnVjdHVyZSBhbmQtdGVhbXdvcmsuCGRmIHw%3D&usg=AFQjCNGraMJtbRDhwnofiJvjcwru-CUCHA

von Stamm, B. (2008). *Managing innovation, design and creativity* (2nd ed.). London, UK: Wiley.

Walton, G. (2008). Theory, research and practice in library management 4: Creativity. *Library Management, 29*(1–2), 125–131. doi:10.1108/01435120810844702

Webb, P., & Page, S. (2015). *Understanding the need for creativity.* Unpublished Working Paper. Page & Webb Creative Management Consultants.

NO DUST IN THE STACKS: CREATING A CUSTOMIZED LOCAL SERIALS COLLECTION ON THE FLY

Derek Marshall, Laurel Sammonds Crawford and Karen Harker

ABSTRACT

Purpose — *The authors present analysis of journal evaluations in creating a customized serials collection specific to veterinary medicine. Readers may apply techniques used for the veterinary medicine library to their own subject specific collections.*

Methodology/approach — *A review of research in journal evaluations and collection assessment was conducted with emphasis on veterinary medicine. This chapter provides a detailed critique of research on journal evaluations for academic libraries as well as the authors' customized approach in creating a subject specific core journal list for a veterinary medicine library.*

Findings — *By utilizing the current research in evaluating library journal collections, librarians can customize their own approach to create core*

Innovation in Libraries and Information Services
Advances in Library Administration and Organization, Volume 35, 277–288
Copyright © 2017 by Emerald Group Publishing Limited
All rights of reproduction in any form reserved
ISSN: 0732-0671/doi:10.1108/S0732-067120160000035019

journal lists specific to the academic departments they serve, allowing for a more effective serials collection.

Originality/value — *Collection assessment and development differs according to user groups based on local needs. Librarians can develop collection development plans specific to their subject areas by using national standards along with local qualitative and quantitative data.*

Keywords: Academic libraries; collection assessment; collection development; electronic journals; journal evaluations; veterinary medicine libraries

INTRODUCTION

Core journal lists are useful tools for the librarian making collection development decisions. However, collection development based on the information needs of the user population not only enhances the library's current collection but also informs decisions during times of budget changes. Librarians have created core lists of serials across the academic curriculum for guidance in selection, retention, and collection assessment (Ugaz, 2011). Members of the Veterinary Medical Libraries Section (VMLS) of the Medical Library Association (MLA) developed a 'Basic List of Veterinary Medical Serials' to assist librarians in building veterinary medicine collections. This list has been a valuable collection management tool for veterinary medicine librarians (Ugaz, Boyd, Croft, Carrigan, & Anderson, 2010).

Although this list is comprehensive and inclusive to all disciplines within veterinary medicine, it may not reflect the nuances of local needs. Consequently, Mississippi State University's College of Veterinary Medicine (MSU-CVM) Library has utilized this list in creating a *customized* core list specific to the local curriculum and research profile at Mississippi State University. For example, the 'Basic List of Veterinary Medical Serials' recommends two lab animal medicine titles in the top 100, but MSU-CVM does not subscribe because none of its researchers are currently studying this sub-set of veterinary medicine. The MSU-CVM Library added several criteria of local importance to those established in the 'Basic List of Veterinary Medical Serials,' and included non-subscribed titles in the analysis, and now applies the modified standards to obtain a better sense of which subscriptions are needed as well as which resources are lacking from the collection.

The authors here describe a method for creating a customized core journal list for a specialized or small academic library collection. Developing a local ranking system based on qualitative and quantitative evidence can be useful for libraries serving a newly created program or evaluating an already established one. Ranking and weighing local needs alongside external measures like standard lists and peer comparisons are important components in a serials collection-evaluation plan. This method, which has been used to evaluate a niche academic branch collection, is ideally suited to solo librarians or others who have little time and few resources. By using this method to make logical collection development decisions through diligent application of gathered evidence, librarians can communicate the reasoning behind collection development decisions to stakeholders, and determine future directions for collection development.

INSTITUTIONAL SETTING

The MSU-CVM Library is a branch library of MSU Libraries that supports the educational programs, research, and the Animal Health Center clinics at the College of Veterinary Medicine, located in Starkville, MS, as well as several diagnostic labs throughout the state.

MSU-CVM offers the Doctor of Veterinary Medicine degree (DVM) as well as graduate programs for Master's or PhD degrees in selected areas of specialization. The college also offers a program in Veterinary Medical Technology. Supporting these academic programs, the MSU-CVM Library provides various services, including collections, technology, and facilities for the academic community and for practicing veterinarians in the state of Mississippi. Recently, the MSU-CVM Library has adopted an electronic-preferred policy in collection development to better support not only onsite researchers, but also researchers offsite at the various diagnostic labs and students entering externships throughout the United States and internationally. MSU-CVM is the only veterinary school, and one of a handful of medical libraries, in the state.

The physical library contains bound volumes of current and previously subscribed journals to supplement the materials available online. These print volumes fill a void caused by the lack of online backfiles not yet purchased by the library. Through consortia partnerships and licensing agreements, however, many currently subscribed journals include coverage over the previous 20 years.

WHY CREATE A CORE LIST?

The Standards Committee of VMLS sets forth recommendations that all academic veterinary medical libraries should follow. The first standard states, 'the library's collection supports the educational, clinical, and research programs of the veterinary medical institution' (Murphy, Bedard, Crawley-Law, Fagen, & Jette, 2005). In order to properly support the educational programs of MSU-CVM, and in response to an overwhelming number of faculty requests, the library has undertaken an analysis of journals to ensure that research and curriculum needs are met.

'The bulk of cited literature in any discipline is published in a core number of journals' (Murphy, 2008). However, this core set of journals may not include or appropriately emphasize those journal titles in specific subdisciplines within an academic department. Hence, a locally customized core list specific to a certain discipline, in our case veterinary medicine, is crucial to meeting the needs of the academic unit. Through evaluation of the library's collection as well as the curriculum and research of the institution, the library's journal collection will more closely support the needs of the patrons rather than if the standard veterinary core list of journals were purchased.

Simply put, an evaluated collection is a better-utilized collection. 'Librarians can build their veterinary science collections based on overall rank or by rank within subject category to best match the research and educational needs of their local institutions' (Ugaz et al., 2010). Evaluating a collection to create a locally ranked core list of serials not only enhances collection development decisions, but it also improves the effectiveness of the library's collection. Since the largest percentage of libraries' budgets are spent on journals, evaluation of the impact of journals is critical. In monitoring their usage, analysis of journals determines if funds are utilized in the best possible way (Tucker, 2013). In the case of budget cuts, or static budgets in a world of increasing costs, a locally defined evaluation will give librarians a proactive approach to collection development. Such an evaluation means that less effective journals can be weeded from the collection during renewal time. A local core list will determine which journals are crucial to the collection and the research produced by the academic department, thus avoiding an arbitrary cancellation decision.

Conversely, an evaluation informed by a local core list can track requested titles, allowing for quick decisions on how to spend any additional funds that might become available. This type of evaluation will enable librarians to make a thorough contextual assessment of requested materials before new purchases are made by considering immediate, substantiated information about journals to which the library should subscribe. It is often cost prohibitive to purchase subscriptions to every journal requested by faculty or researchers. A local core list will support decisions on those requests with data compiled during the evaluation process. When librarians work closely with faculty and ask for their input into the decision-making process, faculty have a larger investment in the collection and a better understanding of how librarians manage collection development. The results of analysis can also form the basis for enhanced communication with faculty by allowing for clear, evidence-based reasoning. Once all of the evaluative information is consolidated, the criteria and results can also be compiled into a collection development plan for future use.

EVALUATION CRITERIA

Many criteria used in other analyses of core journal lists were used in creating the customized list for the MSU-CVM Library. 'Librarians facing a collection-evaluation exercise may select from a variety of techniques described in the voluminous collection development literature. It is important to select both quantitative and qualitative techniques to avoid skewing the results in favor of one or more methods' (Crawley-Low, 2002). As noted above, the authors found it very useful not only to evaluate titles to which the library was currently subscribed, but also unsubscribed titles relevant to the subject area for future consideration.

In compiling the customized local serial core list for MSU-CVM, the authors decided to use the following criteria in evaluating each title:

- Quality
- Relevance
- Subjective faculty input
- Usefulness
- Cost

Librarians evaluating their own collections can apply other criteria, as they deem appropriate.

Quality

In evaluating the quality of a journal, librarians can build upon research already conducted by the experts in the specific discipline. In the case of veterinary medicine, the American Veterinary Medical Association does not have a prescribed list of titles to which each veterinary medicine library should subscribe. However, Veterinary Medicine Librarians are fortunate to have a core list of veterinary medicine titles already published in the 'Basic List of Veterinary Medical Serials.' The methods in compiling this list included expert input, usage, abstracting and indexing coverage, overlapping holdings from veterinary medicine libraries, as well as other criteria (Ugaz et al., 2010). Since this list is inclusive to all disciplines within veterinary medicine, it has been the most beneficial list in creating a customised local collection. The committee creating this 'Basic List' used their own criteria to reach their decisions, which included 'indexing coverage, scholarly ranking from two sources, inclusion on a recommended reading list issued by a veterinary specialty board, and librarian rating' (Ugaz et al., 2010). Many accrediting bodies for other academic departments have their own core lists of journals as well. Other organizations, such as the American Chemical Society, have lists for their associated disciplines of which librarians should be aware; there are also recommended reading lists for board or licensing exams in other areas that may suggest certain journal titles with which students should be familiar.

Relevance

The relevance of a journal is determined by whether the journal fits into the scope of the specific collection. This may be done by the expert librarian, based on the library's collection development policy or simply knowledge of the scope of a given collection. Relevance may also be determined by conducting a more detailed citation analysis − investigating the titles cited by faculty and/or the titles in which they have published. Citation analysis, while not without limitations, 'does provide some indication of the literature that faculty consults for research in their field' (Murphy, 2008). Cory Tucker, in his discussion of citation analysis for collection management, stated 'the primary goals for analyzing literature citations of faculty publications' include determining journals in which faculty publish and identifying the most frequently cited journals (2013). By identifying these journals, librarians can evaluate the relevance of the library's serial collection and determine if the journals cited by faculty are locally owned. Since staff time was limited, the MSU-CVM librarians collected data only on faculty publications, not citations. The librarians also scored each journal for applicability to the collection scope.

Subjective Faculty Input

In determining local needs, librarians should keep track of those titles requested by faculty, students, researchers, and clinicians, and should consider the specific research areas covered by academic departments. For example, MSU-CVM has several researchers focusing on aquaculture, specifically pertaining to the locally important catfish industry, an area of study that may not be as relevant at other institutions. The MSU-CVM Library must contain materials that support this research and be responsive to requests for titles in this area.

Also, in previous years, a journal evaluation project was undertaken by librarians at MSU for the entire campus. Faculty were asked to rate all journals with current subscriptions, using a ranking of A, B, C, or D, with A assigned to the most important journals and D the least. While this information was somewhat outdated by the time the authors compiled the customized local list, these rankings were considered with this caveat. Other libraries may have more up-to-date rankings or survey results conducted at their Universities that would be more relevant in determining local needs.

Usefulness

Electronic use data is the simplest source of information in determining the usefulness of a particular journal. By compiling information on the number of downloads a particular journal has seen or the number of searches conducted within a database, librarians can easily determine the local importance of any given journal. However, in smaller departments with fewer students or researchers, this information is not always reliable. Some journals may see fewer downloads compared to journals from other disciplines, although they still may be the most important journals in their particular field. For those journals without an online component, circulation statistics and in-house use may be helpful in determining their relevance, if statistics are kept accurately and consistently. For journal titles to which the library does not subscribe, interlibrary loan statistics can show which journals are the most requested. If the librarian has time, 'ILL requests can be broken down by material type-such as title, subject, age, format, and language of request-and requestor characteristic-such as status of requestor, degree program, and college or departmental affiliation' (Crawley-Low, 2002). Patron driven acquisition (PDA) is another tool available to determine local needs;

however, programs such as Get-It-Now do not build the collection so much as they provide quick, single-access for an individual patron. Since the collection development mission of MSU-CVM is to build a comprehensive, just-in-case collection for immediate, total access to important literature, PDA programs are not currently utilized.

Cost

The cost of a particular journal is often the most relevant information. The literature is filled with information on analyzing journal costs, package deals, and consortia pricing. However, simply gathering the raw cost of journals is a valuable tool in compiling a list for a locally customized collection. Comparing the price of a journal with the number of downloads it has seen is useful in evaluating the journal. 'Rank ordering of journals by cost per use is a technique that highlights a serial's cost effectiveness. Cost-per-use data are available in many libraries because of past serials cancellation projects; the data included subscription costs and circulation data compiled for a specific time period' (Crawley-Low, 2002). The cost of journal subscriptions can also vary dependent upon package deals, individual subscriptions, or journals obtained through society memberships. These varying prices should be considered and included in the evaluation process. In a climate of tight budgets, the cost of an item can be an influential factor in determining its inclusion in a collection.

CREATING THE LIST

To make a detailed list of serials for evaluation, the authors compiled into a spreadsheet journal titles from current and previous subscriptions, from the 'Basic List of Veterinary Medical Serials,' from current recommended reading lists for board exams, faculty requested titles, and MSU-CVM departmental requirements (required/recommending reading lists based on academic departments and coursework). For each title, the authors noted the aforementioned lists in which the title appeared. For each title included in the 'Basic List of Veterinary Medical Serials,' the authors indicated the individual ranking. Again, many of the titles in the compiled list may not have been currently or previously held by the MSU-CVM Library. This working list, however, became a valuable tool in making future collection development decisions. Once the titles were compiled in an Excel spreadsheet, and bibliographic, order, and local holdings information was added, a detailed analysis was conducted using the criteria described above.

Many librarians already compile cost and usage statistics for their collections. When creating the evaluation list, the authors added this information for each journal subscription the library currently held. The authors also recommend gathering usage statistics over a period of several years to have a more comprehensive analysis of usage for these titles. This is important in some disciplines because course rotations may not occur every year, and some journals may see more use in particular years. The authors used COUNTER JR1 use statistics for the previous 6 calendar years and conducted a cost-per-use evaluation for the most recent subscription year. Librarians may also want to evaluate the cost-per-use over several years for a more comprehensive analysis of data. However, it may be more difficult to track previous years' costs for some journals if this information has not been retained. For the purposes of the MSU-CVM Library, the most recent year was sufficient.

For each title (row) in the spreadsheet, the following criteria were noted in a series of columns, as applicable/available: ranking on the 'Basic List of Veterinary Medical Serials'; inclusion on one or more of the nine specialty board reading lists; whether and how many MSU-CVM-affiliated articles were published in the title; faculty evaluation project average rank; and Journal Citation Reports Impact Factor. Interlibrary loan borrowing statistics were recorded for titles not held by the MSU-CVM Library. Ranks were recorded if applicable, and presence on boards lists were totaled so as to favor those titles on a greater number of lists.

CRUNCHING THE NUMBERS

Elaborate software or programming is not required to compile and analyze the data in creating a customized local serial collection. Using a spreadsheet to compile the data in a logical fashion is an easy way to evaluate the evidence. If desired, weights can be assigned to each criterion by using a whole-number multiplier to enhance the effect of one or more criteria. For MSU-CVM's evaluation, no weights were added to any criteria, effectively making them all equal in importance.

In its first iteration, the MSU-CVM Library's evaluation list was used in renewal decision-making simply by using Excel filters and sorting. For example, the top 50 most-used items were noted and renewed for the next subscription cycle. Then, the authors looked at the titles with the most efficient cost-per-use, and renewed those titles as well. This is a valid, if time-consuming, method to utilize the data compiled.

In the list's next iteration, the authors used built-in Excel functions to display a percentile rank for each criterion and to combine those percentile ranks into an overall composite score. The percentile rank effectively normalizes all of the criteria, making it easier to see at a glance both comparative and summary ranks for each title.

For each criterion, the authors inserted an adjacent column and used the PERCENTRANK.INC function to rank each title among its peers based on that criterion alone. Excel's conditional formatting comes in handy to color-code the cells to indicate the ranks at a glance. Then, the authors used the AVERAGE function to create a composite score for each item based on the percent ranks for all criteria. Lastly, the authors sorted by composite score to create the ranked list.

COMPARING LOCAL RANKING TO NATIONAL "CORE" RANKING

MSU-CVM focuses mainly on small and large animal medicine, and supports a research program that spans the breadth of biological sciences. MSU-CVM emphasizes agricultural and fish medicine, but does not stress avian, primate, or lab animal medicine like some other veterinary schools. It also has a growing veterinary technician program. Would local information re-shuffle the accepted Core title ranking based on the influence of local objective and subjective criteria, or would the original Core List have sufficed for our decision-making?

Fig. 1 shows only the titles ranked in the Core List of Veterinary Serials, comparing the Core List ranking to the relative local ranking. The horizontal axis shows the rank of journals appearing on the 'Basic List of Veterinary Medical Serials' while the vertical axis shows their relative local ranking. A lower rank position indicates increasing importance, so the closer to zero in the chart above, the more important the journal (1 = most important). The top journals, such as the Journal of the American Veterinary Medical Association, are not in dispute and rank highly on both lists (lower left corner with a ranking of 1). Moving away from those indisputable leaders (toward the upper right), the relative

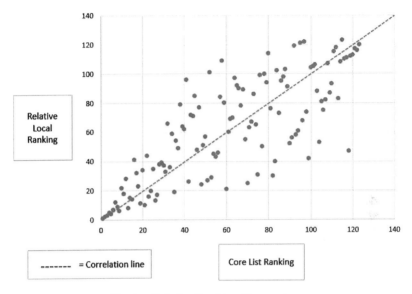

Fig. 1. Relative Ranking Comparison.

importance on a local level becomes debatable. Local data boosted the ranking of some less-important titles related to MSU-CVM's specific programs, including *Veterinary Technician, British Poultry Science*, and *Fish and Shellfish Immunology*. Other, arguably important journals were reduced in rank for no discernible reason: *Revue Scientifique et Technique* and the *Journal of the South African Veterinary Association*. In our test case, 17% of titles moved at least 30 places up or down from their original place in the Core List ranking. This indicated that local criteria influenced the rankings enough to make the list trustworthy and a valid decision-making tool. Using the original Core List would have given us a generic collection not well-tailored to local needs.

CONCLUSION

Taking the time to develop a local ranked core list not only enhances a library's ability to make wise collection development decisions, but also enhances its ability to support decisions with stakeholders and to serve them more effectively. This method uses qualitative and quantitative data to build a more appropriate collection customized to a specific patron population.

The data generated by this process can be quite useful. The analysis itself can form a basis for communication with stakeholders about information needs, usage, and budgetary constraints. Once information is consolidated, the criteria used to evaluate the collection can be compiled into a collection development plan for future use. In the case of static or reduced budgets, evaluation informed by a local core list is a proactive approach to collection development. At MSU-CVM, the authors were able to use this analysis to successfully advocate for a 16% increase in library materials funding. Likewise, this type of analysis can be used to create a 'wish list' in anticipation of an unexpected influx of funding.

Areas for Future Study

The authors anticipate that this method will result in a better-utilized collection, but it will take some time to confirm this hypothesis by analyzing usage data. Additional criteria could be added in future budget cycles, such as analysis of faculty-cited journals and ease of using ILL for a given journal. Further testing of this method on other areas outside of veterinary medicine, particularly non-science areas, is recommended.

REFERENCES

Crawley-Low, J. (2002). Collection analysis techniques used to evaluate graduate-level toxicology collection. *Journal of the Medical Library Association, 90*(3), 310–316.

Murphy, S. (2008). The effects of portfolio purchasing on scientific subject collections. *College & Research Libraries, 69*(4), 332–340.

Murphy, S., Bedard, M., Crawley-Law, J., Fagen, D., & Jette, J. (2005). Standards for the academic veterinary medical library. *Journal of the Medical Library Association, 93*(1), 130–132.

Tucker, C. (2013). Analyzing faculty citations for effective collection management decisions. *Library Collections, Acquisitions, & Technical Services, 37*, 19–33.

Ugaz, A. (2011). Drilling deeper into the core: An analysis of journal evaluation methodologies used to create the 'Basic List of Veterinary Medical Serials' third edition. *Journal of the Medical Library Association, 99*(2), 145–152.

Ugaz, A., Boyd, T., Croft, V., Carrigan, E., & Anderson, K. (2010). Basic list of veterinary medical serials, third edition: Using a decision matrix to update the core list of veterinary journals. *Journal of the Medical Library Association, 98*(4), 282–292.

NEW APPROACHES TO DIGITAL STRATEGY IN THE 21ST CENTURY

Chris Batt

ABSTRACT

Purpose — *To investigate how the United Kingdom's public museums, libraries and archives (collecting institutions) might, in the future, take strategic advantage of the dramatic changes in individual and social behaviours and expectations driven by the socio-technical determinism of the Internet since 2000.*

Methodology/approach — *The chapter summarises the evidence and outcomes of PhD research completed in 2015 that used the tools of hermeneutic phenomenology and systems theory to examine the current state of digital strategy within the United Kingdom's collecting institutions and to compare this with the Internet's fundamental drivers of change and innovation. The research sought not to predict the future, but to define the key opportunities and challenges facing collecting institutions in face of sustained socio-technical change to maintain strategic fit, delivering maximum value in the digital space.*

Findings — *The outcomes of the research demonstrated that libraries, like museums and archives, are ill-prepared to face continued socio-technical determinism. The key drivers of the Internet are single channel*

Innovation in Libraries and Information Services
Advances in Library Administration and Organization, Volume 35, 289–311
Copyright © 2017 by Emerald Group Publishing Limited
All rights of reproduction in any form reserved
ISSN: 0732-0671/doi:10.1108/S0732-067120160000035020

convergence, rapid innovation, instant two-way communication driving social interaction and dramatic change in the relationship between the supplier and the user. Collecting institutions, on the other hand, operate within vertically integrated silos restricting horizontal collaboration that has led to fragmentation of developments and constraints on strategy across and within the various institutional sectors. The major challenges that libraries must consider are summarised.

Originality/value − *The research takes an approach that has never before been attempted, either in scope or depth of analysis. The conclusions may not make comfortable reading for practitioners, but they offer an agenda for new ways of thinking about how public institutions must change to sustain their strategic fit in a digital future.*

Keywords: Collecting institutions; internet; strategic planning; socio-technical determinism; innovation

In the digital world, all of the objects that we have access to via the Web have been imbued with the ability to speak ... This leads to the inescapable conclusion that, in the digital environment, the distinctions between libraries, museums and archives that we take for granted are in fact artificial.

−Martin (2003)

This chapter considers the challenges and opportunities that libraries face in maintaining organisational strategic fit when confronted by the rapid and continuing social and technical change wrought by the Internet. It does not report advances in the organisation of digital strategy within libraries. Indeed, the case will be made that current approaches to the planning and innovation of digital services will restrict future opportunities for libraries to maintain strategic fit in the face of sustained socio-technical change. The chapter's purpose is to shine a searchlight on the state of the use of digital techniques in UK libraries today and to compare it with the key drivers of socio-technical change in Society at large, to propose how libraries might reform their services and structures to develop maximum value to all citizens in the digital space.

BACKGROUND

The chapter presents the evidence and outcomes of PhD research completed in 2015 (Batt, 2015) concerning social and organisational change arising from the socio-technical determinism of the Internet since 2000. *Collecting Institutions in the Network Society's* specific purpose was to investigate how the United Kingdom's public museums, libraries and archives (collecting institutions) might, in the future, take strategic advantage of these dramatic changes in individual and social behaviours and expectations. To maintain strategic fit, all user-facing organisations, public and private, must respond to this rapid and continuing social change. From the evidence of these wide social effects, the research aimed to demonstrate whether current approaches to digital innovation and delivery in collecting institutions would be fit for purpose in the face of continued rapid digital innovation and, if not, what might be the changes necessary to deliver maximum social value. The intention of the research was not to predict some future end state for collecting institutions, rather to establish those aspects of the effects of the Internet in the wider social context that collecting institutions should consider in planning future digital strategy. The research had five separate stages:

Stage 1: Identify a limited number of key Drivers of Internet Change. From analysis of socio-technical change since 2000, identify the fundamental features of the Internet that underpin the socio-technical determinism that has generated rapid and radical change in the lives of individuals and communities.

Stage 2: Examine opportunities and challenges facing collecting institutions in exploiting the long-term potential of the Internet. What are the dominant organisational forms? What is the degree and scope of digital engagement? How prepared are the institutions for sustained socio-technical change? What are the constraints on innovation? What is the extent of strategic collaboration across the collecting institution sector?

Stage 3: Undertake comparative analysis of the evidence. Establish from analysis of Stage 2 the essential opportunities and challenges across all collecting institutions. Synthesise these with the Drivers of Internet Change to produce the high-level opportunities and challenges that collecting institutions will face in the development of online service offers.

Stage 4: Create a conceptual model of how those opportunities might be maximised. Examine what changes would be necessary to the status quo (organisation, collaboration, policy and practices) to enable collecting institutions to take full benefit from the opportunities. Demonstrate the long-term value that would be achieved if the features of the conceptual model could be implemented.

Stage 5: A blueprint for change. Finally, produce a development framework for raising awareness of the research outcomes, proposing an agenda for debating both the opportunities and the challenges identified in the research conclusions.

The evidence presented in the chapter considers the particular situation of UK libraries. However, it is important not to forget that the research addressed the broader context of collecting institutions together, and the overall conclusions of the research, described at the end of the chapter will consider future digital strategic approaches of libraries grounded in the necessity of seeing libraries' approaches as one component in a wider landscape of publicly available digital knowledge assets.

TOWARDS THE NETWORK SOCIETY

> Presence or absence in the network and the dynamics of each network vis-a-vis others are critical sources of dominion and change in our society: a society that, therefore, we may properly call the network society, characterised by the pre-eminence of social morphology over social action. (Castells, 2010)

How far has Castells' prediction of the Network Society, where networks (both the enabling Internet and how it might be used) become the dominant agents of social change? The aim of this stage was to articulate a limited number of drivers of socio-technical innovation and change by analysis of both academic and popular literature from 2000, for subsequent comparison with the purposes, priorities and practices of collecting institutions. Such comparison should provide understanding of the opportunities and challenges compared with the imperatives of the socio-technical determinism of the Internet and digital technologies. There is a rich body of evidence demonstrating the dramatic impact of the Internet since 2000. The Oxford Internet Survey was first published in 2003 and the latest edition presents a picture of United Kingdom trends over a ten-year period. Across what has been a dramatic period of technological innovation the data show consistent increases in the take up of the Internet in all aspects of people's lives. In each edition the Internet reaches further. More people, doing more things. The 2011 edition summed this up simply as:

> The Internet has become an integral part of our lives and our society. (Dutton & Blank, 2011)

While the 2014 Ofcom Communications Review (Ofcom, 2014) reported that the average UK citizen now spends more time using digital technologies than sleeping (8 hours 16 minutes). The analysis was structured around the concept of supply and demand. What changes have taken place in organisations supplying services to society? What opportunities for new business models and the creation of new markets? What challenges have been faced? What has been the impact on commercial risk, on innovation opportunities, on new forms of communication with customers/users? On the demand side, what has been the effect on individual and social behaviours? How has technical innovation influenced broad social trends and expectations? Karpf highlights the dramatic changes that have taken place and suggests that such change is likely to be a continuing phenomenon into the future:

> Consider: in 2002, streaming video was rare, short and choppy. Wireless hotspots were a novelty. Mobile phones were primarily used for (gasp!) phone calls. Commercial GPS applications were still in the early stages of development. Bloggers could be counted by the handful. Social networking sites like Friendster, Myspace and Facebook were still confined to Bay Area networks and technologists' imaginations. A 'tumbler' was a type of drinking glass; a 'tweet' was a type of birdcall. Simply put, the Internet of 2012 is different from the Internet of 2002. What is more, there is little reason to suppose this rapid evolution is finished: the Internet of 2022 will likely be different from the Internet of 2012. (Karpf, 2012)

The review of socio-technical change since 2000 highlighted many examples of tectonic changes in the social fabric, both in supply and demand, ranging from the recorded music industry through online trading and the wide ranging impacts of social networking.

The research mission of enabling strategic comparison between the fundamental drivers of socio-technical change (the digital DNA) and the present operational and strategic engagement of collecting institutions with the Internet and digital technologies called for a very small number of key characteristics that would define *how* and *why* innovation and change take place. The mission was to provide tangible means for practitioners and policymakers to build a bridge between the present and the future. If the digital DNA presents immutable characteristics of all Internet activity they make possible definition of the relationships, structures and operational practices that offer collecting institutions maximum opportunity to develop in the digital space. Analysis of the extensive range of evidence using Grounded Theory (Glaser & Strauss, 1967) to establish dependency relationships produced 36 key themes that could be placed within just two tagged categories:

- Basic features of Internet technology
- Outcome effects arising from the Internet technology

This analysis of the 36 key themes made it possible to identify five basic features of the Internet on which the other 31 key themes depended:

1. Perceptions of time have changed in relation to social behaviours and the speed with which change takes place.
2. Networking has led to the globalisation of the most successful of these services.
3. Frictionless innovation – organisations creating Internet-based consumer offers are able to achieve success without many of the traditional barriers to innovation.
4. The Internet has made possible both the integration of many different channels of communication into one single channel and enabled frictionless two-way communication across that channel.
5. This two-way connectivity has provided opportunities to empower everyone to express themselves, individually or collectively, and thus begin to make more explicit public opinion as well as differing views.

From this list it was possible to derive four Generic Drivers of Internet Change that underpin all aspects of change and innovation (see Table 1).

Table 1. The Four Generic Drivers of Internet Change.

1. The Internet as Digital Common Carrier

- Single channel, simple ubiquitous protocols
- Global network
- Encouraging resource convergence
- Instant two-way communication

2. The Internet Redefines Space and Time

- Every node on the network can be instantly accessible
- Internet time enables fast innovation and rapid social diffusion
- Transmission costs are independent of distance and time
- Instant two-way communication

3. The Internet Possesses Its Own Gravitational Forces

- Successful services grow due to social media and viral marketing
- The big gets bigger
- The gravitational forces affect both supplier and user

4. The Internet Redefines the Relationship between the Supplier and the User

- Low entry barriers mean that the cost of failure is low, encouraging risk taking and experiment
- Success depends on understanding user needs through two-way engagement
- The user can become a contributor to the supply chain

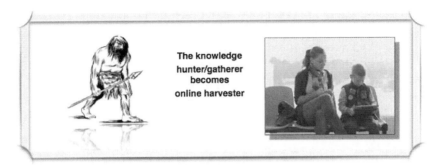

Fig. 1. The Knowledge Revolution.

The evidence from this stage of the research suggests that dramatic social changes have taken place and will continue – a Knowledge Revolution to be compared with the Agrarian Revolution of some 20,000 years ago (Fig. 1).

OPPORTUNITIES AND CHALLENGES ACROSS COLLECTING INSTITUTIONS

The second stage of the research aimed to gain understanding of the present form, components and priorities across collecting institutions that define and direct existing services with two linked purposes. First, from that evidence, to establish common themes and differences of service paradigms across the three institutional types. Second, to demonstrate whether current approaches to digital innovation and delivery in museums, libraries and archives would be fit for purpose in the face of continued rapid digital innovation and, if not, what might be the changes necessary to deliver maximum social value. This stage of the research involved two elements:

1. The examination of the wider public sector within which public collecting institutions operate. This considered the generic organisational structures, policy, power and approaches to innovation to establish whether it might be possible to define a generalised statement – an institutional paradigm – describing the overarching practices and limitations of public service.

2. The application of these generalised concepts of structure, policy and power to collecting institutions to establish the extent to which it might be possible to define a common service paradigm relevant to museums, libraries and archives on which to base a shared strategic future in digital service development and delivery.

The research was based on extensive review of published material ranging from policy documents, academic studies on the nature of public service within 21st century society, strategic studies on collecting institutions, practical case studies of digital service innovation and research studies on the future of digital development in museums, libraries and archives. The analysis produced three outcomes directly relevant to the purpose of the research, summarised in the Tables 2 and 3.

Table 2. Opportunities for Collecting Institutions.

Respected institutions within society

○ Long established with contemporary service practices and processes evolved over more than a hundred years
○ Collecting institutions are deeply embedded within the social fabric
○ Continue to have high social value as trusted and reliable institutions

Rich collections

○ Extensive collections, rich in both scope and depth
○ Traditionally acknowledged as physical collections in fixed locations
○ Collections represent an essential source of memory and understanding with the potential to develop the individual and society in the 21st century

Engagement with learning

○ Learning and education have always been core priorities for collecting institutions
○ Many collecting institutions are components in the organisations and processes of formal education
○ All have the potential to contribute to the promotion and support of informal learning (learning for life)

Digital tools and techniques are widely adopted

○ Extensive use of Web 2.0 tools, techniques of digitisation and digital systems for curation and service management
○ In the digital space the physical differences of collections and their curation needs disappear. They may all be managed and exploited using the same tools and techniques

Table 3. Challenges Facing Collecting Institutions.

The structure of public service

○ *Command and control*: The public sector has a long tradition of policy delivery through vertical integration − organisational silos − as the means of maintaining accountability, command and control

○ *Institutional paradigm*: Across the whole of the public sector, these structures have nurtured an Institutional Paradigm prioritising local management and service delivery over wider horizontal collaboration with organisations beyond the silo (see Table 4)

○ *Physical collections*: Collecting institutions operating within this Institutional Paradigm have had in addition, an important responsibility to curate, preserve, develop and exploit physical collections in fixed locations

○ *Risks of service change*: The joint duties of accountability within the Institutional Paradigm and the need to maintain and exploit physical collections means that significant service changes will have high financial and social costs if they fail

○ *Organisation-friendly innovation*: The consequence is that innovation across collecting institutions is exclusively 'sustaining', grounded in the existing organisational structures, priorities and practices

Fragmentation

○ Over an extended period, the effects on collecting institutions of structural factors has been to create a high level of fragmentation across all museums, libraries and archives where collective strategic collaboration is non-existent

Lack of clarity of purpose

○ An important component of the research was to establish whether museums, libraries and archives present to their users and policymakers a clear and unequivocal statement of their mission. From that evidence to examine whether it might be possible to develop a single mission statement relevant to all collecting institutions in the strategic development of digital services

○ 966 institutional websites and 77 policy documents were analysed and Corpus Linguistic tools used to identify common themes and vocabularies

○ The analysis of institutional websites revealed that across collecting institutions less than 40% had any public statement of mission, and of those that did, many were in policy documents buried deep within the website

Inability to influence national policy

○ The tradition of local service (defined by geography or audience), the hierarchy of vertical integration and the fragmented nature of the three sectors have acted to constrain the ability to exercise collective power at national level to influence and shape digital policy

---

THE INSTITUTIONAL PARADIGM

The outcome of the analysis of the wider public sector produced a model Institutional Paradigm set of common characteristics addressing infrastructure, policy and power. The specific analysis of collecting institutions made evident that the key components of this Institutional Paradigm were equally relevant to the generic activities of public sector museums, libraries and archives, outlined in Table 4.

Command and control through vertical integration has a long tradition in public service. Highly effective when services are clearly differentiated one from another, unsatisfactory when faced with complex service mixes where integration and co-ordination are essential. It is possible to illuminate further this paradigm as a schematic, showing the relationships between the siloed institution as an 'inner world' Organisational Ecosystem sitting within the 'outer world' of wider society (Fig. 2).

This is highly generic schematic attempting to show the organisational setting within which collecting institutions have traditionally operated. The shaded box represents the organisational structure in which the institution sits – local authority, university, or other governing body – with policy sitting partly within that structure and partly in the outer world.

Table 4. The Institutional Paradigm.

Infrastructure

1. *Top/down silos*: Within the vertically integrated structures of public service

2. *Control, not collective action*: While a stable and controlling form of organisation, vertical integration constrains horizontal collaboration

3. *Destinations*: Primarily physical collections and services in places to visit

4. *Fragmentation*: Caused by organisational structures and forms of audiences and collections

5. *Stability*: Neither incremental change nor structural fragmentation seriously hindered service delivery so long as social change was slow, funding levels were maintained and service monopolies uncontested

Policy

6. *Social purpose and practitioner values*: Defined by a long process of incremental evolution

7. *Explicit policy*: Until the end of the 20th century limited to minimal direction for statutory services and some basic standards assessment tools

8. *Tacit policy*: For almost all of collecting institution history incremental evolution sustained a stable, monopolistic service paradigm that provided unchallenged and highly regarded merit good services

Power

9. *Locally*: In the absence of clear national policy direction practitioners may be able to influence priorities and methods within local governance structures

10. *Nationally*: The tradition of local service (defined by geography or audience), the hierarchy of vertical integration and the fragmented nature of the three sectors have acted to constrain the ability to exercise collective power at national level to influence and shape policy

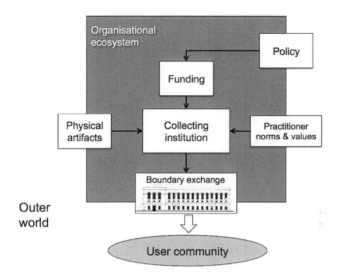

Fig. 2. The Organisational Ecosystem.

Practitioner norms and values will be influenced by education, professional practice and tradition, and the exchange relationship between the institution and the user community delivered through one or more physical locations. The consequence is that there are unconnected Organisational Ecosystems operating independently.

SYNTHESIS: COMPARATIVE ANALYSIS OF EVIDENCE

Stage three of the research included two elements. First, synthesis of the wide range of evidence gathered on collecting institutions – context within the wider public sector, textual analysis of mission statements and policy documents, analysis of strategies and policy documents since 2000 and digital research and innovation since 2000 – to produce a meta-narrative describing the contemporary status and practices of collecting institutions. Second, to compare that meta-narrative with the Four Generic Drivers of Change to produce a limited set of opportunities and challenges for the future.

Creating the Meta-Narrative

This first element contained two parts:

- Using the tools of textual Corpus Linguistics (Kennedy, 2014) and Grounded Theory to draft a mission statement equally relevant to all collecting institutions based on text from a wide range of documentary and other sources;
- Using the evidence of policy documents and digital research to define current collecting institutions' approaches to digital change and innovation.

The Shared Mission Statement
This task aimed to see whether it might be possible to create, from a diverse range of contemporary practitioner and policy evidence to draft a shared mission statement that might provide an enabler of collective advocacy and strategic planning. Two sets of data sources were used to gather relevant text.

1. Documents from professional associations, governmental and other policy bodies across the United Kingdom and a small number of relevant international documents. Some 77 documents were harvested to identify text relating to institutional mission or purpose statement.
2. An audit of the websites of UK public collecting institutions to identify whether institutional mission statements are available to the public and, if so, what is their content. A sample of just under 1,000 websites were searched for purpose or mission statement.

Through the aggregation of synonyms and the tagging of the 26,000 words within a small number of categories a very clear understanding of emergent patterns and differences acquired that could be mapped in word clouds and frequency charts. The two sets of data (mission statements, documentary review) were analysed separately and then mapped together to establish the extent to which institutions used different voices to tell similar stories. Key outcomes of the task were:

- Of the approximately 1,000 websites surveyed, only around 40% of collecting institutions provided a public statement of their mission on the web.
- The analysed text of the mission statements demonstrated that within each of the institutional forms there were shared vocabularies and broadly common priorities.

- Within the documentary review all institutions placed emphasis the presentation of their services for users.
- Broadly the patterns of data of the documentary review and the mission statements were similar.

The result of the textual analysis process was the identification of seven top scoring words (underlined in Table 5) across museums, libraries and archives that might form the basis of a shared mission statement, based on the voices of the institutions.

Approaches to Digital Change and Innovation
The analysis of documents (strategies, policy statements and post 2000 research and innovation) were synthesised using a scorecard enabling comparison across the diverse range of documents. This synthesis aimed to establish the degree to which collecting institutions had changed radically their service propositions since 2000 — how far digital innovation had changed structures, service priorities, practices and practitioner worldviews. On this latter point the research sought to assess the freedom and ability of service managers and their institutions, faced with sustained socio-technical change, to position their services to deliver maximum value to users through digital services.

Table 5. Shared Mission Statement.

The purpose of museums, libraries and archives is to maintain and *promote* collections and *services* to *encourage people's learning* and *enjoyment* and to develop *communities*

The following key issues were identified:

- There were variations in the extent to which strategic proposals were turned into formal plans of action across the four Home Nations (England, Northern Ireland, Scotland, Wales).
- There were differences in strategic priorities proposed for libraries and disparities in the take up of the Internet.
- Lack of collective strategy across different types of libraries in three of the four Home Nations.
- In the research papers, where the Internet was examined, it was to sustain and enhance the Institutional Paradigm: 'industry friendly innovation' (Naughton, 2012).

- Searching the whole 26,000 word database for words relating to innovation, digital technologies and the Internet identified only a very small number of occurrences (0.5% of the 26,000 words searched) of which almost three quarters related to libraries.
- Only one of the nine strategic and policy documents on libraries (Curtis, 2010) demonstrated any reflection on the extent to which socio-technical change might bring radical revision to service paradigms in the future.

Overall, the synthesis demonstrated clearly that, while across the last 14 years there have been both significant increase in focus on policy and strategy for libraries and socio-technical changes, the characteristics of change and innovation in the Institutional Paradigm remain unchanged. The constraints of infrastructure, policy and power, described in Stage 2, continue to be the orthodoxy defining what collecting institutions are able to do. Consequently, innovation is grounded in sustaining current organisational structures. Digital innovation remains an 'add-in' to services rather than an engine to prioritise dynamic change to the relationship between the users and the service offers (see Table 6).

The Organisational Ecosystem schematic (Fig. 2) may be modified to show how the effects of digital technologies in recent years have not changed significantly the organisational practices and structures within which collecting institutions operate (Fig. 3).

This Organisational Ecosystem 2.0 schematic, which is ubiquitous across all collecting institutions, shows that service delivery changes have focused

Table 6.   Change and Innovation within Collecting Institutions.

1. *Risks of strategic change*: the price of making mistakes include both financial and social penalties engendering a culture of risk aversion in bureaucratic structures.
2. *Organisational constraints*: Strategic change is constrained since, traditionally, vertical integration restricts inter-organisational planning and implementation.
3. *Collecting institution specific needs*: maintaining and exploiting physical collections overtime places additional constraints on radical change due to traditional user expectations and sunk investment.
4. *Incremental change*: In consequence generally innovation has been incremental, undertaken within existing organisational structures of power and procedure. It has been 'sustain innovation' to maintain a status quo that does not challenge existing service paradigms.
5. *Limits of incremental change*: The increasing speed of change and complexity of social needs means that an incremental approach to strategy and change may become increasingly disconnected from the needs (behaviours and expectations) of the user. While most change and innovation continues to take place within traditional practices and structures, public sector examples of strategic projects and long-term planning activities were identified.

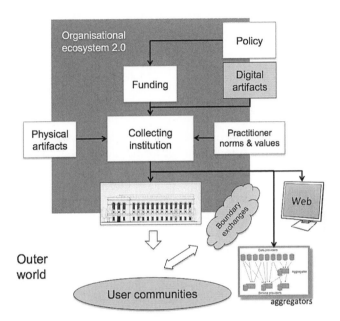

Fig. 3. Organisational Ecosystem 2.0.

on the adoption of digital artefacts (commercial knowledge services, born digital items, institutional digitised collections), and the delivery of collection information, images and documents using the organisation's website or through aggregator services. This 'local-centric' approach sustains, in the digital space, the institutional fragmentation described earlier.

The Dialectic of Change: Opportunities and Challenges for Collecting Institutions in Developing Digital Strategy

This component of Stage 3 of the research compared the features of the Four Generic Drivers of Change (Table 1) with those of the Institutional Paradigm (Tables 4 and 6) to produce a limited number of opportunities that all collecting institutions must face in their future exploitation of digital technologies and the Internet. This involved extensive use of Grounded Theory to establish from the very wide range of factors embedded within the Four Generic Drivers and the Institutional Paradigm a set of all-embracing opportunities and challenges.

The implications of the Generic Drivers of Change point towards collecting institutions presenting to the user as a single digital supply chain rather than the heterodox landscape that is to be observed today – akin to the way that the government portal GOV.UK has changed the relationship between the online user and government services. Before the Internet visiting physical collections was the norm. Today, for the knowledge harvester, travel can be a preference rather than a necessity, while ease of discovery and fulfilment are sovereign. This research does not suggest an either/or choice between place and space in future developments. Its purpose is to demonstrate that the Institutional Paradigm does not fit well with the development of user-friendly online services and to propose a more strategic and collaborative pathway for the delivery of maximum value and long-term sustainability online.

It is helpful to consider differences between the physical and the virtual within the phenomenology of Hegel's dialectic, where the resolution of the tension between thesis and antithesis should lead to aufheben, literally to lift up (Redding, 2014). Through dialogue between thesis and antithesis the intention is not simply to find an acceptable compromise, but to overcome (rise above) the differences by identifying what is significant to retain and what to set aside. The interpretation of aufheben in this context has generated significant academic study since in Hegel's use of it he implies the double meaning of both changing and preserving (Derrida, 1982; Palm, 2009). Wikipedia attempts a simple definition:

> preserving the useful portion of an idea, thing, society, etc., while moving beyond its limitations.

The essential opportunities and challenges of the Institutional Paradigm were compared the Generic Drivers using Grounded Theory to produce the summary in Table 7.

Table 7 does not resolve uncertainties about the future. Rather it provides a series of agenda topics for reflective and collective consideration by practitioners and policymakers, to achieve Aufhebung (lifting up) – what to preserve and what limitations to move beyond. The concept is relevant to this research since moving beyond the present fragmented landscape is an essential feature of a future strategy for collecting institutions' engagement with the digital space. The first step on the journey must be collective ownership by those directly involved with policy and management. Stage 4 describes the development of a conceptual model based on the Dialectic of Change.

Table 7. The Dialectic of Change.

Thesis – what do the Generic Drivers offer for future strategic innovation?	*Antithesis* – what institutional barriers must be overcome?
Potential of the Internet to increase the social value of collecting institutions	The characteristics of the Institutional Paradigm and lack of strategic planning
New relationships between supplier and user; new business models	Importance of the status quo; long-established service patterns
The importance of presence in the digital space to meet emergent behaviours and build wider audiences	The value of the institution as physical destination
Rapid innovation and diffusion	The risks of radical change
Implications of strategic change	Constraints of structure and resources
Digital channel convergence	Organisational fragmentation
Globalisation from gravitational forces	Localism and vertical integration
Need for one voice and one message to promote collective value nationally	Absence of explicit shared mission across collecting institutions

CREATING A CONCEPTUAL MODEL: FROM ORGANISATIONAL ECOSYSTEM TO DIGITAL KNOWLEDGE ECOLOGY

The purpose of this stage of the research was to produce a set of key issues evinced from Stage 3 that would provide stimulus for debate. This called for tangible and practical examples of the strategic challenges implicit within Table 7 and to model the kind of organisational arrangements that might offer the means of achieving maximum public value from the digital disclosure of collections. Moving beyond the present fragmented landscape is an essential task for collecting institutions' engagement with the digital space. Such radical change must begin with collective ownership of the challenges by those directly involved with policy and management.

Three Strategic Challenges

The research identified three Strategic Challenges that call for urgent reflective debate as a precursor to collective advocacy, strategic planning and action:

- *The quest for common purpose*
  - Overcome the fragmentation across collecting institutions;
  - Agree a common vision and finding a single voice for digital engagement;
  - Create a collaborative structure for channel convergence to build critical mass;
  - Work outside (or round) the Institutional Paradigm box.
- *The boundary exchange: from hunter/gatherer to harvester*
  - Place the user at the heart of all service developments and delivery;
  - Build scale, convenience and uniqueness in the face of competition;
  - Have confidence about the differences between the physical object and the virtual object and their utility for users;
  - All service innovation to place formal and/or informal learning at its heart with far greater understanding of the complex nature of the relationship between learning and the individual (e.g. emergent learning theory).
- *The speed of innovation and change*
  - How can collecting institutions manage innovation to ensure strategic fit today and in the future?
  - Balance the long-term value of collections and their presentation with the changing social behaviours and expectations in digital use.

Modelling Future Possibilities

The summary of the present relationship between collecting institutions and the Internet (see section 'Creating the Meta-Narrative') indicated that while there is wide use of digital tools and techniques, the underlying institutional structures, practices and processes remain rooted in the traditional Institutional Paradigm. At various stages in the research a simple ecosystem model was used to demonstrate the relationships within the vertically integrated organisation and with the outside world. Below, this model shows a schematic of the present relationship between collecting institutions and the digital. The conclusion to be drawn from this process of comparison of the Generic Drivers and the Institutional Paradigm is that best value for society will be achieved through radical change in strategic approaches to digital innovation and delivery. If advantage is to be taken from the common form of digital objects, if the benefits of agile innovation are to be achieved and if strong digital advocacy is to be presented at national level then the diversity of the organisational ecosystem

2.0 will require a very different ecological model. The point of departure for such change must be *Do it Once, Do it Right.*

Below a theoretical model – the Digital Knowledge Ecology – shows the degree of change that might be required to gain maximum benefit. It is an example of one possibility and there may be others. However, it is clear that in the long term the present arrangements are likely to lead to the sub-optimisation of opportunity. Rather than several thousand Organisational Ecosystems 2.0, it presents all of those ecosystems and components of a single Digital Knowledge Ecology. While the institutions remain separate for the provision of their physical collections, all of the digital processes are drawn together in a Digital Knowledge Ecosystem that coordinates policy, delivery, advocacy, research and innovation (Fig. 4).

The Digital Knowledge Ecology is not a solution. It is intended as an incentive for practitioners and policymakers to consider a digital future based on the Generic Drivers rather than the Institutional Paradigm.

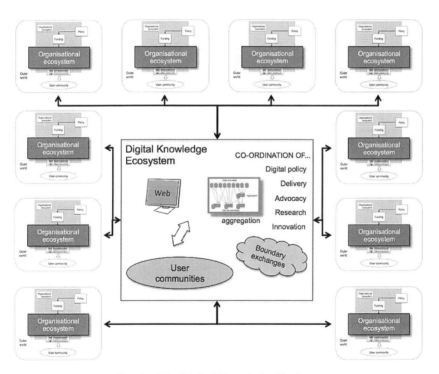

Fig. 4. The Digital Knowledge Ecology.

To face up to tough questions about future digital strategy, demonstrating what long-term success might require, stimulating new ways of thinking about future strategies and possibilities.

The implications of such a change should not be underestimated in terms of practitioner commitment to the task of changing public policy at national and local level to enable this approach. Yet if the implications for future digital strategy defined by the Dialectic of Change, the Digital Knowledge Ecology and the Three Strategic Challenges appear possibilities, then action must surely be debated.

> I envision a digital community where a person can gather the information they need regardless of what kind of institution the resources are owned by. The person will not have to know where he or she is getting the information. Regardless of what role you have, a student, researcher, mother, tourist you should be able to get the right sort of resources you need at the time and in the role you have. (Geser & Pereira, 2004)

Long-Term Potential of the Digital Knowledge Ecology

Despite the fact that the Digital Knowledge Ecology represents a mechanism to encourage a collective debate cross museums, libraries and archives, encouraging practitioners and policymakers to consider the strength of joint action for the digital future and how it might be developed, it is relevant to suggest what might be some of the long-term benefits evidenced by the research outcomes:

The Citizen Offer − The creation of digital collections alters radically the relationship between the object and the user. All digital objects share the same virtual form and are therefore released from the bounds of the physical destination. Digital objects are all electrons. Convergence of digital innovation and disclosure across collecting institutions into single-channel delivery within a shared strategy − the Digital Knowledge Ecology − would provide maximum accessibility to collections regardless of their location and form.

New Relationships with Individuals and with Communities − Resource convergence would enable both specialists and citizens to contribute new learning resources and subject themes linking objects together in new ways, increasing two-way user engagement and creating new knowledge. The results would be a high profile, organic and evolving service enriching learning, education and enjoyment for all.

Agile Innovation − Responding effectively to the rate of development and diffusion of Internet-based services and user expectations requires agility in testing and implementation. A single, co-ordinated approach to digital innovation is the only means of sustaining maximum value to users in the face of external competition and change by reducing risk and enabling co-ordinated diffusion across all institutions.

Power and Influence through Stronger Advocacy − For collecting institutions to have impact on policy at national level they must have a single 'voice' advocating the collective value of collecting institutions' resources to 21st century life and the ways in which a shared digital strategy would be a cost effective way of addressing a wide range of national policy agendas.

Rethinking Professional Practice and Development − Digital innovation and development are already changing the skills needed by practitioners in the creation, curation and delivery to users of digital assets. A single, shared digital strategy could facilitate the skills sharing across different institutional forms and redefine the education and training of those practitioners around disciplines and skills rather than solely by institution type.

Redefining the Concept of Collections for the 21st Century − While in many situations the physical collection may remain a fundamental part of collecting institutions' armoury, the Internet offers a number of significant opportunities to extend the reach of collections and their value to everyone. Digital assets would be accessible to audiences remote from the physical collection while the interactivity enabled by the Internet would allow new connections to be made between objects in different institutions, building new knowledge. Social value would be maximised through single-channel access to the collective worth of all assets bringing greater clarity to the distinctive roles of the physical and of the digital.

A BLUEPRINT FOR CHANGE

The final chapter of *Collecting Institutions in the Network Society* − A Blueprint for Change − makes clear that the radical changes in digital service development and delivery implied by the research outcomes should not be seen as a 'plug and play' solution. Rather they should be seen as the means of making explicit the chasm that exists between how museums, libraries and archives currently approach digital innovation and change and the fundamental features of the Internet defined by the four Generic Drivers of Internet Change. A Blueprint for Change therefore presents suggestions for the first steps in building collective debate, using the evidence and models of the research as a mechanism for encouraging practitioners to think reflectively about the long-term future and how best to maximise the value of their digital assets for all citizens. The Digital Knowledge Ecology offers a means to articulate the organisational transformation that will be required, but the strategic and operational solutions necessary to a Blueprint must be resolved by collective debate and action.

The reader of *Advances in Library Administration and Organization* might reasonably expect to read about advances that have taken place, when this chapter has focused specifically on advances that have not taken place, but should do so within the broader landscape of museums, libraries and archives. However, the present fragmented approach to digital developments seems unlikely to achieve the synergies offered by collective 'collecting institution' action and setting aside the wider messages that Blueprint presents, the research highlighted that the UK libraries sector is, itself, highly fragmented by national boundaries, library types and a wide range of separate parent agencies. So, while collective action across all collecting institutions may take a long time coming, if at all, there is no reason why the libraries sector cannot consider how a common sense of purpose for future digital strategy might be nourished.

Libraries of all types are active in the adoption of digital techniques, albeit to enrich traditional delivery models. They have engaged with the Open Access movement and have a long history of service presentation focused more on individual need than general, static collections of objects or documentary records. There is absolutely every reason, therefore, for librarians to make a commitment to spend time thinking radically about the future.

The outcomes of Collecting Institutions in the Network Society present the means to redefine not just how digital collections are managed, but the worldview of practitioners. The Four Generic Drivers provide the foundation on which to build effective and sustainable digital services placing the user at the heart of all activities. Rising to the challenges that the thesis has identified must empower practitioners and policymakers to reflect far more radically about the broader, long-term future of collecting institutions in the 21st century.

> The dogmas of the quiet past are inadequate to the stormy present. The occasion is piled high with difficulty, and we must rise with the occasion. As our case is new, so we must think anew and act anew. (Lincoln, 1862)

REFERENCES

Batt, C. (2015). *Collecting institutions in the network society*. Retrieved from http://www.digitalfutures.org/Digital_Futures/Collecting_Institutions_in_the_Network_Society.html

Castells, M. (2010). *The rise of the network society: The information age: Economy, society and culture* (Vol. 1, 2nd ed. & rev.). Chichester: Wiley-Blackwell.

Curtis, G. (2010). *Academic libraries of the future: Scenarios beyond 2020*. Guildford: Curtis and Cartwright.

Derrida, J. (1982). *Margins of philosophy*. Chicago, IL: University of Chicago Press.

Dutton, W., & Blank, G. (2011). *Next generation users: The internet in Britain*. Oxford: Oxford Internet Institute.

Geser, G., & Pereira, J. (2004). *The future digital heritage space: An expedition report thematic issue 7*. Salzburg: Digicult Consortium.

Glaser, B. G., & Strauss, A. L. (1967). *The discovery of grounded theory: Strategies for qualitative research*. Piscataway: Aldine Transaction.

Karpf, D. (2012). Social science research methods in internet time. *Information, Communication and Society*, *15*(5), 639–661.

Kennedy, G. (2014). *An introduction to corpus linguistics*. Oxford: Routledge.

Lincoln, A. (1862). Second annual message, December 1, 1862. In G. Peters & J. T. Woolley (Eds.), *The American presidency project* [online]. Retrieved from http://www.presidency.ucsb.edu/ws/?pid=29503

Martin, R. S. (2003). *Cooperation and change: Archives, libraries and museums in the United States*. The Hague: IFLA.

Naughton, J. (2012). *From Gutenberg to Zuckerberg: What you really need to know about the internet*. London: Quercus Publishing.

Ofcom. (2014). *Communications market report*. London: Ofcom.

Palm, R. (2009). *Hegel's concept of sublation: A critical interpretation*. Leuven: Leuven Catholic University.

Redding, P. (2014). Georg Wilhelm Friedrich Hegel. In E. N. Zalta (Ed.), *The Stanford encyclopedia of philosophy* [online] Spring (2014 ed.). Stanford, CA: Stanford University. Retrieved from http://plato.stanford.edu/archives/spr2014/entries/hegel/

ABOUT THE AUTHORS

David Baker was Principal of University College Plymouth St Mark & St John (now the University of St Mark & St John) 2003–2009. He is Emeritus Professor of Strategic Information Management there. He has published widely in the field of Library and Information Studies, with 18 monographs and some 100 articles to his credit. He has spoken at numerous conferences, led workshops and seminars and has undertaken consultancy work in most countries in the European Union, along with work in Ethiopia, Kuwait, Nigeria and the Sudan. He was Deputy Chair of the Joint Information Systems Committee (now Jisc) until December 2012, also having led a number of large technology-based projects, both in relation to digital and hybrid library development and content creation for teaching and learning. He has published the following books with Chandos: *Strategic Information Management, Strategic Change Management in Public Sector Organisations* and (with Bernadette Casey) *Eve on Top: Women's Experience of Success in the Public Sector* and coproduced (with Wendy Evans) *Digital Library Economics: An Academic Perspective, Libraries and Society: Role, Responsibility and Future in an Age of Change, Trends, Discovery and People in the Digital Age, A Handbook of Digital Library Economics: Operations, Collections and Services* and *Digital Information Strategies: from Applications and Content to Libraries and People.*

Chris Batt was Chief Executive of the Museums, Libraries and Archives Council (MLA), the development agency for the sector until September 2007. Following its creation in 2000 the MLA had a pivotal role in many aspects of cultural heritage and ICT strategy. Chris originally joined national government in 1999 to lead the implementation of the highly successful £170m People's Network project and while in the role of MLA's Chief Executive continued to ensure involvement in digital strategy.

Between late 2007 and 2010, as a director of Chris Batt Consulting Ltd, he led research projects for the Joint Information Systems Committee (now Jisc) on audience analysis and modelling in digital content. International projects and speaking engagements have included work in

Australia, New Zealand, Singapore, Canada, the United States, Iceland and a dozen countries across Europe.

In 2015 Chris was awarded a PhD by University College London for his research thesis: Collecting Institutions in the Network Society.

Laurel Sammonds Crawford is the Coordinator of Collection Development at University of North Texas Libraries. Laurel holds a Master's degree in Library and Information Science from Louisiana State University, and has extensive experience in academic library collection development. She has presented at local, state, and national conferences on collection analysis, organisational strategies, and assessment. Laurel's research areas include library leadership and collection assessment.

Wendy Evans is Head of Library and Data Protection and Freedom of Information Officer at the University of St Mark & St John in Plymouth. She has a keen interest in electronic resources and in particular access to journals and databases. Wendy has published, lectured, and researched in the field of electronic journal and database usage and also access versus ownership of journals. She has co-authored and co-edited *Digital Library Economics: An Academic Perspective, Libraries and Society: Role, Responsibility and Future in an Age of Change, Trends, Discovery and People in the Digital Age* and *A Handbook of Digital Library Economics: Operations, Collections and Services*. Wendy is a Chartered Librarian, an Associate Member of the Higher Education Academy and has been awarded an Associate Teaching Fellowship from the University of St Mark & St John. Also a part-time student at the University of St Mark & St John, Wendy is working toward an Executive MBA.

Karen Harker earned her Master of Library Science Degree (MLS) from Texas Woman's University in 1999 and her Master of Public Health (MPH) from University of Texas (UT) School of Public Health in 2007. From 2000 to 2009, she evaluated and developed Web-based information systems for UT Southwestern Medical Center Library. After three years as biostatistician for a psychiatry clinical trial, she returned to librarianship in 2012 to serve as Collection Assessment Librarian for the University of North Texas Libraries. She has applied her skills in research methods, statistical analysis, and data management to the broad evaluation of library collections.

Masanori Koizumi wears many hats in his life: an assistant professor, researcher, teacher, entrepreneur, advisor/consultant, mountaineer, husband,

and father. He is currently an assistant professor of the Faculty of Library, Information and Media Science (iSchool) at the University of Tsukuba in Japan. Formerly he was a visiting scholar at the School of Information Sciences, University of Pittsburgh until March 2015. His research focuses on how libraries or other similar institutions provide information resources and services to citizens, and how they solve social problems by using their resources in local communities. In particular, he examines those questions based on three levels, (1) Government (public policy and public sphere), (2) Libraries (strategic management), (3) Citizens (library users), from the perspectives of management or governance. He is regarded as one of the top Japanese experts on library management, innovation and growth of libraries. He was awarded his Masters thesis from Keio University in 2009 and became a faculty member there the same year. He was also given awards for business consulting for international markets, as well as business consulting for domestic markets at KDDI Corporation (Second Largest Telecommunications Company in Japan) in 2004, Institution of highest degree, Ph.D. Keio University, Library and Information Science in 2013.

Tibor Koltay is Professor at the Institute of Learning Technologies of Eszterházy Károly University (formerly Department of Information and Library Studies of Szent István University), Hungary.

One of his main professional interests, where he has also published papers extensively, includes information literacy and related fields, including information overload and − more recently − data literacy and the role of academic libraries in Research 2.0.

Derek Law is Emeritus Professor of Informatics in the University of Strathclyde. His career was spent in library and latterly university management. He has published extensively on policy issues and continues to act as a speaker author and consultant.

Derek Marshall is the Coordinator of the College of Veterinary Medicine Library at Mississippi State University. His experience in branch libraries includes both public and academic libraries. Having served many years as a branch manager of several public libraries, Derek has made the transition to academic libraries, beginning as a serials librarian and now serving the College of Veterinary Medicine. In his 15 plus years as a librarian, his responsibilities have included collection development, management, and assessment, as well as end-user experience.

Mike McGrath started work in Brymbo steelworks in 1961 in operational research. He then changed course and worked as a bricklayer before joining the Department of Egyptian Antiquities in the British Museum in 1969, where he worked on the 1972 Tutankhamun exhibition and catalogued the department's collection of 70,000 objects. He joined the British Library on its inception in 1973. He retired in 2001 as Head of UK Marketing having also worked for some years internationally. In semi-retirement he edits the *Interlending and Document Supply* journal and remains active in document supply matters and has a particular interest in open access. He has presented at many conferences over the last 25 years. Mike can be contacted at mike@mikemcgrath.org.uk.

Chloe Persian Mills MLIS, MA, is Associate Professor of Learning Resources at Robert Morris University Library in Pennsylvania. Her research interests include librarian involvement with professional unions, academic library special populations, and supporting research and education in economics, business, and the social sciences. Chloe can be contacted at millsc@rmu.edu.

Valentini Moniarou-Papaconstantinou is Emeritus Professor at the Department of Library Science and Information Systems of the Technological Educational Institute of Athens, Greece. She was teaching information services management and collection management and had given lectures on these topics in courses organised by various organisations in Greece. Her research interests include a theorisation of changes in the information field and information services management, LIS students' educational choices and their learning careers, as well as the understanding of information technology acceptance by LIS students. She has given talks and presentations at several international conferences and her research publications have appeared in international journals such as *Education for Information, Aslib Journal of Information Management, Library and Information Science Research, New Library World and Library Management*.

John Robinson joined SOAS in 2009, having worked in a variety of roles in the university sector since 1974. He is Director of the SOAS Library (the UK National Research Library for Asia, Africa and the Middle East) and is responsible for SOAS' Information Systems, ICT, MultiMedia and Print Services, supporting SOAS staff, students and external visitors. From 2005 to 2009 John was Jisc Director of Services, responsible for the Jisc services portfolio which included JANET (the national academic network),

Jisc Collections and Jisc's support and advisory services. A member of the SOAS Academic Board and its Board of Trustees, John also sits on the Boards of a number of external bodies including Research Libraries UK (RLUK), the OLE Partnership and the London Metropolitan Network. He represents the SOAS Library and RLUK at national and international advisory groups and conferences. He has published articles and given conference papers on the subject of Digital Library economics, Open Source software systems and shared services.

Jo Smedley is Professor of Learning Innovation at the University of South Wales, UK. In a career spanning over 30 years with experience in Further and Higher Education in the United Kingdom and Europe, she specialises in enabling innovative learning and teaching through appropriate uses of technology. The effective management of data and information to maximise impact from practice and process along the learner journey are other areas of her work.

Evgenia Vassilakaki is Scientific Associate at the Department of Library Science and Information Systems of the Technological Educational Institute of Athens, Greece. She received her PhD in 2011 from Manchester Metropolitan University, Department of Information & Communications and her Masters in Information Science in 2006 from Ionian University, Department of Archive and Library Sciences, Corfu, Greece. She currently teaches information literacy and records management and her research interests lie in Multilingual Information Retrieval, Digital Libraries, and Information Seeking Behaviour. She has recently published part of her research work in the journals of *Library and Information Science Research*, *Information Research*, and *The International Information & Library Review*. Evgenia can be contacted at evasilakaki@yahoo.gr.

Graham Walton has over 30 years' experience in higher education libraries in the United Kingdom. He has worked at Northumbria University where he oversaw services to health students and three campus libraries. Between 2004 and 2016, he was employed at Loughborough University as Assistant Director (Academic and User Services) in the University Library. He is an Honorary Research Fellow in the Centre for Information Management at Loughborough University's Business School. He has published over 50 journal articles and edited 6 books. His most recent book focuses on informal learning spaces in universities and was published in 2016. Graham is currently Editor of the *New Review of Academic Librarianship*.

Innovation and creativity within libraries have been an area of interest for a number of years informed by the Creative Management course he completed as part of his MBA (Master of Business Administration). He attended secondary school with the co-author (Paul Webb).

Paul Webb initially graduated with a BSc in the life sciences and then worked in the biotechnology/scientific instrumentation sector primarily in International marketing roles.

Since undertaking his MBA at Durham University he has worked in various University Business Schools. From 2000 to 2015 Paul worked full time at the University of Chester where he was responsible at various times for the Full Time and Part Time MBA programmes as well as a bespoke MBA provided to Liverpool City Council managers. He has in the past worked as an Associate teaching basis for Durham University, Hull University and the Open University Business School. Since retiring from his full time position Paul has continued to undertake Associate teaching roles at Bradford, Salford, Sheffield & Sheffield Hallam Universities, as well as delivering 'Creative Thinking Courses' to Housing Association managers. He has published widely in the areas of International Marketing and strategy and has a particular interest in aspects relating to Internationalism of the HE market. He attended secondary school with the other co-author (Graham Walton).